W9-BHD-960

ECONOMY,
ENVIRONMENT,
AND
TECHNOLOGY

Studies in Socio-Economics

MORALITY, RATIONALITY, AND EFFICIENCY
NEW PERSPECTIVES ON SOCIO-ECONOMICS
Richard M. Coughlin, editor

SOCIO-ECONOMICS
TOWARD A NEW SYNTHESIS
Amitai Etzioni and Paul R. Lawrence, editors

INSTITUTIONAL CHANGE
THEORY AND EMPIRICAL FINDINGS
Sven-Erik Sjöstrand, editor

THE MORAL PHILOSOPHY OF MANAGEMENT
FROM QUESNAY TO KEYNES
Pierre Guillet de Monthoux

THE SOCIO-ECONOMICS OF CRIME AND JUSTICE
Brian Forst, editor

ECONOMY, ENVIRONMENT, AND TECHNOLOGY
A SOCIOECONOMIC APPROACH
Beat Bürgenmeier, editor

ECONOMY, ENVIRONMENT, AND TECHNOLOGY

A Socio-Economic Approach

EDITOR
Beat Bürgenmeier

M.E. Sharpe
80 Business Park Drive
Armonk, New York 10504

Copyright © 1994 by M. E. Sharpe, Inc.

Library of Congress Cataloging-in-Publication Data

Economy, environment, and technology : a socioeconomic
approach / edited by Beat Bürgenmeier.
p.cm. — (Studies in socio-economics)
Includes index.
ISBN 1-56324-413-6.—ISBN 1-56324-414-4 (pbk.)
1. Environmental policy—Economic aspects.
2. Environmental policy—Social aspects.
3. Environmental economics.
I. Bürgenmeier, Beat.   II. Series.
HC79.E5E287 1994
363.7—dc20   94-1913
CIP

Printed in the United States of America

The paper used in this publication meets the minimum requirements of
American National Standard for Information Sciences—
Permanence of Paper for Printed Library Materials,
ANSI Z 39.48-1984.

∞

BM (c)   10   9   8   7   6   5   4   3   2   1
BM (p)   10   9   8   7   6   5   4   3   2   1

To

Floriane, Nathalie, and Stéphanie

Contents

List of Tables and Figures   ix

Introduction   3

PART I: THE BEHAVIORAL SCIENCES FACING ENVIRONMENTAL PROTECTION

1   Estimating Nonuse Values Requires Interdisciplinary Research
Gardner Brown   11

2   Understanding Environmental Problems: A Sociological Perspective
Riley E. Dunlap, Loren A. Lutzenhiser, and Eugene A. Rosa   27

3   Recycling Consumer Waste: A Behavioral Science Approach to Environmental Protection Policy
John Thøgersen   51

PART II: BIOECONOMICS

4   New Approaches in Ecological Economics: Energy Analysis and the Socioeconomic Elements of Environmental Economics
Sylvie Faucheux   77

5   Economic-Ethical and Bioeconomic Elements of "Practical" Economics
Eberhard K. Seifert   107

PART III: SUSTAINABLE DEVELOPMENT

6   Sustainable Development and the Economic Growth Debate
Paul Ekins   121

7   The Physical and Biological Environment—The Socioeconomy
    of Sustainable Development
    Andrea Baranzini and Gonzague Pillet   139

PART IV: THE POLICY IMPLICATION

8   Nearly Uncontrollable Pollution of an Agrarian System:
    A Socioeconomic Case Study
    Jean-Louis Le Moigne and Magali Orillard   165

9   Environmental Policy: Beyond the Economic Dimension
    Beat Bürgenmeier   175

10 The Challenge of Economics to Political Modernity: Some
    Views on the Limits of Collective Action and Power
    Charles Roig   191

Index   209

Contributors   217

About the Editor   219

List of Tables and Figures

Tables

1.1   Testing Embeddedness   15

3.1   Willingness to Participate in a Source Separation Program and
      Beliefs about Trouble and Nuisance, in Tarup, Denmark   59

3.2   The Percentage of Participants Experiencing ''No Trouble'' from
      Source Separation of Food Waste in Aalborg, Denmark, by Age   63

3.3   Extra Work and Collection Effectiveness in Farum, Denmark   66

7.1   Payoff Matrix of Technological Choices   144

9.1   Environmental Policy Instruments: Advantages and Disadvantages   177

9.2   Objections to the Competitive-Market Model in
      Environmental Policy   179

Figures

1.1   Relationship between Judged and Statistical Frequencies for
      Forty-one Causes of Death   19

2.1   Ecological Complex   30

2.2   Causes of Environmental Problems   32

2.3   Expanded Model of Major Causes   34

2.4   Impacts of Environmental Problems   44

3.1   A Behavioral Science Frame of Reference   56

3.2   Motivation Unfolded   57

3.3   Personal Abilities and the Execution of Intentions   62

3.4   Conditions for the Execution of Intentions   65

7.1   Economic Functions of the Environment   143

7.2   A General Model of Economic-Environmental Interactions   152

ECONOMY,
ENVIRONMENT,
AND
TECHNOLOGY

Introduction

Environmental protection calls for a strategy of unprecedented proportions. Not only is our knowledge of the numerous interactions between the natural environment, society, and the economy incomplete, but our understanding has to reach far beyond the usual limits of our time horizon. Confronted by so much uncertainty, we may consequently be tempted to apply well-known remedies that recall an old antagonism in policy making: market incentives as opposed to direct control. This opposition reflects a frame of mind in which economic constraints remain in the forefront.

Therefore, we are tempted to look at the problems of environmental protection in the light of economic reasoning, in order to conceptualize them along usual market lines. This view is complemented by an attempt to deal with these problems from the exclusive perspective of the natural sciences. This reflects the positivist wisdom of a society that rests on a strong connection between economics and technology. One of the early scientists (Thomas 1956), aware of the ecological consequences of human activity, pointed out that the problem is also rooted in the social sciences. Another voice (White 1967) recalled the historical roots of today's environmental crisis. In spite of such clarity of thought, our society continues to favor economic and technological approaches to pollution control. An example can be found in the concept of sustainable development, which became popular with the publication in 1987 of the report by the World Commission on Environment and Development (The Brundtland Report) (WCED 1987). Sustainable development is defined as

> . . . a process of change in which the exploitation of resources, the direction of investments, the orientation of technological development, and institutional change are made consistent with future as well as present needs. (Chap. 2, p. 4.)

The general nature of this definition does not indicate how the goal of sustainable development can be achieved, but in actual policy discussions (e.g., Tietenberg 1989), market incentives and technical progress are viewed as the most promising means of doing so.

A socioeconomic approach to the environment is an attempt to reduce the imbalance between policies based on economic and technological applications and those based on a broader and deeper understanding of the social fabric. This leads to an emphasis on the ongoing change in values. Economic analysis acknowledges only values formed on the marketplace. Without supply and demand, natural resources are a free good. Litter and waste are deemed as lacking value and cost unless they can be expressed by a price. The social sciences have always been interested in the process of value formation outside the economic sphere. Value judgments emerge from a socioeconomic analysis which, by its very nature, is not only interdisciplinary and multimethodological but also geared toward operational decision making. Economic models reduce value judgments to the sum of individual marginal adjustments. As a result, institutions are seen as independent entities. Their role is underestimated by denying the interdependence between institutions and human behavior and by assuming that social structures are immutable.

Any attempt to combine the economy and the environment in a single framework requires an unprecedented shift in our value system. Therefore, norms must be given a far more important role in the study of sustainable development than a purely economic approach will allow.

A broader approach to the environment is being developed in two main directions, which are presented in this book. The first takes into account human behavior, institutions, and collective decision making in relation to environmental protection policies. It extends our understanding of the issues raised in the humanities and social sciences by focusing on the process of value transformation and on the symbols used by society in order for its members to be able to communicate with each other. Value transformation ultimately legitimizes any action in the realm of environmental protection. New policies represent a new form of government intervention in the economy and disturb links that had slowly become institutionalized over time in order to overcome conflicts between special interest groups. New policies lead to a redistribution of established rent situation and require a rearrangement of the web of coalitions in order to make room for the ecological dimension within established social and economic relationships. The old debate about value formation emerges again.

The second direction casts some light on the existing interface between the economy and the biosphere and tries to take the physical and biological environment into account in economic analysis. The discipline that explicitly explores this avenue is now called ecological economy (Constanza 1989). Its aims are to cover the domains of ecology, environmental economy, and natural resources in order to solve rising problems that are not studied by any specific discipline, such as acid rain, global warming, and the preservation of species.

These two directions of research not only represent an important move toward an interdisciplinary synthesis in environmental studies, but also lead to operational policy considerations. The implementation of any effective environment policy is a far more normalized process than economic theories on the internalization of external costs are prepared to admit. The breaking down of barriers between the various disciplines studying the environment is the aim of this book, in which values are discussed. Such a discussion makes sense only if it sets out from an ethical set of references about which there is an implicit social consensus. Before new values can be introduced to fully take environmental protection into account, the prevailing value system on which traditional public policy is based needs to be clarified. This raises the issue of society's perception of the government. The need to protect the environment emphasizes the distinction between general and individual interests. Without a doubt, environmental protection policies underscore the boundaries between the public and private spheres.

This fundamental issue is addressed in four different sections. The various contributions cover human behavior and institutions in relation to bioeconomics in order to discuss the process that legitimizes operational environmental protection policies.

Part I recalls the contributions of the behavioral sciences to the understanding of environmental protection and contains three contributions. Chapter 1, by Gardner Brown, stresses the need for the involvement of social scientists in research programs in several critical areas of environmental protection and demonstrates how cognitive psychologists can usefully contribute to the debate on the estimation of nonmarket and nonuse values. Brown presents problems of embedding, of framing, of objective versus subjective probability, and of discrete versus continuous methods of consumer choice that arise with contingent valuation methods. The trade-off between values set by the market and those formed in the mind of the consumer is an unsolved problem and clearly stresses the need for interdisciplinary research. Chapter 2, by Riley E. Dunlap, Loren A. Lutzenhiser, and Eugene A. Rosa, brings a sociological perspective to the understanding of environmental problems. Their approach gives an account of the new field of environmental sociology, which focuses on the causes of, solutions to, and impacts of environmental problems. Emphasis is not so much on major explanatory variables of pollution, such as population growth and technology, as on the interaction between such variables in recognizing the societal significance of the ecological sphere. A sociological approach to the environment proves to be very useful in examining aspects of social organization such as the marketplace. It complements the socioeconomic perspective by insisting on power, institutions, and social values. This helps to point out the shortcomings of an approach that blames environmental problems solely on supposed free choice of the consumer. The same critical perspective is also adopted in the third chapter, by John Thøgersen, who discusses a behavioral science approach to one particular aspect of environmental protection policy, namely, recycling consumer waste. Using data collected in Denmark, Thøgersen explains consumer behavior in terms of motivation, capability, and the actual possibility of carrying out the actor's intentions. These three variables define a frame of reference rooted in behavioral science; they are also discussed with respect to the importance of social norms in a source separation program for household waste. However, real outcomes often fail to reflect the attitudes revealed by surveys. If that has not happened in the data presented, it can be explained by moral values that are part of the behavioral assumptions used in socioeconomics.

Part II focuses on another line of research, namely, bioeconomics. Chapter 4, by Sylvie Faucheux, uses the case of energy analysis to illustrate new approaches in ecological economics. By reminding us of the need for a multidimensional approach to the study of the relationships between economics and the biosphere (which also includes the social sphere), Faucheux warns against simply replacing monetary evaluations by others expressed in energy units, because this is just another form of reductionism. Such replacement not only leaves out the social sphere, where nonmarket and nonuse values are also formed, but also does not take into account the entropy approach to production, which may serve as an indicator of the degree of pollution caused by various substances. Therefore, an ecoenergy analysis has to be developed in order to define a tool of broader scope, which would be of help in measuring the pollution potential of the inputs used in a production process. The concept of sustainable development cannot be a mere extension of economic theory. This conclusion is discussed in a broader sense by Eberhard K. Seifert in chapter 5, which presents five theses on the history and present-day relevance of an alternative to the dominant engineering approach to economics. Seifert's first thesis stresses the importance of the historical-ethical dimension. The second recalls that economics is indeed a moral science. The third establishes the link between the Enlightenment and ethics in order to formulate a fourth thesis stating that the Enlightenment is distinct from Aristotle's practical philosophy, which also included economics. Finally, the fifth thesis reminds us that industrial production not only cannot change the laws of nature but increases entropy as well.

Part III discusses the concept of sustainable development and attempts to combine in a unified framework many of the variables discussed in parts I and II. Chapter 6, by Paul Ekins, discusses the consistency of the link between sustainable development and economic growth, and it reviews the debate surrounding this issue. In discussing how sustainability can be achieved, Ekins clarifies the relationship between economic growth and environmental as well as social sustainability. The policy shift from growth targets to environmental protection is exemplified by the Ehrlich equation, which links sustainability to population growth and technology, two variables that are also discussed in part I in a sociological perspective. Chapter 7, by Andrea Baranzini and Gonzague Pillet, extends the concept of sustainable development not only to the economic but also to the physical and biological environment, establishing a link with the discussion in part II. Baranzini and Pillet clearly show that the physical viability of systems has to be guaranteed before discussing how sustainability can be achieved. To analyze sustainable development, enlarged models of growth and natural resource management are reviewed. However, the practical applications of these models are very limited because of the methodological problems they raise, scientific uncertainties, and lack of data. In order to assess sustainability, physical indicators, which are imperfect and generally limited in scope, are proposed. Baranzini and Pillet show that sustainable development implies a broader notion of welfare than the one presented in a neoclassical model.

Part IV deals with the policy implications of a socioeconomic approach to the environment. Chapter 8, by Jean-Louis Le Moigne and Magali Orillard, presents a case study of a French company that sells mineral water and is confronted with increasing levels of nitrates. A systems modeling approach is used to study this problem in an ecological, economic, and social perspective. This case study assesses the socioeconomic paradigm and underscores the virtues of procedural forms of rationality, as opposed to the usual behavioral assumptions of mainstream economics. The need for an approach broader than a purely economic one to the environment is also demonstrated in chapter 9, by Beat Bürgenmeier, which assesses the advantages and drawbacks of environmental policy instruments. It shows the complementary nature of direct controls and incentives and lists the main objections to market-oriented policies. The broadening of our view beyond the economic dimension is illustrated in the fields of psychology, law, sociology, and political science, leading to environmental policy designs that combine incentives and direct controls and that take into account changing attitudes to environmental values. Chapter 10, by Charles Roig, expresses some views on the legitimacy crisis emerging in the present debate on environmental protection. This crisis is seen in a historical and philosophical perspective, where economics is presented as a challenge to political modernity. Starting from the politics of the Enlightenment, it shows how economics has emerged as a political choice leading to a societal polarity inherent to modernity. A definition of societal polarity and its effects can be based on the characteristics of community as opposed to society. This opposition leads to political crisis, loss of control, and countereffects. Environmental protection policies cannot escape similar consequences.

Based on a conference held at the University of Geneva in 1991 on behalf of the Society for the Advancement of Socio-Economics, this book brings together the first independent socioeconomic analysis of the most acute problems for the survival of humankind.

References

Constanza, R. 1989. "What is ecological economics?" *Ecological Economics* 1(1): 1–7.
Thomas, W. L. (ed.); C.O. Saver, M. Bates (collaborators). 1956. *Man's role in changing the face of the earth.* Chicago: University of Chicago Press.
Tietenberg, T. H. 1989. "Marketable permits in the U.S.A.: A decade of experiences." In *Public finance and the performance of enterprise,* ed. K.W. Roskamp. Detroit: Wayne State University Press.
White, L., Jr. 1967. "The historical roots of our ecological crisis." *Science* 155: 1203–7.
World Commission on Environment and Development (WCED). 1987. *Our common future* (The Brundtland report). Oxford: Oxford University Press.

Part I

The Behavioral Sciences Facing
Environmental Protection

1

Gardner Brown

Estimating Nonuse Values Requires Interdisciplinary Research

Introduction

There is a sea change under way, driven by forces unlikely to diminish in magnitude or direction for a good many years. The phenomenon I refer to is the need for and inclusion of other social scientists in research programs in several critical areas of environmental economics. Such research programs involve estimating nonmarket and nonuse values and conducting risk assessment or risk-benefit analysis. Other social scientists include cognitive psychologists who know how people perceive and make decisions and survey or market researchers who have special knowledge about survey design instruments.

In recent years, population growth, technology, and tastes have conspired to place enormous and increasing economic importance on goods and services not traded in markets. Water and air quality or hazardous waste disposal from a local and international perspective, as well as the specter of rapidly vanishing species, are public policy issues in which the underlying externalities and public goods militate against straightforward marketlike solutions. One such example is the design of a property rights scheme to facilitate optimal resource allocation and distribute the rights in an equitably acceptable fashion. Even if such a property rights system is feasible, in some instances quantitative measurements of the gains and opportunity costs would be required in order to know how many rights to issue. The estimated value of the right surely will play a role, in many cases, in deciding how the rights should be distributed, that is, in deciding who should or should not get the rights and limits, if any, or whether to use per capita distribution.

By the very nature of these goods, there is no organized or approximate market in which we can accurately register our willingness to pay for nonmarket goods such as preservation of the blue whale. Thus, we must turn to indirect methods such as contingent valuation (CV) studies in which values are elicited by survey methods.[1]

When we leave the realm of the market, we can no longer estimate demand or marginal values from observed behavior but must confront people with hypothetical situations and elicit or coax marginal values from them. It is an adventure into realms in which economists have had woefully inadequate professional preparation. While it is possible to use travel cost and hedonic methods to recover *use* values not traded in the market, the frequently very significant *nonuse* values (existence and bequest) simply have no reliable reflection in behavior, so surveylike CV methods are unavoidable. In the ensuing pages I will show how badly we need noneconomists by sketching the four problems I think are of utmost importance for CV survey methods. Arguments about the comparative advantages and gains of specialization dictate that we call on those with specialized knowledge about how to elicit nonuse values from the mental constructs of the sampled population.

The problems in order of presentation are embedding, framing, subjective versus objective probability, and discrete versus continuous methods of consumer choice (matching the way people think about and choose between options with the appropriate estimation techniques).

Embedding

Embedding is perhaps the most serious difficulty confronting practitioners of the CV method. Embedding occurs when a subject, asked to value a particular good or service, in fact gives a response that reflects the value of a more general good that embraces the constituent element. There are several explanations for embedding. If I were asked to value the quality of a specific groundwater aquifer in the context of hazardous waste contamination of the aquifer, I may be unable to make a clear mental distinction between the more general problem of environmental water quality and my valuation of the particular aquifer. Therefore, the value I report is for a more inclusive good and therefore yields an overestimation of the value of the particular good.

Kahneman and Knetsch (1992) argue that when moral satisfaction is an important part of the welfare gain, the willingness-to-pay (WTP) value of a public good is not the equivalent of the value of a private consumption good. While suggestively valid, it cannot be precisely correct because people voluntarily purchase higher-priced consumer goods that differ from the lower-priced counterparts only in their kindness to the environment, such as greater biodegradability or use of recycled materials.

One reason for the mental joint product is that the amenity in question symbolizes or is part of one's more general moral concern for a better environment. Utility is increased directly by contributing to the improvement of a particular amenity and indirectly by improving the aggregate component, environmental integrity, in the utility functions. Often the substantial symbolic content of an issue gives rise to CV studies: oil spills, hazardous waste contamination, habitat destruction that endangers species, and activities that cause large-scale water or air pollution. In these circumstances survey design is crucial; for example, the order of the questions greatly matters. Smith (1991a) paraphrases Cummings's (1989) conjecture that individuals will " 'dump . . . the contents of their good cause account' on the first valued cause posed to them in a [contingent value] CVM question."

Finally McClelland et al. (1991a) argue that survey respondents may believe that a public program will necessarily have a broader compass than the survey designers state. McClelland et al. (1991a) found in their debriefing of subjects that some "viewed health and visibility improvements as joint products" (p. 9), thus corroborating the arguments of cognitive psychologists Fischhoff and Furby (1988). Thus, any contribution that improves one element (say, visibility) would necessarily improve other things positively valued in the utility function of the program. Despite attempts of researchers to identify and separate goods, respondents may believe and respond as if there is a technological interdependence, which, to emphasize the parallelism, is distinct from the mental joint product and the interdependence of tastes cited above. One can understand why the phenomenon addressed here is also called part-whole, symbolic, or disaggregation effect (Cummings, Brookshire, and Schulze 1986; Mitchell and Carson 1989).[2]

Before illustrating the quantitative significance of embedding, which some may wish to skip, the key point of this section should be set forth. Embedding is the grist for the cognitive psychologists' mill. It has long been a worrisome topic of concern for them. Economists are latecomers to this dialogue. Conceptually, embedding is founded in the mind, a realm in which economists have traditionally been proud to disclaim any expertise. Economists study *observable* behavior. Its empirical dimensions turn on proper survey design, which is very much the domain of noneconomists, as Mitchell and Carson (1989), Smith (1991a), and others make clear.

In an unpublished study (Rowe et al. 1991), subjects were asked how much they would be willing to pay for a public program that prevents the occurrence of a particular environmental impact on a particular natural resource in a particular region. Subjects were subsequently asked to comment, if they wished, and to judge the accuracy of their response. (The survey researchers suggested—on the basis of focus groups and intensive debriefing of subjects who had filled out earlier versions of the questionnaire—that some subjects may find it difficult to think about paying for a very specific pollution prevention program.) Each subject was asked (the percentage response to each motivation is included parenthetically; the numbers do not sum to 100 due to rounding) if the amount reported earlier was:

for the specific event described earlier (22)
partly for that event and partly for all similar events in a broader region (36)
partly for the generic event and broader environmental causes (20)
primarily a contribution to all good causes (23)

Only 22 percent of the respondents stated that their answer was consistent with the question asked. All others responded as though there was embedding. Respondents were then given an opportunity to apportion the share of the reported value in the earlier question to the specific abatement program. Embedding accounted for 42 percent of the original total value.

In a second study (Doyle et al. 1991), eighty subjects filled out a survey about groundwater values in a laboratory situation. Each subject was asked his (her) willingness to pay through an increase in water charges for groundwater treatment. After an intervening question, subjects were asked the following two questions:

Q-46   In questions Q-41 and Q-44 you were asked to state the dollar amounts you would be willing to pay for COMPLETE GROUNDWATER TREATMENT. Would you say that the dollar amounts you stated were

(2/3)   1.   JUST FOR THE STATED GROUNDWATER PROGRAM...

       2.   SOMEWHAT FOR THE GROUNDWATER REFERENDUM AND SOMEWHAT A GENERAL CONTRIBUTION TO ALL ENVIRONMENTAL CAUSES.

       3.   BASICALLY   A   CONTRIBUTION   TO   ALL ENVIRONMENTAL CAUSES.

       4.   OTHER   (Please   specify)
_____.

Q-47   About what percent of your dollar amount was just for the stated groundwater program?

NONE	SOME	HALF	MOST	ALL
0	10% 20% 30%	40% 50% 60%	70% 80% 90%	100%

The responses indicate that one-third of the subjects were embedding.[3] Adjusting for the embedding reduced the value by 15 to 20 percent (p. 30).

The quantitative results of these two studies differ for a variety of reasons. One may be that the payment vehicle in the groundwater survey involves an increase in water charges, which a subject may perceive she (he) is more likely to bear, compared to an industry product price increase occasioned by increased pollution abatement costs, the payment vehicle in the first example. However, the qualitative conclusion remains: Embedding is often very significant.

The following examples of embedding are controversial, as we shall see. Kahneman, a psychologist, and Knetsch, an economist (Kahneman in Cummings, Brookshire, and Schulze 1986), surveyed residents in Toronto, asking them how much they were willing to have their taxes increased to preserve fishing success, first in a part of the province (Muskota or Haliburton), *then* for the whole province (Ontario). The willingness to pay for either of the smaller regions was nearly the same as the willingness to pay for the province. Kahneman and Knetsch (1992) recently tested the embedding hypothesis by asking one

Table 1.1

Testing Embeddedness (dollars)

	Group 1 $n = 66$	Group 2 $n = 78$	Group 3 $n = 74$
	WTP: Improved Environmental Services		
Mean	135.91		
Mode	50.00		
	WTP: Greater Preparedness for Disasters		
Mean	29.06	151.60	
Mode	10.10	50.00	
	WTP: Equipment and Trained Personnel		
Mean	13.57	76.65	122.64
Mode	1.00	16.10	25.00

WTP: Willingness to pay.
Source: Kahnman and Knetsch, *Journal of Environmental Economics and Management,*
22: p. 61.

set of subjects their willingness to pay for *improved environmental services*
through taxes, higher product prices, and user fees. Next they were asked the part
of the total amount they were willing to pay for a specific service, *greater
preparedness for disasters.* (The San Francisco earthquake of 1989 had just
occurred.) Finally, they were asked the part of the total amount that should be
allocated for *equipment and trained* personnel for rescue operations in connection with disasters. Each subsequent service is thus nested in the previous service. Kahneman and Knetsch (1992) then surveyed a second group, omitting the
first all-encompassing question. Finally, each subject in a third group was asked
his (her) willingness to pay into a special fund to provide for the most nested
public service in the sequence, equipment and trained personnel for rescue operations.

Results of this survey (Kahneman and Knetsch 1992), summarized below, are
striking. First, the value of a given service depends dramatically on the order in
which the question is asked. The median value of greater preparedness for disasters was $50, or five times higher, when it was the first question rather than the
second. The median value of equipment and trained personnel was $25, $16, or
$1, depending on whether it was the first, second, or third question, respectively,
in the order of questions asked. (See the last row of Table 1.1.) Second, the mean
and median response to the first question asked was not significantly different
across the first three questions (for example, $135.91, $151.60, and $122.64),
despite the fact that the service differs for each question.

Not surprisingly, there is a distribution of views about the fundamental importance of embedding. Critics, many of whom are cognitive psychologists, conclude that it is a serious issue. Others, including many economists, are more hopeful and believe that good study design will greatly reduce the problem. Mitchell and Carson (1989, pp. 250–51, 302) argue for (1) personal interviews rather than mail or telephone surveys to permit a more complex design of the survey instrument which more sharply delineates and more precisely describes the type of valuation desired; (2) descriptions of more inclusive and specific entities with visuals such as maps to emphasize the differences; (3) warnings not to confuse the smaller with the larger concept; (4) valuing the "total resource, even if that is not the subject of the study, and then . . . [allocating] their total WTP amounts for the component of interest", (pp. 251–52); (5) informing the respondent of the sequence or nested nature of the valuations before the first question is asked; and (6) allowing an opportunity to review and revise responses. Smith (1991a) devotes an entire article to an attack of the Kahneman and Knetsch (1992) paper, arguing that "all" of the conclusions are incorrect, citing Mitchell and Carson's arguments as well as others.

For the purposes of this chapter, it isn't necessary to take sides, for it is clear that many contemporary well-financed studies, designed by a team representing economics, cognitive psychology, and survey research, have encountered the embedding phenomenon, and it will require more interdisciplinary cooperation to ameliorate this vexing problem in the years to come.

Framing

Framing refers to the way the hypothetical payment scheme in CV applications is constructed and administered. It has a rich vector of dimensions which I'll pursue only in sufficient detail to provide a sense of the relative inadequacy of economists to address the issues.

$WTP (\Delta X) \neq WTP (\Delta X)$. Technically we know that a half-full glass is the same as a half-empty glass in the sense that if you prefer the half-full glass to an alternative option (here unspecified), you should also prefer the half-empty glass to the alternative (unspecified) option. That is not what happens in surveys.[4] In the following vivid example, Arrow (1983) draws from McNeil et al. (1982). Physicians were asked to choose between two cancer therapies. Surgery had a risk of mortality during the operation but, on balance, had a longer expected survival compared to radiation therapy at that time. When physicians were presented with probabilities of survival for five years, one year, and during treatment, 84 percent of the physicians preferred surgery (over radiation therapy). But when the data were simply transformed into probabilities of dying—instead of probabilities of survival—physicians reduced their preference for surgery to 50 percent from 84 percent.

Smith and Desvousges (1986) found that a sample of households around Boston reported values for a given risk *reduction* that differed by a factor of ten compared to the value of avoiding an equivalent *increase* in risk. The change in risk was not large enough to explain order-of-magnitude differences in the absolute value.

Payment vehicles. Practitioners of the CV method know that a WTP question based on a product price increase elicits a significantly different answer from one framed in terms of a tax increase.

Often one can frame the valuation question as close as possible to the wording used in the referendum. The idea is that since people in the United States, by voting on referenda, commonly make binding financial commitments for new schools, hospitals, and other public facilities and services, the form will be understandable and routine to them. Generally, a referendum format will elicit different values from either the tax or price change vehicle. However, Doyle et al. (1991, app. A, table 3, p. 37) found that there was no significant difference between responses from a referendum format and those from a price increase format. It remains to be explained what exactly gives rise to similar responses.

Context of information. Survey researchers must decide how much information to provide subjects. Generally the estimated WTP varies, depending on the amount of information provided. If a subject is provided with extensive information on, say, the mechanism of groundwater flow, the type and extent of damage, and the way to remedy the damage, will this allow respondents to act as they would in a market context? Some believe that providing a richer background of information will substitute for market experience and elicit better values (Fischhoff and Furby 1988; Mitchell and Carson 1989). However, Coursey, Hovis, and Schulze (1987) found no change in values when they conducted a sequential survey in which subjects were given increasing amounts of information.

Specifically, an innocuous bitter liquid was carefully described and subjects were asked their WTP to avoid tasting. The mean reported value with no experience (and the variance, in parentheses) was $2.60 ($15.80). Next, the subjects directly experienced the taste; afterward they reported a mean WTP of $1.95 ($5.06). Finally, the subjects engaged in a competitive auction designed to mimic a market in which they bid to avoid the commodity. In this third experiment, the mean value was $1.95 ($5.23). Interestingly, while the mean response did not change with greater experience, the variance did change in a statistically significant manner. McClelland et al. (1991b) report other experiments in which bidding variance declines with both market size and reward size. Even if these experiments were grounds for optimism, many dimensions of the framing issue are not resolved.

It has been argued that the sensitivity of respondents to framing issues depends on how crystallized respondents' values are (Schuman and Presser 1981). If one has repeatedly experienced purchasing a particular good, hypothetical CV studies with different framing devices are unlikely to dislodge the values that habit has firmly set in one's perceptions. Indeed, CV studies have performed best when people were offered the opportunity in a laboratory setting to buy market goods, such as strawberries, for which they have direct experience.

If, however, monetary values are not crystallized because the goods are fundamentally nonmarket, as are so many of the amenity goods (viz., air quality and visibility), then framing is likely to matter. Framing enters into the process one uses to understand the physical dimensions of the environmental amenity to be valued and impinges on the process by which one transforms these physical dimensions into a monetary value. All of this exchange takes place in the mental marketplace, not the economic marketplace. The need for mental market specialists—cognitive psychologists—is or should be self-evident.

Subjective versus Objective Probability

Rational consumers, faced with uncertainty, are assumed to maximize a good's expected utility. Arrow (1983) presents an exceptionally simple characterization. Suppose an individual experiences utility (U) from consumption (C) if he (she) is alive, but the product has no utility if the individual is dead. Expected utility is

$$PU(C)$$

where P = the probability of survival. The WTP per unit of survival (utility held constant) is

$$WTP = \frac{U(C)}{PU'(C)} \tag{1.1}$$

The probability of an event clearly plays a prominent role in any expected utility maximization formulation.[5]

The psychology profession has never been very keen on the ground truth of expected utility maximization. Experimental testing in which the theory fails dates back to the very excellent research completed almost four decades ago by psychologists Davidson, Suppes, and Siegel (1957). Shiller (1981) draws on stock market data to show that stock price movement is incompatible with the rational expectations hypothesis. Grether and Plott (1979) attempted to discredit the psychologists' works as applied to economics and conclusively failed.

Many features of expected utility theory are vulnerable. For this section my attention is confined to the probabilistic element. Should objective or subjective probabilities be used for policy analysis? I'll argue that this is not merely a conceptual matter because subjective and objective probabilities often differ vastly, so that which we use will often be decisive in a policy context.

We imagine that individuals start out with prior probabilities about the occurrence of events, then update them as new experience and information arrive. In the fullness of time we expect subjective probabilities to approach true probabilities.[6] Typically they don't. Worse, decision makers often don't use Bayes's rule correctly, according to Arrow (1983), who cites Tversky and Kahneman (1974) and Eddy (1980).[7] In the latter study, physicians vastly overestimated the likelihood of cancer when diagnostic tests indicated a malignancy, because they failed to adjust for the underlying low a priori probability of cancer. Magat, Viscusi, and Huber (1988) found that subjects valued hand burns from liquid drain opener at $1.24 million and avoidance of bleach gassing at $1.38 million. Since these values are more representative of the risk of

Figure 1.1. **Relationship between Judged and Statistical Frequencies for Forty-one Causes of Death**

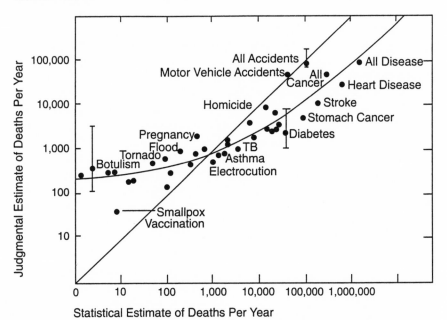

Source: Lichtenstein et al., *Journal of Experimental Psychology: Human Learning and Memory*, 4, 1978.

death, not morbidity, the authors conclude that respondents did not understand the low probabilities, so the result would "not provide a good normative guide to the appropriate level of risk-dollar trade-off for benefit assessment purposes" (p. 407).[8] The authors are simply applying a widely held view that people overestimate the chance of lower risk events and underestimate the chance of higher likelihood events. The observed phenomenon is illustrated by the curved (logarithmic) line in the figure (see Figure 1.1), reproduced from Slovic, Fischhoff, and Lichtenstein (1985). The authors further argue that the probability of easily recalled events, such as natural disasters or homicides, are likely to be inflated.

Another reason subjective and objective probabilities differ is that the information portraying the risk or risk reduction may be difficult to understand. In one study (Smith 1988, pp. 7–8), participants in a focus group could not comprehend how government could reduce the risk of death from hazardous wastes. Additionally, subjects simply may reject the scientists' estimates of the probability of important environmental risks, such as the chance of another earthquake in San Francisco of the magnitude of that which occurred in 1989. The rejection comes even if great effort is made to explain the basis of the probabilities.[9] Whether from incredulity about the chance of a natural event or the likelihood of a man-made change, the result is the same. Individuals substitute their own for the professional's probability, and reported values reflect this typically subjective but unknown probability.

Risk unavoidably is a substantial driving force underlying many of the vital issues in empirical environmental economics today. Once again, how we help those whom we interview to perceive more accurately the probability of alternative outcomes is a task that will require professionals skilled in understanding how individuals perceive events and make judgments. The necessary interdisciplinary task is unenviable since cognitive psychologists seem predisposed to reject the rationality embedded in the constitution of most economists.

A further, intradisciplinary debate that is fascinating is whether to use subjective or objective probabilities in our computations of WTP. Arrow (1983, p. 27) says that we should honor the individual's utility function but reject subjective probabilities, but Arrow gives no reasons for his position. Smith (1991b) occupies a middle ground when he attaches weights to both the objective and the subjective probabilities. My inclination is to favor using subjective probabilities on the grounds that these are what consumers use when they make private consumption decisions. The food I eat or don't eat and the car (safety) I drive (enjoyment) are determined by my judgment, however imperfect, of the risks entailed in making these or similar decisions. Rejecting subjective probabilities is not much different, in my judgment, from rejecting consumer sovereignty, which I am reluctant to do.

However, I do have a nagging feeling that when a public decision is being made, objective probabilities may have a role to play. Why shouldn't the public's probability count, and why can't it be an informed probability? Should information incorporated in objective probabilities be excluded? Suppose, for example, a public agency is thinking about providing a public service such as floodplain insurance. Longtime series data enable one to estimate the probability of given sized floods and to translate the physical event into economic damages. It is also known that people systematically overestimate flood frequencies (see Figure 1.1). The government could offer the proper actuarial price for insurance based on objective probabilities. Suppose the public agency knows that it will be prohibitively expensive to educate the public about the true probabilities. Instead of setting actuarial prices, the public agency, knowing (for analytical purposes) the demand function for the public service based on subjective probabilities, could maximize the expected utility of the consumer's using objective probabilities but be constrained by the aggregate of each individual's subjective response function. The agency would compute the price that maximizes in this second-best world. Clearly the alternative to this formulation is quantity allocation if one eschews using a price policy for public services. This second-best solution uses all the information, both objective and subjective probabilities, but its welfare implications remain unstudied.

Discrete versus Continuous Methods of Consumer Choice

Suppose we were interested in automobile safety legislation or in developing policies to regulate the sale, storage, or disposal of products containing some hazardous material. In order to know how severe or permissive our policies should be, we require information on the trade-off between a slightly changed probability of death and the extra cost or loss of marginal consumption, assuming additional safety measures are expensive. More concretely, suppose that greater safety can be purchased at increased public cost, that is, the increased marginal cost of safety. The policy maker asks the researcher what level of expenditure can be justified by the benefits consumers receive from the safety provided. Since market observations don't exist, indirect methods of estimating value must be used. Two generic methods of eliciting value are the choice method and the matching method.

To illustrate the method cognitive psychologists call choice, a researcher can design a very careful study in which respondents are asked to choose between or rank a few options—for example, a comprehensive cleanup after an oil spill which restores the habitat and makes swimming and boating possible at a cost of $1 billion to the taxpayer or a partial cleanup and a delay of swimming and boating for several years at a cost of $300 million.

Another example is for prospective consumers to choose between several slightly different versions of a consumer product that vary only in cost and safety dimensions. From a well-conceived study that confronts the respondent with discrete alternatives, the best choice can be made. As a further example to provide a close comparison with the matching option, respondents could be asked to choose which of two bleach products described below they prefer:

Current Bleach	New Bleach
Cost per year: $10	Cost per year: $15
Injury Level:	Injury Level:
50 gas poisonings for every 2 million homes	50% decrease in gas poisonings compared to current product

The researcher varies the value inserted for cost per year of the new bleach, across the sample of subjects, so that each subject sees only one value.

Now suppose, as a check, the research economists adopt the matching survey method in which the respondent is asked to make a decision involving a quantitative and more exact computation of the marginal risk reduction–value trade-off. Magat, Viscusi, and Huber (1988) provide a good example. The U.S. Environmental Protection Agency was interested in how consumers valued reduced risks of poisoning resulting from the use of household products. To this end, the authors presented several hundred subjects with a questionnaire in which the subjects were given the following information and asked, "How high would the price of the new bleach have to be before you would rather buy the current bleach?"

The subjects entered their responses into the computer provided them. Proper statistical analysis of these two data sets yields an average value for reduced risk.

The unsuspecting research economist should anticipate equivalent answers from these two approaches because the value responses should be invariant to the procedure used to elicit them. Our textbooks don't condition the ordering, reflexivity, and transitivity assumptions about preferences or the method by which preferences are revealed. Indeed, in both economics (Arrow 1983) and psychology (Kahneman and Tversky 1984), the rational theory of choice requires "procedure invariance."[10] On the other hand, cognitive psychologists have known for some time (Slovic 1975) that reported values depend on whether choice or matching procedures are used. We should not expect "procedure invariance." Consequently, economists need cognitive psychologists and their literature to help choose the appropriate elicitation procedure.

Cognitive psychologists don't have all the answers, and this chapter is not intended to be a primer on the subject, but a few comments illustrate how their literature may be a useful guide. When respondents are faced with choosing between (ordering) two options that differ in cost and health risks, they are likely to rank first the option that has the highest value for the attribute most important to the subject. Use of this lexicographic ordering is called the prominence hypothesis (Tversky, Sattath, and Slovic 1988). Health risks would seem to be the primary dimension in the questions set forth above (dollars second in importance as the questions were framed). Tversky, Sattath, and Slovic (1988) cite literature in support of the prominence hypothesis. Pragmatically, a researcher in favor of more safety can show relatively larger values for desirable public safety expenditures by using a choice procedure. The matching option brings dollars more prominently into the mind's eye and typically leads to a reduced marginal value of risk.

A second insight is that procedural invariance is more likely to be observed when people are familiar with the comparisons in question or when similar exchanges are routinely made so that preferences are crystallized. Unfortunately, the big environmental issues of the day are novel—willingness to pay for programs that ensure species preservation, avoid future oil spills, decrease acid rain, and the like. Yet these are the very questions currently attracting the most research interest and dollars for nonmarket valuation in North America. So choice of elicitation method is critically important for environmental economists.

There is a natural way to think about framing questions.[11] Consumers may customarily think about making discrete choices between certain goods or services because that is the way their options or opportunity set customarily is presented to them. There are both a taste and a technology component to a consumer's mental ordering. Even if there are continuous options available, habit, mental economizing, or other factors may have made the availability set discrete. If the method of eliciting preferences is compatible with the way subjects traditionally make actual choices, then there is greater familiarity with the task. It takes less time and energy to understand what is asked for, and it may even be viewed as a less risky—because better understood—situation. We should therefore expect the accuracy of values elicited to depend on the procedure adopted unless the way in which respondents reach actual and hypothetical decisions is independent of the way nature, technology, and enterprise present the options to us.

Good study design requires that we use a discrete choice approach such as a random utility model when the options are lumpy—or when respondents think in a predominantly discrete, ordinalist manner—and that we use a continuous, cardinalist framework when respondents are comfortable mentally tracing marginal rates of substitution functions and matching them with the budget surface. The appropriate method of elicitation can be identified by initially determining whether respondents prefer a binary-type choice or a matching, cardinalist task framework. Schematically the desirable match of procedure and mental organization is illustrated below.

Mental Organization

Procedure	Discrete Ordering	Continuous Trade-offs Possible
Matching	Inaccurate values elicited	Appropriate
Choice	Appropriate	Inaccurate values elicited

Conclusion

Current legislation in the United States, exemplified by the new Clean Air Act and the regulations regarding damage assessment due to hazardous waste, essentially requires that nonuse values of the environment be estimated. It is all too easy when perspective is foreshortened to mistakenly believe that a contemporary phenomenon is a permanent institution. Nevertheless, I believe that the necessity to estimate nonuse values will grow in the United States and begin to permeate European consciousness and policy. Applied economists will have to address the substantial shortcomings of nonmarket valuation techniques, particularly contingent valuation methods. The purpose of this chapter has been to indicate that nonmarket values are formed in the mind. By their nature, these values will not be expressed by observable market behavior but must be coaxed out of the subjects' mental accounts by cognitive psychologists, survey researchers, and other social scientists whose expertise is in this area of inquiry. My conclusion should hold as long as economists continue to subscribe to the ancient dictum dating back to Adam Smith, that there are gains from specialization. Economists will necessarily play a key role in nonuse value research because we are very clever about setting the analytical framework for and estimating marginal values, but we can do nothing practical until the basic data are found. That is the province of other social scientists. The sooner we acknowledge their comparative advantage, the faster we can make progress in establishing the true economic importance of environmental resources.

Notes

1. An elitist position not put forward here is to argue that the tastes of the citizenry should not be trusted to properly value higher pleasures such as budgets for opera or wilderness programs.

2. As is customary in new research areas, researchers may attach different labels to essentially the same phenomenon, or, with time, small differences may prove important enough to warrant different names. Mitchell and Carson (1989, pp. 249–51) argue that a part-whole bias arises when subjects misperceive the geographic extent of the amenity change or its composition (nonuse value versus total value, for example), rather than its symbolic content.

3. Some of those not embedding were incensed that their understanding of the original question should have been impugned.

4. See Tversky and Kahneman (1981) for many illustrations of this behavior.

5. Arrow (1983) acknowledges Allais's more general formulation that consumers maximize $U(C,P)$, which leads to $WTP = UP/UC$. Most policy issues cause marginal changes in the probability of survival, in which case the linear approximation of WTP from Allais's formulation is approximately the product of equation (1).

6. This Bayesian approach can be expressed more formally as

$$\frac{\text{The Posterior Probability}}{\text{of the Event}} = \frac{(\text{The Likelihood of Data}) (\text{Prior Probability of the Event})}{\text{Marginal Likelihood of Data}}$$

7. However, Smith (1988) cites a study by Grether (1980) indicating that financial incentives and experience reduce, if not eliminate, departure from the Bayesian updating process, and Camerer (1987) also finds that experience helps to reduce the discrepancy between objective and perceived payoffs.

8. The authors believe the respondents may not have understood the base number of at-risk households, 2 million, so the risk rate with a large denominator was confusing. However, if one reduces the denominator, the probability becomes even smaller and this may make the problem worse.

9. Slovic, Fischhoff, and Lichtenstein (1985) argue that people cling tenaciously to their judgments. When respondents were asked to judge the odds of correctly choosing which of two lethal events occurs more frequently (Fischhoff, Slovic, and Lichtenstein 1977), odds of at least 100 to 1 were given one-fourth of the time. Yet one-eighth of these answers were wrong. Slovic, Fischhoff, and Lichtenstein (1985) cite studies that establish that people think they can estimate risks with much greater precision than they actually can.

10. See Tversky, Sattath, and Slovic (1988) for further discussion of procedure invariance.

11. I credit Smith (1991) with the genesis of this idea and take responsibility for errors in detail.

References

Arrow, K. J. 1983. "Behavior under uncertainty and its implications for policy." In *Foundations of utility and risk theory with applications,* ed. B. P. Stigum and F. Wenstop. Norwell, MA: D. Reidel Publishing Co.

————. 1982. "Risk perception in psychology and economics." *Economic Inquiry:* 201–9.

Camerer, C. F. 1987. "Do biases in probability judgment matter in markets? Experimental evidence." *American Economic Review* 77 (December): 981–87.

Coursey, D., J. Hovis, and W. D. Schulze. 1987. "On the supposed disparity between willingness to accept and willingness to pay measures of value." *Quarterly Journal of Economics* 102: 679–90.

Cummings, R. 1989. Letter to the Office of Environmental Project Review, Department of the Interior, November 10, 1989.

Cummings, R. G., D. S. Brookshire, and W. D. Schulze, eds. 1986. *Valuing environmental goods: An assessment of the contingent valuation method.* Totowa, NJ: Rowman and Allanheld.

Davidson, D., P. Suppes, and S. Siegel. 1957. *Decision making: An experimental approach,* Palo Alto, CA: Stanford University Press.

Doyle, J. K., S. R. Elliott, G. H. McClelland, and W. D. Schulze. 1991. "Valuing the benefits of groundwater cleanup: Interim report." Washington, DC.: Environmental Protection Agency (January).

Eddy, D. 1980. *Screening for cancer: Theory, analysis, and design.* Englewood Cliffs, NJ: Prentice-Hall.

Fischhoff, B., P. Slovic, and S. Lichtenstein. 1977. "Knowing with certainty: The appropriateness of extreme confidence." *Journal of Experimental Psychology: Human Perception and Performance* 3: 552–64.

Fischhoff, B., and L. Furby. 1988. "Measuring values: A conceptual framework for interpreting transactions with special reference to contingent valuation of visibility." *Journal of Risk and Uncertainty* 1: 147–84.

Grether, D. M. 1980. "Bayes rules as a descriptive model: The representativeness heuristic." *Quarterly Journal of Economics* 95 (November): 537–58.

Grether, D., and C. Plott. 1979. "Economic theory of choice and the preference reversal phenomenon." *American Economic Review* 69: 623–38.

Horgarth, R. M., and M. W. Reder. 1986. "Editor's comments: Perspectives from economics and psychology." *Journal of Business* 59 [Special issue: "The behavioral foundations of economic theory"] (October): S105–S426.

Kahneman, D. 1986. "Comments on the contingent valuation method." In *Valuing environmental goods,* ed. R. G. Cummings, D. S. Brookshire, and W. D. Schulze, Totowa, NJ: Rowman and Allanheld.

Kahneman, D., and J. L. Knetsch. 1992. "Valuing public goods: The purchase of moral satisfaction." *Journal of Environmental Economics and Management* 22: 57–70.

Kahneman, D., and A. Tversky. 1984. "Choices, values and frames." *American Psychologist* 39: 341, 50.

Lichtenstein, S., P. Slovic, B. Fischhoff, M. Layman, and B. Combs. 1978. "Judged frequency of lethal events." *Journal of Experimental Psychology: Human Learning and Memory* 4: 551–78.

Magat, W. A., W. K. Viscusi, and J. Huber. 1988. "Consumer processing of hazard warning information." *Journal of Risk and Uncertainty* 1 (June): 201–32.

McClelland, G., W. Schulze, D. Waldman, J. Irwin, and D. Schenk. 1991a. "Sources of error in contingent valuation." Washington, DC: Environmental Protection Agency (January).

McClelland, G., W. Schulze, D. Waldman, J. Irwin, D. Schenk, T. Stewart, L. Deck, and M. Thayer. 1991b. "Valuing Eastern visibility: A field test of the contingent valuation method." Washington, DC: Environmental Protection Agency (January).

McNeil, B. J., S. G. Pauker, H. C. Sox, Jr., and A. Tversky. 1982. "On the elicitation of preferences for alternative therapies." *New England Journal of Medicine* 306: 1259–62.

Mitchell, R. C., and R. T. Carson. 1989. *Using surveys to value public goods: The contingent valuation method.* Washington, DC: Resources for the Future.

Rowe, R. D., W. D. Schulze, W. D. Shaw, P. Schenk, and L. G. Chestnut. 1991. "Contingent valuation of natural resource damage due to the Nestucca oil spill, final report," prepared for Department of Wildlife, State of Washington, and British Columbia Ministry of Environment, Canada.

Schuman, H., and S. Presser. 1981. *Questions and answers in attitude surveys: Experiments of question form, working and context.* New York: Academic Press, Inc., Harcourt Brace Jovanovich.

Shiller, R. J. 1981. "Do stock prices move too much to be justified by subsequent changes in dividends?" *American Economic Review* 71: 421–36.

Slovic, P. 1975. "Choice between equally valued alternatives." *Journal of Experimental Psychology: Human Perception and Performance* 1: 280–87.

Slovic, P., B. Fischhoff, and S. Lichtenstein. 1985. "Regulation of risk." In *Regulatory policy and the social sciences,* ed. Roger Noll. Berkeley, CA: University of California Press.

Smith, V. K. 1988. "Public choice and private risks: The role of economic analysis." Benjamin Hibbard Memorial Lecture Series, University of Wisconsin, October.

———. 1991a. "Arbitrary values, good causes, and premature verdicts: A reaction to Kahneman and Knetsch." *Journal of Environmental Economics and Management.* Forthcoming.

———. 1991b. "Environmental risk perception and valuation: Conventional versus prospective reference theory." April 8. Unpublished manuscript.

Smith, V. K., and W. H. Desvousges. 1986. "Asymmetries in the valuation of risk and the siting of hazardous waste disposal facilities." *American Economic Review* 72 (papers and proceedings) (May): 291–94.

Smith, V. K., W. H. Desvousges, and A. M. Freeman III. 1985. *Valuing changes and hazardous waste risks: A contingent valuation analysis,* vol. 1 (Report to U.S. Environmental Protection Agency under Cooperative Agreement No. CR–811075). Nashville, TN: Vanderbilt University (February).

Tversky, A., and D. Kahneman. 1974. "Judgment under uncertainty: Heuristics and biases." *Science* 185: 1124–31.

———. 1981. "The framing of decisions and the psychology of choice." *Science 211:* 453–58.

Tversky, A., S. Sattath, and P. Slovic. 1988. "Contingent weighting in judgment and choice." *Psychological Review* 95: 371–84.

2

RILEY E. DUNLAP, LOREN A. LUTZENHISER, AND EUGENE A. ROSA

Understanding Environmental Problems: A Sociological Perspective

Introduction

The imperfect correspondence between objectively measured levels of environmental deterioration and societal awareness and concern over such deterioration has frequently been noted. In past decades, for example, environmental pollution sometimes reached severe levels without generating much public concern, while more recently societal attention to problems such as air pollution has varied considerably even when measured levels of pollution changed very little. In pointing to and highlighting this incongruence between physical conditions and societal response, social scientists have provided insights into the socially constructed nature of environmental problems (Albrecht and Mauss 1975; Yearly 1991). Sociologists in particular have emphasized the role of environmental activists and the media in generating societal awareness of the problem of environmental degradation (Mazur and Lee 1993) and the role of competing interests in subsequently providing contrasting explanations of the origins of and prescriptions for the solutions of such problems (Dietz, Stern, and Rycroft 1989).

Studies that compare the perspectives of industrialists and environmentalists (Cotgrove 1982) or of scientists representing industry, government, and environmental organizations (Dietz and Rycroft 1987) provide important insights into the inherent social dimensions of environmental problems. Similarly, theoretical analyses that deconstruct the meaning of environmental problems shed light on the intimate connections between contemporary social life and the physical world (Taylor and Buttel 1992). Such examinations of the nature and roots of differing perspectives on environmental problems, which at a more mundane level may simply involve comparisons of perceptions of and opinions about the environment across major social strata (by class, gender, and cohort, for example), are eminently sociological and can provide important insights and useful information (see, e.g., Van Liere and Dunlap 1980).

There is, however, a tendency among sociologists and other social scientists to assume that since environmental problems are to some degree socially constructed, the task of the social sciences is to focus on the process of construction to the exclusion of the biophysical conditions that prompted the societal attention. Thus, one finds sociological analyses of the 1970s debate over the limits to growth that focused on the roles and motivations of the competing interests in that debate with little interest in the societal implications of such limits (Sandbach 1978). Some social scientists go even further and argue that since the social definition of conditions can differ so much from the objective physical conditions, there is little if any relationship between physical reality and societal perceptions of this reality (Fox 1991). And, finally, others go to the extreme of attributing societal preoccupation with the threat of environmental problems solely to social and cultural conditions, in essence denying the reality of problematic environmental conditions (Douglas and Wildavsky 1882).

Emphasizing the social aspects of environmental problems, and downplaying the physical conditions themselves, are common tendencies within mainstream social science. Because the social sciences developed during an era of enormous resource abundance (due to Europeans' discovery of the New World), tremendous technological advances and, consequently, abnormal material progress, the social sciences have assumed that modern industrial societies are not constrained by physical conditions (Catton 1980). Unlike other species, which are bound by the laws of nature, *Homo sapiens* has been assumed by social scientists to be exempt from nature's constraints because of the species' exceptional characteristics of language, culture, science, and so forth (Catton and Dunlap 1980; Dunlap and Catton 1992–93). This human exemptionalism paradigm, having pervaded modern social science, is apparent in each discipline's tendency to assume that industrialized societies can readily adapt to environmental conditions such as resource limits. Thus, sociologists place faith in social organization (such as the division of labor), anthropologists in culture (including technology), political scientists in the polity, and economists in the operation of the marketplace (plus technological substitution) as mechanisms for ensuring that adequate resources will always be obtained to sustain human societies (Dunlap 1980). The same mechanisms that are seen as ensuring adequate resources are also seen as able to solve problems of pollution, with the result that modern societies are no longer viewed as dependent on their ecosystems.

While its exemptionalist orientation has led mainstream social science largely to ignore environmental problems over the past two decades—or at most to emphasize the socially constructed nature of these problems—a small but growing number of social scientists have adopted an alternative focus. Although not denying the existence of a socially defined element in most environmental problems, or the unique qualities of *Homo sapiens,* specialists in new areas, such as environmental sociology, ecological economics, environmental history, and environmental psychology, have acknowledged the ecosystem-dependence of human societies. Such dependence is made increasingly obvious by the accelerating pace and broadening scale of anthropogenic changes in environmental conditions and the resulting problems posed for societies by these changing conditions (Stern, Young, and Druckman 1992).

The aim of this chapter is to provide an overview of the approach to environmental problems embodied in one of these new fields—environmental sociology. This newly emergent field combines the societal focus of its parent discipline, a focus that complements socioeconomics, with the ecological orientation shared by other environmental/ecological social sciences such as ecological economics. Thus, despite their awareness of differing interests in the definition and interpretation of environmental problems, environmental sociologists tend to go beyond simply identifying the nature of these interests and their social origins. Instead, environmental sociologists are apt to focus on three fundamental issues still largely ignored within mainstream sociology: what are the basic "causes" of changing environmental conditions, how might the problematic changes be halted, and what are the likely social impacts of the changes and their possible solutions. These three issues—the causes of, solutions to, and impacts of environmental problems—are the major foci of this chapter, and we will endeavor to show how an environmental sociology perspective is useful in shedding light on each issue. In the process we will point to parallels between the perspectives of environmental sociology and those of socioeconomics.

The Causes of Environmental Problems

By the early 1970s there was considerable debate over the major causes of environmental problems, primarily pollution of various types—especially air and water—but also resource scarcity. Natural scientists were the central parties in these debates, as social scientists were fairly slow in coming to recognize the reality and societal significance of environmental problems. Perhaps most notable was the vitriolic debate between Barry Commoner, who emphasized the role played by technological developments since World War II, and Paul Ehrlich, who downplayed technology in lieu of overpopulation, as the fundamental cause of environmental problems (see their exchanges reprinted in Marden and Hodgson 1975). A number of other factors were also emphasized by various environmental analysts, ranging from the Judeo-Christian ethic to capitalism to industrialization to excess consumerism (see, e.g., Harvey and Hallet 1977; Wenner 1976). A key role played by environmental sociologists has been to emphasize the oversimplification involved in all of these unicausal arguments, in large part due to the interdependences between these causal factors and the

Figure 2.1. **Ecological Complex**

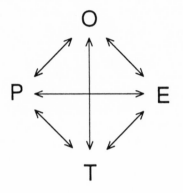

P = Human Population
O = Organization (Social Organization)
E = Environment (all non-human components)
T = Technology

consequent difficulty of isolating their independent linkages to environmental degradation.

A Socioecological Perspective

In examining the debates over the causes of environmental problems, environmental sociologists have often drawn upon a human ecological perspective. This perspective was originally advanced by the subfield of sociological human ecology, but in recent years it has been virtually abandoned by that field in lieu of more mainstream sociological investigations that minimize the importance of the physical environment relative to social conditions as a cause of social phenomena such as migration (Beus 1993; Dunlap and Catton 1983). One sociological human ecologist who early on recognized the societal significance of environmental problems as well as the utility of examining such problems from an ecological perspective was Otis Dudley Duncan.

Duncan's (1964) formulation of the ecological complex as a means of analyzing human societies has proved to offer a fruitful framework to environmental sociology. While recognizing its vast oversimplification, Duncan demonstrated the analytic utility of examining human societies via a model comprising of four interrelated components: human populations (P), their technology (T) and social organization (O), and their physical environment (E) (see Figure 2.1). Because the last component is basically a residual category, encompassing all nonhuman life and nonliving components of the ecosystem, Duncan's ecological complex— or POET model, as it is known—is a very oversimplified and anthropocentric version of what bioecologists mean by *ecosystem*. Nonetheless, not only did it enable Duncan to emphasize that human populations adapt to their physical environments by means of social organization (e.g., division of labor) and technology (tools and techniques employed for extracting and using natural resources), but it also allowed him to suggest that (1) each of three human-based elements, *P*, *T*, and *O*, can directly impact the environment and (2) they may interact in complex ways in producing such impacts. This conceptualization has proven to be a most valuable insight for environmental sociologists (Dunlap and Catton 1979, 1983).[1]

Among environmental sociologists, Schnaiberg (1980) has most explicitly focused on the debates over the causes of environmental problems, particularly the roles played by population and technology (see also Humphrey and Buttel 1982). Schnaiberg's (1980) analysis shows the limitations of emphasizing either population or technology as the crucial causal force in environmental degradation. In terms of population, he points out the enormous variation in environmental impact between residents of the rich and poor nations as well as that across socioeconomic strata within individual nations, both of which make it difficult to compare the impacts of population size and growth per se. More importantly, he emphasizes the degree to which population growth is interrelated with social organization, especially how poverty within poor nations contributes to population growth—for example, it encourages parents to have as many children as possible to work on farms or otherwise contribute to family income and to serve as insurance when the parents are too old to work. Similarly, Schnaiberg criticizes the view of technology as an independent force, stressing the degree to which technological developments are driven by decisions in the political and especially economic realms. Thus, rather than focus on technology as the villain, Schnaiberg stresses the importance of understanding the socioeconomic forces that encourage technological progress, particularly the competitive pressure of capitalism that constantly seeks technological substitution for costly labor inputs in the productive process.

In short, Schnaiberg criticizes the tendency to view either population or technology as autonomous factors affecting the environment, highlighting the degree to which both population growth and technological development are embedded within the larger socioeconomic context. In other words, he suggests that the high degree of interrelation or interaction between the three nonenvironmental components of the ecological complex makes it difficult to isolate the direct impacts of either population or technology on the environment (see Figure 2.2). In addition, Schnaiberg goes on to suggest that social organization may in fact be the most crucial factor affecting the environment, both directly and indirectly via its influence on population growth and technology, and deserves far more attention than it is typically given by bioecologists such as Ehrlich and Commoner.

Figure 2.2. **Causes of Environmental Problems**

Simplistic Model   Realistic Model

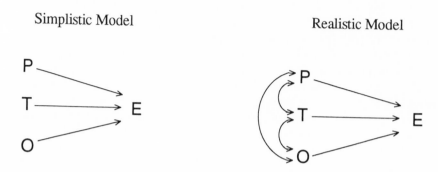

The insights of Schnaiberg, and an environmental sociological perspective more generally, in clarifying the causes of environmental problems can best be appreciated by looking at the Ehrlich-Commoner debate a bit more closely. As the debate evolved and sharpened, both sides gave increasing recognition to the fact that the other's preferred cause could not be ignored and to the social dimensions of environmental problems. Yet their views remained dramatically different and became encapsulated in differing interpretations of a very simple formulation, the IPAT equation. Formulated as Environmental Impact = Population × Affluence × Technology, this heuristic device is logically compatible with the POET model.[2] The equation serves to illustrate that, all other things remaining equal, either an increase in population or an increase in resource consuming/polluting technology would lead to an increase in environmental degradation and a recognition that human lifestyles or levels of affluence likewise have an impact on the environment. The debate, then as now, rests on the relative weights given to these three factors, with Ehrlich and his colleagues stressing population (see, e.g., Ehrlich and Ehrlich 1990) and (Commoner 1990) emphasizing technology.

Some environmental sociologists have sought to clarify the complex interrelations between population, technology, and affluence, especially as they interact to produce an increasing load on ecological carrying capacity (Catton 1980). Others have begun to use the IPAT equation in the study of global warming and rain forest destruction, examining the relative contributions of population, technology, and affluence to these problems (Dietz and Rosa 1991; Rudel 1989). It is the affluence variable that has probably attracted the most attention from sociologists. The degree to which this variable oversimplifies the social organizational component of the ecological complex, and the fact that focusing on per capita affluence ignores huge variations in levels of affluence within most societies, have been emphasized by environmental sociologists (Schnaiberg 1980). Furthermore, although Lacy (1985) concluded that the increase in energy consumption in the United States in the twentieth century seemed attributable more to a rise in affluence than to population growth or technological development, he argued that the increased affluence was more apparent than real—much of it was needed to compensate for a degraded socioeconomic environment or decline in quality of life.

The very term *affluence* seems tilted toward a particular perspective on the role of people, as it calls attention to their lifestyle or consumption behavior. The notion of a materialistic consumer as the primary cause of environmental problems has long been a popular one, at least within the wealthy nations. Thus, the famous Pogo cartoon that proclaimed, "We have met the enemy, and it is us!" became a popular slogan among environmental analysts and served to readily portray individual consumers as the prime villains in the environmental crisis. Schnaiberg (1980), along with other environmental sociologists (e.g., Humphrey and Buttel 1982), takes issue with this perspective. First, he distinguishes between *production* and *consumption*, and then he argues that it is the former aspect of social organization that is the prime factor in creating environmental problems. Schnaiberg accomplished this by clarifying what he terms the treadmill of production, or the inherent need of a capitalist system (and any other system that seeks to compete economically with capitalism) to continually yield a profit—primarily by creating a never-ending demand for its products and by producing the products ever more efficiently and cheaply. In other words, he stresses the creation of consumer demand via advertising and, more generally, socialization into a materialistic culture, and the enormous limitations of the marketplace as a determinant of basic human needs. In short, Schnaiberg argues that it is the affluence (and power) of a very narrow segment of the public, those who control the production process, rather than the lifestyle of the majority that is the crucial causal force in generating environmental deterioration.

Whether or not one agrees with Schnaiberg's neo-Marxist analysis (for a more explicitly Marxist perspective, see O'Connor 1991), which we have admittedly oversimplified in the interest of brevity, it points to the necessity of acknowledging the role of social organization in generating environmental problems as well as the inherent complexity of dealing with this component of the ecological complex (including its relationship to the other two components: population and technology). Simply acknowledging the role of affluence, for example, ignores the fundamental distinction between the production and consumption realms. It also leads to an insensitivity to the existence of vast disparities between the impacts of decisions made by those in charge of the production process and those made by mere consumers, as well as to the differing environmental impacts of the lifestyles of the more and less affluent sectors of society.

Although the distinction between the production and consumption spheres of society is of fundamental importance, an alternative decomposition of social organization yields additional insights. Many sociologists, most notably Talcott Parsons, have distinguished between the psychological, social, and cultural systems as analytically separable realms of human social life and hold that substituting these three realms for social organization within the ecological complex

Figure 2.3. Expanded Model of Major Causes

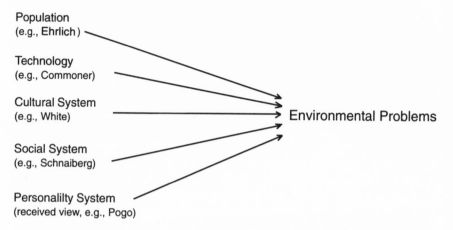

Population
(e.g., Ehrlich)

Technology
(e.g., Commoner)

Cultural System
(e.g., White)   Environmental Problems

Social System
(e.g., Schnaiberg)

Personalilty System
(received view, e.g., Pogo)

provides some additional insights into the origins of environmental problems.[2] As shown in Figure 2.3, we can conceptualize environmental problems as having their origins in any of five distinguishable sources—human population, technology, culture, social systems, and personality systems—or, more realistically, as resulting from interactions between two or more of these factors.

Indeed, to our knowledge, virtually all existing arguments about *the* cause of environmental problems can be classified into one of these five categories (see, e.g., Harvey and Hallet 1977, chap. 4, and Wenner 1976, chap. 6). We have already discussed the debate over the relative importance of population and technology, probably the two most widely debated causes, and mentioned several other hypothesized causes in passing. For example, White's (1967) emphasis on the Judeo-Christian ethic granting humans exalted status over the rest of nature and contributing to the absolute separation of humans from nature, is widely cited (albeit also often criticized—see, e.g., Moncrief 1970). Similarly, commentary on the materialistic character of modern industrialized societies points to the cultural realm into which individuals are socialized. Conversely, other analysts—epitomized by Pogo—focus their attention on individual consumers, stressing the acquisitive pursuit of wants as opposed to needs as a manifestation of personality flaws (Harvey and Hallet 1977).

Finally, the concept of social system is remarkably flexible, encompassing various scales of organization and differing realms of society. For example, Schnaiberg's (1980) and O'Connor's (1991) emphasis on capitalism clearly stresses the role of the economic system or sector of the social system, while others pointed long ago to the fact that other types of economic systems have led to even worse environmental problems (Goldman 1973). This, in turn, has led some to place the onus of environmental deterioration on economic growth, industrialization, or industrial society in general (Harvey and Hallet 1977).

Political scientists, in turn, often point to the inadequate nature of the polity, or political system, in coping with environmental problems (Ophuls 1977), while economists frequently note the importance of common property resources, the limitations of the free market, and so forth (Wenner 1976).

In short, as a classificatory scheme the expanded model of the ecological complex would seem to encompass virtually all arguments about the primary factor(s) responsible for environmental degradation, and such classification can itself be useful in clarifying and distinguishing between arguments. However, of greater significance is the facts that we must keep in mind that these five factors are only analytically separable and that in reality all five are highly interrelated. The linkage between culture and personality is perhaps most obvious, but we have already discussed the linkages between the economy and both population and technology—and clearly the latter two are themselves interrelated, as witness the impacts of birth control technologies on population growth. Similarly, one critique of White's (1967) thesis has been that Western religions have produced a culture amenable to the development of modern science, which in turn has had a major impact on the environment via technology (Moncrief 1970). And, of course, a founding father of sociology, Max Weber, is famous for attributing the rise of capitalism to fundamental aspects of Protestant Christianity.

Thus, we see that by using an ecological perspective, environmental sociology can shed light on the vast number of inevitably partial and often conflicting analyses of the primary sources of contemporary environmental problems. Although showing that the situation is typically more complex than first imagined is not always a welcome contribution, it is nonetheless important. For example, those who would derive simplistic policy prescriptions from the various arguments, whether enforced population control, shifts to appropriate technology, or higher taxes on consumer products, need to ground their prescriptions in a fuller understanding of the complex roots of environmental problems.

Fortunately, however, an environmental sociological perspective on the causes of environmental problems can yield insights over and above pointing to the inherent complexity of such causes and the simplicity involved in singling out population or technology. Not surprisingly, the utility of a sociological approach can perhaps best be illustrated by a careful examination of aspects of social organization. In particular, we shall focus on the economy and compare a sociological approach with the common emphasis on affluence or, more specifically, consumer behavior in the marketplace—the focus of standard economic approaches to environmental problems. Not surprisingly, three phenomena that are seen as central to socioeconomics are also central to sociological perspectives on environmental problems: power, context, and values (Etzioni 1991).

A Socioeconomic Perspective

In criticizing the mainstream (neoclassical) economic image of human beings as rational, maximizing *individuals'* freely making decisions in the marketplace,

Etzioni (1991; also see 1988) emphasizes the neglect of power, social context, and social values by economists. In the process of developing an alternative, socioeconomic perspective on human society, Etzioni offers crucial insights that are helpful in clarifying the vague concepts of social organization and in pointing to the shortcomings of identifying affluence as the prime culprit in environmental deterioration.

Like Schnaiberg, Etzioni (1991) stresses the power differentials between producers and consumers in modern societies, emphasizing that the former have considerable say over what gets consumed as well as what is produced in industrialized societies. In the United States, for example, the general public was never invited to take part in a referendum on whether many urban areas would be designed primarily for private automobile use and would thus have inadequate public transportation available. Likewise, despite economists' emphasis on consumer choice in the marketplace, it seems likely that Detroit's desire to build large, profitable cars has at least as much impact on the widespread use of energy-inefficient autos in the United States as does pure consumer preference. Similarly, it is very difficult for individual consumers to make food purchases that will change agribusiness's heavy use of chemicals in modern food production. These and numerous other areas suggest that both economists and many environmental analysts treat in an overly simplistic fashion the lifestyles of affluent consumers and the choices that stem from this affluence.

In societies dominated by large, multinational corporations that are free to engage in oligopolistic practices, it seems unwise to single out the sovereign consumer as a key source of environmental problems. When one considers the ability of large producers to set prices, profits, and choices, one begins to see the *power* of corporate producers in influencing the kinds of choices that consumers make in the marketplace. Thus, simply blaming consumers for our current environmental problems is a gross distortion, from the perspective of both environmental sociology and socioeconomics.

In addition to ignoring the role of power, modern economists and many environmental analysts also ignore the importance of the social context in which the economic system operates. As Etzioni (1988) puts it, the market is embedded in a broader socioeconomic system, and this context can exert a powerful impact on both individual preferences and purchases. Economists, environmental analysts, and policymakers often ignore the degree to which our sociocultural system shapes consumer behavior, and thereby the environmental impacts of modern lifestyles. Not only has the corporate world considerable power to create wants (as opposed to mere needs—see Etzioni 1988) and preferences via an immensely influential advertising industry, but this power is abetted by the widespread socialization of youth into a system that emphasizes the importance of possessions as determinants of status and satisfaction. In other words, the culture of industrialized nations equates material goods with happiness (Ekins 1986). To argue, therefore, that pollution exists because consumers want various goods whose production inevitably results in pollution ignores the existence of a preexisting cultural system that exerts a profound impact on the supposedly free, marketplace choices of citizens.

Finally, Etzioni (1988) points to economics' inadequate treatment of the role of values in human behavior. Indeed, economists prefer to ignore values altogether, using the concept of revealed preference (preferences presumably revealed by purchases in the marketplace) as an indicator of consumer values. Yet we have just seen that production interests can influence and constrain the choices that consumers make—thus distorting considerably our ability to infer values from those choices—and that consumers' values themselves can be influenced tremendously by the productive sector's influence on modern culture. Consumer behavior is a result of many sociocultural processes that are interpersonal as well as intrapersonal, and to assume that it is a direct reflection on the individual's personal values is very naive (Etzioni, 1988).

In short, a socioeconomic perspective on environmental issues nicely complements an environmental sociology perspective by clarifying some of the inherent complexity of the social-organizational component of the ecological complex. Use of concepts such as power, social context, and values clarifies the shortcomings of attributing environmental problems to the free choices of affluent consumers (as economists are prone to do). As social scientists we need to emphasize the constraints operating on the marketplace and caution against using individual purchasing decisions as valid indicators of consumers' lack of concern about the quality of the environment. Indeed, one interpretation of the presumed anomaly between polls in the industrialized nations that find large majorities placing a high value on environmental quality but not engaging in strong proenvironment behaviors is that it is often difficult for citizens to translate their concern for the environment into everyday behaviors—due to lack of choices, inadequate information, poor incentives, the costs (in conveniences as well as money) of "doing the right thing," the belief that individual action is not efficacious, and so forth (Dunlap 1991). In other words, were it not for powerful interests that prevent the development of stronger proenvironment policies and limit the availability of affordable, environmentally sound choices, many citizens might do a much more effective job of translating their personal values into actual behaviors.

To sum up our discussion thus far, environmental sociology and socioeconomics are useful in elucidating the complex nature of the causes of environmental problems. Natural scientists have traditionally emphasized the importance of population and/or technology in generating environmental degradation and have generally failed to acknowledge fully the complex linkages between these two as well as between these and other aspects of society. When social factors are taken into account, there is a tendency to focus on affluence, or lifestyle, and thereby at least implicitly to emphasize the actions of individual consumers, rather than acknowledge such fundamental issues as the relative power of producers and consumers in determining the choices that cumulatively constitute lifestyle.

Recognizing the impacts of culture and personal values and how both are shaped by the larger socioeconomic context, as well as the interrelations between all of these factors and population and technology, makes it difficult to point to *the* cause of environmental problems. However, building solutions on the bases of simplistic diagnoses of causality may only worsen the problem. Our analysis suggests that in the absence of better information, efforts to reduce the impact of human societies on the environment ought to take into account as many levers of probable causality as possible. Thus, slowing population growth, shifting toward renewable and environmentally benign technologies, developing regulations and incentives to promote environmentally sound behaviors at both the corporate and individual levels, and instilling an environmental consciousness and ethic in citizens via education would all be worthwhile activities. Of course, the relative emphasis given to each might be varied across societies and within sectors of individual societies. For example, among poor nations experiencing rapid population growth, emphasizing the dissemination of birth control might be given high priority, while among wealthy nations, greater emphasis might be placed on strategies designed to change industrial and consumer behaviors. A crucial role for social scientists is to call attention to the variations in the relative impact of differing causal forces in environmental degradation in various situations.

Solutions to Environmental Problems

As the seriousness of environmental problems becomes ever more apparent, increasing attention is being paid to possible solutions. Since the mid-nineteenth century, the industrial societies (and to a considerable extent, their colonies and trading partners) have been transformed substantially by technology. In the West, particularly in the United States, the changes wrought by mechanization, mass production (and mass consumption), electrification, and the new science-driven chemical and communications technologies represented a widely celebrated form of social progress (Hughes 1989). Although the wisdom of transforming societies into complex technological systems has periodically been questioned both by segments of the public (e.g., the Luddites) and by scholars (e.g., Ellul 1990), Western sentiments have generally supported the technologists. It comes as no surprise, then, that once the negative environmental consequences of technological progress came to be recognized, only a limited number of choices have been seriously considered as solutions—and they all involve technology. These include (1) the technological fix, or using more technology to solve pollution problems or to find new energy sources; (2) appropriate technology, changing the scale of technical systems and designing technologies to fit preexisting cultural patterns; and (3) what we might call technological simplification, which was embodied in communal and more individual back-to-the-land movements in the early 1970s.[4] Only the first prospered in the 1970s and

1980s. Indeed, relying on newer technological systems to fix the problems created by older ones is the backbone of industrialized societies' current efforts to solve environmental problems.

At present, the search for technological solutions involves new energy technologies (primarily nuclear), effective use of computer and information technologies, and various forms of bioengineering (e.g., creating toxin-consuming microbes). These technological fixes are attractive for several reasons. They fit nicely with the widespread belief in progress embedded in Western culture; they are widely supported by government, scientific, and corporate institutions and interests; and they appear to obviate the need for inducing changes in human behavior and social life—changes that are widely believed to be difficult to achieve and often go against the grain in societies that emphasize personal (and corporate) freedom from government intervention (Heberlein 1974).

In recent decades it has become increasingly clear, however, that technological fixes often fail to accomplish their ends, either because the ends were not clear at the outset or because the fixes were confounded by environmental and social dynamics that were not originally taken into account (such as widespread public opposition, as in the cases of nuclear power and, to a lesser degree, bioengineering). New technologies also frequently create new, unintended problems that may become more serious than those they were designed to solve. For these reasons, increasing attention is being paid to the possibilities of changing both human behavior and various aspects of social organization—for example, through interventions ranging from environmental regulations on industry, to educational efforts aimed at promoting recycling and conservation among consumers, to environmental agreements between nations. Although policy makers are not known for soliciting the expertise of social scientists before formulating such policies, a good deal of attention has been paid by social scientists to issues surrounding environmental policy formulation and implementation.

Political scientists and economists seem most interested and involved in environmental policy issues, the latter concerned that policies be economically sound and the former with analyzing the process by which policies are developed and implemented. Nonetheless, environmental sociologists and social psychologists have conducted a fair amount of applied research aimed at shedding light on environmental policy and have attempted to apply basic knowledge from the social and behavioral sciences to environmental policy problems. In particular, sociologists have examined the theoretical and empirical bases for various broad strategies aimed at promoting environmental protection (e.g., Heberlein 1974; Nelson and Honnold 1976). Central to this effort is the recognition that at least three nontechnological social fixes seem to be implicit in most policy debates and initiatives (Dunlap 1983; Olsen 1978).

A particularly popular intervention strategy in industrialized nations is the cognitive fix, or knowledge fix (Dunlap 1983; Heberlein 1974; Olsen 1978). This approach assumes that information and persuasion will suffice to convince individuals of the dangers of environmental pollution and the necessity of acting in environmentally responsible ways. It is well regarded by policy makers because it is voluntaristic—amounting to "educating the public"—and because it fits with an image of consumers as the crucial source (and therefore the logical solution) of environmental problems. It is also consonant with the rational consumer model which conceives of behavior as driven by individual choice rather than social and cultural processes. In the United States the old "don't be fuelish" publicity campaigns to save gasoline epitomized this approach. The empirical evidence suggests, however, that this kind of appeal seldom works very effectively.

The cognitive strategy rests on three assumptions about individual behavior: first, that attitudes and cognitions are tightly linked to behaviors; second, that attitudes and cognitions can be changed; and third, that such cognitive change will lead to behavioral change. With regard to the first, there is considerable evidence that attitudes and beliefs are only modestly correlated with behavior (Heberlein 1974). Among the reasons for this modest linkage between attitudes and behavior are some of the social-organizational factors discussed earlier, such as the lack of adequate public transportation for people who might see the importance of cutting down on driving, or the additional expense of "green" products that prevent environmentally aware (but financially limited) persons from purchasing them. Second, there is little evidence that large-scale efforts to change societal attitudes outside small, laboratory settings can be effectively designed. And third, even if attitude change could be induced on a wide-scale basis, the tenuous link between attitudes and behaviors suggests that we cannot therefore assume that changing the former will lead to changes in the latter.

The findings of public opinion research over the past two decades consistently show high levels of support for environmental protection within industrialized nations. But consumers are also sensitive to the social contexts within which their consumption and environmental choices occur. Polling data suggest, for example, that persons who might otherwise be willing to change their consumption behavior in order to protect the environment may not do so because they believe that industry is primarily responsible for the problems, that government (rather than consumers) should act to solve these problems, or that individual behaviors won't make much difference. In fact, significant portions of the public say that they will change behaviors only when laws are passed that ensure that all individuals comply (e.g., Dunlap 1991).

At the opposite end of the continuum of fixes is the structural strategy, which rejects voluntarism in favor of pressure (some would say "coercion")—that is, laws and regulations designed to induce the desired change (Heberlein 1974; Dunlap 1983; Olsen 1978). These laws may be directed at individuals (such as speed limits designed to promote energy conservation) or at organizations (such as requirements that car manufacturers achieve fuel efficiency goals). While regulations aimed at organizations probably engender less resistance among the public, they are often more difficult to implement because of the political power of those who would be subjected to them—for example, the automobile and electric power industries. Thus, in Western nations, relying on structural strategies to promote environmental protection has proven to be a difficult path to follow.

However, when politically feasible, the structural approach can be effective—witness the effects of simply banning nonreturnable containers for soft drinks. Furthermore, there is some evidence that changes in behavior induced by regulations can, under some circumstances, lead to cognitive changes (Heberlein 1974). In the United States, for example, as pressure to design more fuel-efficient automobiles has increased and consumers have bought smaller cars, there seems to have been a move toward greater social acceptability of smaller cars and even something of a stigmatization of larger, luxury models. Furthermore, because some individual (and corporate) actors are often hesitant to engage in environmentally responsible behavior unless it is mandated—individuals because they want to make sure their actions won't be wasted, and corporations because they don't want to be put at a competitive disadvantage—there may be more support for regulatory programs than many politicians assume to be the case.

The third, and possibly most feasible approach in many societies is the behavioral fix (Olsen 1978; Dunlap 1983). It uses positive or negative reinforcers or both (what political economists call selective incentives) to promote environmentally responsible behavior. Individuals, corporations, and other entities are rewarded for good behavior and penalized for bad behavior. At the corporate level, both pollution taxes (penalties) and tax credits (rewards) for installing pollution abatement technologies have been widely used. At the individual level, this strategy is reflected in taxes that encourage recycling of bottles and in economic incentives for other forms of recycling. Theoretically, it could be applied even more rigorously. For example, the once-common declining-block rate-system for electricity pricing (in which higher levels of consumption were rewarded with lower unit prices) has now been displaced in many localities by inclining-block-rate schemes (in which larger quantities are more costly per unit of energy consumed). This approach could be extended into other areas where high consumption levels and particular technologies have demonstrable environmental impacts (e.g., higher taxes on less-efficient cars or special taxes on air-conditioned cars).

On an ideological level, the behavioral fix has considerable appeal in free-market economies because it preserves individual choice and avoids coercion. Perhaps for this reason, it also seems highly recommended by mainstream economists and favored by many politicians. In general, the behavioral approach does seem to offer considerable hope for altering environmentally harmful behaviors at both the individual and corporate levels. It may meet less resistance by consumers, who, when given the opportunity to behave in economically rational ways that are also environmentally beneficial, will gladly choose to do so (such as recycling beverage containers for which they have paid deposits).

Experience with energy conservation programs suggests, however, that consumers may respond erratically (or not at all) to price signals, such as the proposed carbon tax as a means of discouraging fossil fuel consumption that contributes to the greenhouse effect. The magnitude of the signal necessary to induce desired change may depend on a host of factors that are beyond the present abilities of economists and environmental policy analysts to evaluate—for example, the availability and knowledge of alternative technologies and behaviors, the relative cost of consumption, and the meaning of cost increases to consumers at different price levels (Lutzenhiser 1993). Consumers, and firms for that matter, often display unreasonably high discount rates for energy- and resource-conserving investments (e.g., requiring new technologies to pay for themselves with savings in less than a year, although their ultimate savings make these investments better than any blue chip alternative available in the financial market). On the other hand, small price increases, if they are above some symbolically important level, will sometimes precipitate dramatic consumption declines—as in the case of electric utilities' raising the specter of a death spiral, wherein declines in consumption in response to price increases require additional price increases to cover fixed costs.

The dramatic increases in the efficiency of energy use in the United States—which is still only half as efficient as in Japan and the European nations—in the 1970s and early 1980s have yet to be accounted for and cannot be attributed solely to higher prices. In addition to price increases, patriotic appeals for conservation, stringent building codes, environmental consciousness, increased foreign automobile imports, and a host of other factors undoubtedly contributed to increased conservation, but the effects of these influences, and of their interactions, have yet to be sorted out (Lutzenhiser 1993). Furthermore, we know that changes in one part of society can spur changes elsewhere. For example, the threat of stringent appliance-efficiency standards in California could lead to a collaboration between environmental advocates and appliance manufacturers to persuade an otherwise uninterested federal government to adopt uniform nationwide efficiency standards as the lesser of two evils (the worse being the prospect of fifty different state standards) from the manufacturers' standpoint.

The behavioral fix also has some very significant built-in biases. Significant distributional consequences arise, for example, from interventions that levy taxes on consumers (or on producers who pass them on to consumers), as well as from efforts to provide incentives to behave in environmentally beneficial ways. Not only are the costs and benefits of market-based interventions often inequitably distributed, but the strategy ignores the vast differences in ability to pay and invest (among both individuals and firms) present in most societies. It is for this reason that environmental policies have often been criticized as regressive, harming the poor and the working class more than others (Morrison and Dunlap 1986). For example, increasing the tax on oil will clearly hurt a lower-class family, especially one renting a poorly built, uninsulated house, more than an upper-class family—in terms of both the percentage of budget devoted to home heating and the fact that the upper-class family is much more likely to be able to invest in home insulation and other efficiency improvements (Dillman, Rosa, and Dillman 1983). Also, families with higher incomes are the most likely to occupy newer homes built under energy efficiency codes and are also the most likely to purchase newer, more efficient appliances (Lutzenhiser and Hackett 1993). The irony here is that those consumer groups who are the best able to respond to price signals, and to take advantage of tax incentives, are precisely those whose income elasticities of demand are the lowest.

Making effective use of the behavioral approach requires government action, political support, and the cooperation of producers and consumers. This suggests the importance of using all three strategies in various combinations. In other words, a cognitive approach may work to some degree to engender public support for governmental regulations to protect the environment, while in some areas a structural approach may be seen as more effective and equitable and therefore receive more support. (For example, there is evidence that the public is more supportive of speed limits than higher fuel taxes to reduce gasoline consumption and carbon gas pollution.) A crucial goal of social scientists, therefore, ought to be to establish the most effective mix of the three approaches. A socioeconomic perspective—with its sensitivity to the multifaceted nature of the causal forces motivating both individual and corporate action—provides an excellent framework for examining this mix.

While we have focused on broad policy approaches that can be used in efforts to solve environmental problems in general, our environmental sociology perspective suggests that it will be important to disaggregate the causes before formulating specific solutions. For example, an approach that might be useful in promoting a decline in population growth might be less useful in altering consumer behavior or in modifying industrial technology. In general, it appears that in many nations there would be opposition to a structural solution to population problems, although the Chinese used it effectively (Lamott 1977). However, it has often been suggested that behavioral approaches such as changing pronatalist tax policies might be effective, and it seems likely that the "two is enough" education campaign (and eventual shift in social norms) has had some effect within the industrialized countries. Conversely, it appears unlikely that a cognitive approach will suffice for inducing corporations to shift to more environmentally benign technologies and likely that a behavioral and possibly structural strategy will be necessary. Clearly, considerable effort should be given to identifying the critical causal elements underlying a particular problem before strategies are designed for ameliorating the problem. The previous section's discussion of the complex causal roots of many environmental problems suggests that this will be no easy task.

Figure 2.4. **Impacts of Environmental Problems**

Simplistic Model   Realistic Model

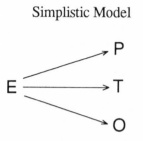   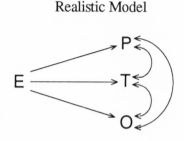

The Impacts of Environmental Problems

We have saved the topic of impacts for last, in part because social scientists have devoted as much attention to the impacts of the policies designed to solve environmental problems as they have to the impacts of the problems themselves. In fact, there has probably been more attention to policy impacts, perhaps because examining the impacts of specific policies seems to be a more manageable task than that of discerning the impacts of environmental problems per se. Some idea of the complexity involved in the latter is illustrated in Figure 2.4, which basically reverses the causal order of Figure 2.2. As was the case for examining the causes of environmental problems, there is a tendency to adopt a simplistic model of the impacts. However, as shown in the realistic model of impacts, environmental problems (typically, environmental changes induced by humans) often not only affect all of the other components of the ecological complex—human populations, technologies, and social organization—but the effects between the latter are interrelated (especially as higher-order effects). Thus, determining the specific impacts of particular environmental problems is likely to be a difficult task to accomplish.

Even in the cases of small-scale and geographically bounded problems, such as the toxic contamination of communities such as Love Canal in New York, the personal and social repercussions have been found to be very complex and far-reaching. Not only was the psychological and physical well-being of some individuals affected, but family and community integration were as well (Levine 1982). And, of course, eventually the impacted population itself was moved from the locale. Likewise, the considerable amount of social science research on the energy crisis of the 1970s, along with a good deal of speculation, has led to detailed forecasts of the complex social impacts of resource scarcity in general (Finsterbusch 1981). Not surprisingly, then, recent awareness of human-induced global environmental change has led to calls for social scientists to mount the unprecedented research efforts that will be necessary to understand the far-reaching impacts of global warming, ozone depletion, and related changes (Stern, Young, and Druckman 1992).

Rather than add to speculations about the widespread social impacts that global environmental problems portend, or try to review the sizable amount of research on the impacts of specific environmental policies, we will focus instead on a topic of critical importance to environmental sociology and social science more generally—the distributional impacts of environmental problems and policies. The fact that the effects of both environmental problems and the policies developed to solve them are typically felt unequally across differing social strata has been the subject of considerable attention. What follows are some of the more central findings.

Despite the fact that the poor typically contribute less to environmental problems due to their lower consumption levels, they often bear the brunt of these problems because they live in the worst conditions due to the operation of a housing market that puts a premium on attractive locales (Bullard 1990). Ironically, however, since the policies designed to deal with the problems often involve higher taxes or prices (such as requiring the installation of air pollution devices in automobiles and charging higher prices for heating oil), the solutions are often regressive as well. In other words, relying on either the market or taxes, both classic examples of the behavioral fix, often creates unfair burdens on those segments of society that contribute least to negative environmental impacts because of their limited levels of affluence (Morrison and Dunlap 1986).

A similar pattern is clearly developing at the international level. The poorer nations, which have suffered and continue to suffer from having their resources exported at low prices to richer nations, are increasingly becoming the favored sites not only for heavily polluting industries but for waste dumps as well (Redclift 1984). At the same time, they are being asked to help shoulder the burden of halting the global environmental problems (problems that have been created primarily by the rich, highly industrialized nations) and will undoubtedly share in the negative impacts of these problems.

To complicate the matter further, these issues of intra- and international equity are being compounded by questions of intergenerational equity as well. The potential calamities that major climatic change or ozone destruction might deliver upon future generations make the standard economic practice of discounting the future particularly inappropriate—from both an ethical and a policy perspective. Yet, taking the interests of future generations into account makes the design of equitable solutions to environmental problems even more difficult. All of these equity problems are highly interrelated and again illustrate the enormous complexity of clarifying the social-organizational component of both the causes and the impacts of environmental problems. Yet it is essential to keep in mind that the environment does not simply impact society at large but that these impacts are inevitably mediated by the existing social-organizational system and are likely to be distributed in a nonrandom fashion across differing strata of society (Schnaiberg 1980).

Summary and Conclusion

We have attempted to show the utility of viewing environmental problems from the perspective of environmental sociology. This relatively new area of study basically combines the insights into social phenomena developed by its parent discipline with the insights into ecological phenomena developed by contemporary human ecology, or "bioecology" (see, e.g., Ehrlich and Ehrlich 1990; Commoner 1990; Catton 1980). In particular, it attempts to clarify the critical role played by technology and especially social organization in mediating the relationship between human populations and their environments. Consequently, to some degree, environmental sociology inevitably shows the limitations of arguments concerning the primary cause of environmental problems, particularly those that single out population or technology (and thus the limitations of policies based on these overly simplistic diagnoses). In the process of emphasizing the complex nature of the human causes—and potential consequences—of environmental problems, environmental sociology implicitly points to the limitations of treating humans as simply another species population (Schnaiberg 1980; Buttel 1987).

Yet, it must be emphasized that environmental sociology also rejects mainstream sociology's implicit assumption that the special features of our species (especially organization and technology) exempt us from ecological constraints (Catton and Dunlap 1980; Dunlap and Catton 1992–93). In fact, environmental sociologists argue that the dynamics of industrialized societies (to say nothing of the world as a whole) can no longer be understood without paying careful attention to the inherent, and increasingly problematic, dependence of human societies upon their physical environment. Thus, not only do environmental sociologists criticize the parent discipline's ignorance of the growing societal significance of environmental problems, but they also caution that mainstream sociology may become increasingly irrelevant in an age of growing ecological constraints on human beings (Catton and Dunlap 1980).

Because of its combination of sociological and ecological perspectives, environmental sociology has sometimes been termed the new human ecology (Buttel 1987), but it might equally be called ecological sociology (as recently suggested by Dunlap and Catton 1992–93). Indeed, in many respects the field seems quite analogous to ecological economics, seeking to blend its parent discipline's knowledge of social phenomena with the rapidly emerging knowledge of the changing nature of the human impact on the environment (from local to global ecosystems), just as ecological economics seeks to integrate insights about economic phenomena with ecological realities (Costanza 1989).

Of course, environmental sociology and ecological economics also overlap in their concern with *both* social and economic phenomena, a convergence that clearly comes under the rubric of socioeconomics. However, while the new field of socioeconomics seeks to integrate knowledge from economics and sociology (and the behavioral sciences in general) for a more adequate understanding of human behavior and societies (Etzioni 1988), this integration is not sufficient in an age of ecological constraints. Just as environmental sociologists and ecological economists have had to free themselves from the disciplinary blinders that continue to lead most of their colleagues to ignore the ecological constraints facing modern human societies, so it is important for socioeconomists to ground their new field on a firm ecological base. What is needed for examining contemporary human life is a socioecological economics, or simply an ecological socioeconomics. Fortunately, ecologically grounded socioeconomics is already visible within The Other Economic Summit, or TOES (Ekins 1986), and the Society for a Human Economy, or SHE.[5] Integrating this work with that of the Society for the Advancement of Socio-Economics offers great promise for developing an understanding of the current status and probable future of *Homo sapiens.*

Notes

1. Although sociological human ecologists have widely employed the ecological complex, and while some have emphasized the key roles of organization and technology in human adaptation to the environment, most sociological human ecologists have ignored Duncan's (1964) insights into the origins of environmental problems. First, sociological human ecology has followed the larger discipline in emphasizing the importance of the social as opposed to the physical environment, thus leading them to ignore physical conditions such as pollution. Second, and relatedly, they have followed the larger discipline in endorsing the human exemptionalism paradigm. The result is a tendency to assume that human adaptation to the environment is nonproblematic because advances in technology and/or social organization will always enable a growing population to obtain adequate sustenance from the environment. In other words, most sociological human ecologists assume that P and E will always reach equilibrium due to the mediating roles of T and O, both of which are under human control (see Beus 1993; Dunlap and Catton 1979, 1983).

2. The "impact" in the former refers to humans' impact on the environment (E in the latter), while P and T refer to the same variables in both, and affluence (A in the equation) is a specific aspect of social organization (O in the POET model).

3. One could further divide social systems into the crucial institutional realms of economy, polity, religion, education, family, and so forth.

4. One might also see risk assessment and environmental impact assessment as types of technological response to environmental problems. However, technically they are both methods of assessing the risks posed by the problems, rather than means of solving such problems.

5. SHE publishes the *Human Economy Newsletter,* while TOES publishes *TOES/Americas.*

References

Albrecht, S. L., and A. L. Mauss. 1975. "The environment as a social problem." In A. L. Mauss, ed., *Social problems as social movements.* Philadelphia: J. B. Lippincott.
Beus, C. 1993. "Sociology, human ecology and ecology." In L. Fresse, ed., *Advances in human ecology,* vol. 2, 93–132. Greenwich, CT: JAI Press.

Bullard, R. D. 1990. *Dumping in Dixie: Race, class, and environmental quality.* Boulder, CO: Westview.

Buttel, F. H. 1987. "New directions in environmental sociology." *Annual Review of Sociology* 13: 465–88.

Catton, W. R., Jr. 1980. *Overshoot: The ecological basis of revolutionary change.* Urbana, IL: University of Illinois Press.

Catton, W. R., Jr., and R. E. Dunlap. 1980. "A new ecological paradigm for post-exuberant sociology." *American Behavioral Scientist* 24: 15–47.

Commoner, B. 1990. *Making peace with the planet.* New York: Pantheon.

Costanza, R. 1989. "What is ecological economics?" *Ecological Economics* 1: 1–7.

Cotgrove, S. 1982. *Catastrophe or cornucopia.* New York: John Wiley & Sons.

Dietz, T. M., and R. W. Rycroft. 1987. *The risk professionals.* New York: Russell Sage.

Dietz, T. M., P. Stern, and R. W. Rycroft. 1989. "Definitions of conflict and the legitimation of resources: The case of environmental risk." *Sociological Forum* 4: 47–70.

Dietz, T. M., and E. A. Rosa. 1991. "Global environmental impacts of economic and population growth: The case of CO_2 emissions." Paper presented at the annual meeting of the Society for Risk Assessment, Baltimore, Maryland.

Dillman, D. A., E. A. Rosa, and J. Dillman. 1983. "Lifestyle and home energy conservation in the United States: The poor accept lifestyle cutbacks while the wealthy invest in conservation." *Journal of Economic Psychology* 3: 299–313.

Douglas, M., and A. Wildavsky. 1982. *Risk and culture: An essay on the selection of technical and environmental dangers.* Berkeley, CA: University of California Press.

Duncan, O. D. 1964. "From social system to ecosystem." *Sociological Inquiry* 31: 140–49.

Dunlap, R. E. 1980. "Paradigmatic change in social science: From human exemptionalism to an ecological paradigm." *American Behavioral Scientist* 24: 5–14.

———. 1983. "Promoting collective action for human survival." In *Environment and population: Problems of adaptation,* ed. J. C. Calhoun (pp. 58–60). New York: Praeger.

———. 1991. "Public opinion in the 1980s: Clear consensus, ambiguous commitment." *Environment* 33 (October): 10–15, 32–37.

Dunlap, R. E., and W. R. Catton, Jr. 1979. "Environmental sociology." *Annual Review of Sociology* 5: 243–73.

———. 1983. "What environmental sociologists have in common (whether concerned with 'built' or 'natural' environments)." *Sociological Inquiry* 53: 113–35.

Dunlap, R. E., and W. R. Catton. 1992–93. "Toward an ecological sociology." *Annals of the International Institute of Sociology* 3: 263–84.

Ehrlich, P. R., and A. H. Ehrlich. 1990. *The population explosion.* New York: Touchstone.

Ekins, P. ed. 1986. *The living economy: A new economics in the making.* London and New York: Routledge & Kegan Paul.

Ellul, J. 1990. *The technological bluff.* G.W. Bromiley, trans. Grand Rapids, MI: W. B. Erdmans.

Etzioni, A. 1988. *The moral dimension: Toward a new economics.* New York: Free Press.

———. 1991. "Socio-economics revisited." *Sociological Inquiry* 64: 68–73.

Finsterbusch, K. 1981. "Consequences of increasing scarcity on affluent countries." *Technological Forecasting and Social Change* 23: 59–73.

Fox, N. 1991. "Green sociology." *Network* (newsletter of the British Sociological Association) 50 (May): 24–25.

Goldman, M. I. 1973. "Growth and environmental problems of noncapitalist nations." *Challenge* (July–August): 45–51.

Harvey, B., and J. D. Hallet. 1977. *Environment and society: An introductory analysis.* Cambridge, MA: MIT Press.

Heberlein, T. 1974. "The three fixes: Technological, cognitive and structural." In *Water and community development: Social and economic perspectives,* ed. D. R. Field, J. C. Barron, and B. F. Long. Ann Arbor: MI: Ann Arbor Science Publishers.

Hughes, T. P. 1989. *American genesis: A century of invention and technological enthusiasm.* New York: Viking Penguin.

Humphrey, C. R., and F. H. Buttel. 1982. *Environment, energy and society.* Belmont, CA: Wadsworth.

Lacy, M. G. 1985. "Apparent and genuine affluence: Their relation to energy consumption." *Sociological Perspectives* 28: 117–43.

Lamott, K. 1977. "The Mao solution." *Human Behavior* 6: 17–21.

Levine, A. G. 1982. *Love Canal: Science, politics and people.* Lexington, MA: Lexington Books.

Lutzenhiser, L. 1993. "Social and behavioral aspects of energy use." *Annual Review of Energy and the Environment* 18: 247–89.

Lutzenhiser, L., and B. Hackett. 1993. "Social stratification and environmental degradation: Understanding household CO_2 production." *Social Problems* 40: 50–73.

Marden, P. G., and D. Hodgson, eds. 1975. *Population, environment, and the quality of life.* New York: Halsted.

Mazur, A., and J. Lee. 1993. "Sounding the global alarm: Environmental issues in the U.S. national news." *Social Studies of Science* 23: 681–720.

Moncrief, L. W. 1970. "The cultural basis for our environmental crisis." *Science* 170 (October 30): 508–12.

Morrison, D. E., and R. E. Dunlap. 1986. "Environmentalism and elitism: A conceptual and empirical analysis." *Environmental Management* 10: 581–89.

Nelson, L. D., and J. A. Honnold. 1976. "Planning for resource scarcity: A critique of prevalent proposals." *Social Science Quarterly* 57: 339–49.

O'Connor, J. 1991. *Conference papers: Capitalism, nature, socialism.* Santa Cruz, CA: Center for Ecological Socialism.

Olsen, M. E. 1978. "Public acceptance of energy conservation." In *Energy Policy in the United States,* ed. S. Warkov (pp. 91–106). New York: Praeger.

Ophuls, W. 1977. *Ecology and the politics of scarcity.* San Francisco: W. H. Freeman.

Redclift, M. 1984. *Development and the environmental crisis.* New York: Methuen.

Sandbach, F. 1978. "The rise and fall of the *Limits to Growth* debate." *Social Studies of Science* 8: 495–520.

Schnaiberg, A. 1980. *The environment: From surplus to scarcity.* New York: Oxford University Press.

Stern, P., O. Young, and D. Druckman, eds. 1992. *Global environment change: Understanding the human dimension.* Washington, DC: National Academy Press.

Taylor, P. J., and F. H. Buttel. 1992. "How do we know we have global environmental problems?" *Geoforum* 23: 405–16.

Van Liere, K., and R. E. Dunlap. 1980. "The social bases of environmental concern: A review of hypotheses, explanations, and empirical evidence." *Public Opinion Quarterly* 44: 181–97.

Wenner, L. M. 1976. *One environment under law: A public-policy dilemma.* Pacific Palisades, CA: Goodyear.

White, L., Jr. 1967. "The historic roots of our ecologic crisis." *Science* 155 (March 10): 1203–7.

Yearly, S. 1991. *The green case: A sociology of environmental issues, arguments and politics.* London and New York: HarperCollins Academic.

3

John Thøgersen

Recycling Consumer Waste: A Behavioral Science Approach to Environmental Protection Policy*

Abstract

Evaluations of programs whose purpose is to increase recycling in Denmark through changing consumer waste handling practices are reviewed and the results discussed in a behavioral science framework. Denmark is one of the fastest-moving European countries with regard to policies targeting consumer waste handling. Danish authorities have succeeded in motivating consumers to source separate waste. Possible explanations for the positive attitudes are discussed. The good intentions of seemingly well-motivated citizens are not always borne out in adequate action. Possible reasons and implications for policy are discussed.

The Problem and Its Setting

The growing mountains of refuse are one of the most conspicuous and urgent environmental problems in modern society. Most Western European countries face a shortage of disposal capacity for solid waste (landfills and waste incineration plants). It is becoming increasingly difficult to find new, suitable locations for landfills that do not threaten the future supply of such basic amenities as pure drinking water and recreational areas. Incineration plants are met with serious reservations because of the construction costs and the fear of emissions of heavy metals, acids, and dioxins, among other toxins.

*The research reported in this chapter was part of a project titled "A Behavioral Science Framework for Source Separation Systems for Household Waste." Besides the author, the project team included research fellow Michael G. Johansson. The project was financed by the Danish Social Science Research Council and the Aarhus School of Business.

In the late 1980s the per capita production of municipal solid waste in the Organization for Economic Cooperation and Development (OECD) area surpassed half a ton per year, growing at a yearly rate of approximately 2 percent (OECD 1991).[1] Most of it was consumer waste; the rest came from shops and offices. Because of its composition and its diverse and numerous sources, consumer waste is the most complex waste fraction to handle and control.

Recycling is increasingly seen as the—at least short-term—rescue for removing large quantities of waste from the traditional waste disposal system. Most Western European countries aim at dramatically increasing the recycling rate before the turn of the millennium.

Commingled waste cannot be recycled. The by-themselves-usable materials in the commingled waste pollute each other and create a useless mess. That is why recycling and source separation have in recent times become nearly inseparable terms. The means to increased recycling is source separation of waste.

Various approaches have been tried in order to make recycling effective. Buy-back arrangements and deposits are examples of approaches that rely on economic incentives. Some of these instruments have been very effective, but only for a narrow array of materials (primarily beverage containers). In order to catch a wider array, multimaterial source separation schemes are increasingly applied in Western Europe and North America, on a mandatory or a voluntary basis.

In its mandatory form this instrument resembles a traditional regulation approach to environmental policy. However, because of the large number of sources, control and sanctioning are nearly impracticable. Hence, there is a need to create a positive motivation in mandatory as well as voluntary source separation schemes.

Economists normally classify environmental policy instruments as either "direct control" or "incentives." Clearly, the crucial characteristics of the kind of environmental policy treated in this chapter are not caught by any of these headings. Source separation schemes represent a wider approach, combining positive reinforcement (with an emphasis on collective rather than personal benefits), education, and infrastructure policy.

This chapter describes one example of this approach: municipal recycling policy in Denmark. Evaluations of source separation programs are reviewed, first with regard to the effectiveness of the programs as a means to motivate and activate consumers, and second as an explanation of the levels and variations of effectiveness.

In spite of increases in the waste collection assessment, source separation programs have generally been well received by the public. The authorities seem to have succeeded in motivating consumers to act for conservation and a clean environment.[2] However, it seems to be more difficult to establish conditions that facilitate carrying out the good intentions of environmentally motivated citizens. Also, the Danish experience shows that even well-motivated citizens may lack appropriate knowledge to carry out the specific source separation tasks. Hence, the actual outcomes in terms of source-separated materials tend to be smaller than promised by the enthusiasm expressed in surveys.

Municipal Recycling Policy in Denmark

With regard to policies that target consumer waste handling, Denmark is one of the fastest-moving countries in Europe. By now nearly every Danish municipality employs source separation programs for household waste, offering some or all of its citizens the opportunity to deliver waste materials to recycling centers, or (for hazardous waste) to environmentally sound treatment plants, instead of just "getting rid" of it. Source separation of waste is a rapidly expanding enterprise, covering increasing numbers of households and materials.

Waste handling in Denmark is the responsibility of the municipalities. In many municipalities collection is carried out by private contractors, although landfills and incinerators are public. Increased recycling is mandated by state law. It is the goal of the Danish Ministry of the Environment to increase recycling from approximately 30 percent[3] to 50 percent of all landfill-designated refuse during the course of this decade (Ministry of the Environment 1989). The subgoal for recycling consumer waste at the end of the decade is a less precise 40 to 50 percent, up from less than 10 percent when the decade started. Traditionally, voluntary organizations have collected some waste materials for recycling, but infrequently and on a small scale. Today, nearly every recycling program is municipal or under contract from the municipality and integrated (more or less) in its overall waste management system.

The introduction of source separation programs has led to increases in the assessment for waste collection, in some cases 100 percent or more. Generally, the assessment is not differentiated with regard to participation in a source separation program or the amount of garbage delivered. (That is, the municipalities do not use financial incentives to increase recycling of consumer waste.)

Participation in Source Separation Programs

In evaluating the degree of consumer participation created by source separation programs, participation in the programs is estimated. Participation has been measured either by self-reports (e.g., Gendan 1985; Rambøll and Hannemann 1990) or by observation (e.g., Enviroplan A/S 1983; Enviroplan A/S 1988; Jysk Teknologisk Institut 1985b). Participation measured by self-reports varies from a low of 10 percent of the target population in an early test program (Gendan 1985) to around 95 percent in newer programs (e.g., Bov Municipality 1989; Rambøll and Hannemann 1990). When participation is inferred from the percentage of the potential of target materials collected, the best programs exceed 90 percent (Enviroplan A/S 1983; Albertslund Municipality 1989).

Few evaluations combine self-reports and observation measures of behavior. The ones that do so find that the former measure shows a higher participation than the latter (Enviroplan A/S 1988; Gendan 1983; Gendan et al. 1990), as illustrated by the following example:

In Møn, a partly urban, partly rural municipality, glass and newspapers were collected for recycling six times a year. Households were asked to put the recyclables in bags distributed free of charge by the municipality and to place the bags at curbside on collection days. In a survey, 73 percent of the sample answered that they put out glass, and 54 percent newspapers, on every collection day. However, on the following collection day only 15 to 20 percent of rural households and 37 to 47 percent of urban households had put out bags for collection (Enviroplan A/S 1988).

The discrepancy between the two measures confirms the assessment by Pieters (1989b) and others that self-reported behavior in this field is far from reliable. On the other hand, the observation measures should also be interpreted with caution (Pieters and Verplanken 1991). Households that did not put out bags with recyclables on a particular collection day may still source separate some or all of their newspapers and glass. The discrepancy may be due to the estimation of the frequency of delivery in the program rather than to source separation per se (see, e.g., Gruder-Adams 1990).

Attitudes toward Source Separation and Recycling

Attitudes are often used as a proxy for motivation. In several evaluations, the attitudes of actual or potential participants toward recycling, source separation in general, or a specific program have been measured (Christiansen et al. 1987; Enviroplan A/S 1983, 1988; Gendan 1983; Gendan et al. 1990; Gregersen and Poulsen 1990, 1991; Grenaa Municipality 1989). All evaluations conclude that the attitudes are overwhelmingly positive, more so in recent than in earlier evaluations.

However, some reservations about the quality of these measures should be considered. For example, there seems to be an inverse relationship between the percentage of the respondents who express a positive attitude and the specificity of the question. For instance, in an evaluation in Farum, a suburb of Copenhagen (Enviroplan A/S 1988), 99 percent of the respondents agreed that "it is a good idea to recycle newspapers and glass packaging," while "only" 79 percent were positive without reservation toward the specific source separation program. This evaluation (like most others) asked questions about attitudes toward recycling in general or toward a source separation program, that is, toward an object rather than an activity. When what is needed is information about the motivation to *act* in a certain way, the attitude toward *carrying out* the behavior in question (e.g., participating in a source separation program) should be measured (Ajzen and Fishbein 1977, 1980). Unfortunately, among the applied measures, the most specific ones are most likely to have been understood by the respondents as questions about the attitude toward participation in the source separation program. This could mean that the least positive measures are the best predictors of behavior.

Additionally, when interpreting the numbers it should be kept in mind that surveys like these are likely to be biased because nonrespondents have less positive attitudes than respondents have (cf. e.g., Fowler 1991, about nonresponse bias in general, and Pieters 1989b, about nonresponse bias in evaluations of source separation programs).

Summary

In spite of the reservations, the general impression from the data at hand is that Danish municipalities have had considerable success with creating a positive attitude toward source separation and getting citizens to participate in programs, even though the programs have often led to increases in waste assessments. In a later section, the evaluations are reviewed with regard to explanations for the positive attitudes and the possible reasons why seemingly good intentions do not always result in adequate behavior. But first a frame of reference is introduced.

The Frame of Reference

In Figures 3.1 and 3.2, a frame of reference for assessing possible explanations for a source separation program's success with regard to changing attitudes and behavior is outlined, integrating elements from cognitive and behavioral psychology. Considering only the concepts emphasized in Figure 3.1, the model is little more than a classification scheme based on few, relaxed assumptions. Basically, consumer waste handling practice is explained by three main determinants (or classes of determinants) of consumer behavior:

1. The motivation of the actor to choose one or another alternative action. Motivation has its roots in values, beliefs about outcomes, attitudes, and norms. These variables are core constructs in cognitive psychology.

2. The actor's ability to carry out his or her intentions. Here, I focus on task knowledge and habits (but other relevant resources at the actor's command could be discussed under this heading too). These variables have primarily been researched by developmental psychologists.

3. The outer-determined opportunities for carrying out intentions. For example, a commuter may be highly motivated to save energy and may know that the most effective way to do so would be to use public transportation. But the commuter who lives in an area with inadequate public transportation services may feel that a private car is the only option available (Dholakia, Dholakia, and Firat 1983). Opportunities are seated in the person's environment. The study of

Figure 3.1. **A Behavioral Science Frame of Reference**

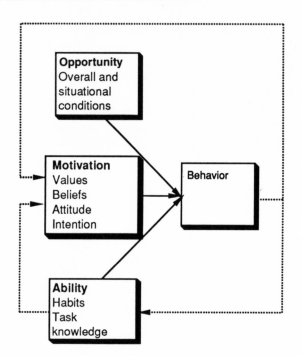

environmental effects on behavior has engaged primarily applied behavior analysts. (However, the consumer's perception of opportunities is within the traditional domain of cognitive psychologists.)

The feedback arrows illustrate that beliefs about an activity often change because of experience. A change may develop after the first (or first few) trial(s) if expectations about costs or benefits are exaggerated (a direct arrow), or it may develop after a while, when learning has made the task easier (an indirect arrow).

The assumptions of this frame of reference deviate from the neoclassical paradigm at one important point. By implication, it is assumed that consumers have limited mental capacity. This is a so-called assumption because in reality it is a relaxation of an assumption which serves as a basis for a large volume of neoclassical economic reasoning, but which probably nobody would consider realistic.

If consumers have limited mental capacity, the development of new knowledge and new behavior is a gradual process. "Being informed" is not a synonym of "understanding." A learning process is often needed. Further, a limited mental capacity means that a consumer must "economize" with mental resources. The most important "economizing" technique is habit building.

Figure 3.2. **Motivation Unfolded**

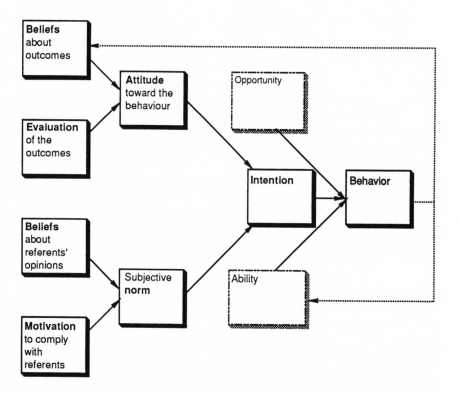

We "automize" repetitive activities so that they can be performed without straining our mental capacity (see, e.g., Peter and Olson 1990; Pieters 1988). A change in habitual activities requires reprogramming and hence is a time-consuming process.

More in line with neoclassical economic thinking, it is assumed that the behavioral resources commanded by an individual are limited. Behavioral resources are money and time, but also physical and psychic energy (Verhallen and Pieters 1984).

No assumptions are made about the motives driving behavior. They may reside in self-interest or altruism (or both).

Unfolding Motivation

Many models have been developed for the study of motivation. Fishbein's reasoned action model is one of the most popular in consumer research because of its simplicity and high applicability. I will not go into detail about the theory here (see instead Fishbein and Ajzen 1975; Ajzen and Fishbein 1980) but will instead concentrate on the empirical findings that illuminate the character of the Danish consumer's motivation to source separate household waste.

Attitudes or Social Norms?

The importance of social norms for source separation has not yet been studied in Denmark. In the Netherlands, Rik Pieters (1989a) of Erasmus University, Rotterdam, found that attitudes, but not social norms, have a strong impact on intentions about source separation. This result, I believe, is dependent on the cultural setting as well as on the visibility of the behavior. In reports on source separation in the United States (e.g., Glenn 1988), the importance of peer pressure for participation in source separation programs using curbside collection is often stressed. Denmark is culturally closer to the Netherlands than to the United States, and the typical Danish source separation system uses either backyard collection or containers at public places, and hence offers discretion to the user. There is reason, therefore, to expect intentions about source separation in Denmark to be determined primarily by attitudes.

I mentioned earlier that a large majority of Danish citizens seem to hold positive attitudes toward source separation. Now the results of the reviewed evaluations are summarized with regard to perceptions of costs and benefits connected with source separation.

Financial Costs

In many cases the introduction of source separation is followed by an increase in waste assessment (because of higher collection costs and the need to invest in new equipment). Such increases are usually accompanied by a message from the waste management authorities that without source separation the waste assessment would rise even more in the long run. Although increased assessments may put the source separation program in a bad light, available surveys reveal that economic costs have little bearing on the attitude toward source separation.[4]

In surveys where the respondents were asked if they had reservations about the costs of recycling, only 8 percent (Kaysen 1988) to 14 percent (Enviroplan A/S 1983) of the respondents made their support for the idea dependent only on recycling's paying off financially.

Payment for waste services in Denmark is practically independent of individual behavior, so no conclusions concerning the sensitivity of recycling behavior to economic incentives can be drawn from these surveys. All that may be concluded is that most consumers seem to agree that it is fair that they should contribute to the remedy of waste problems. The consumer's perception of this question may be conditioned by the low cost of waste services in Denmark and the fact that, due to its integration with other levies, the cost is barely visible.[5]

Table 3.1

Willingness to Participate in a Source Separation Program and Beliefs about Trouble and Nuisance, in Tarup, Denmark

	% Source Separation ⇒ More Work	% Source Separation ⇒ Hygienic Problem	% Interested in Permanent Program
Participants	9	8	77
Nonparticipants	33	37	12

Source: R. Eriksen, *Spørgeskemaundersøgelse: Genbrug i Tarup 1984–1985* (Questionnaire analysis: Recycling in Tarup 1984–1985). Danish Data Archive (Odense: Odense University, 1985).

Behavior Costs

In several evaluations participants were asked whether source separation is more demanding than the old, single-stream waste handling (Albertslund Municipality 1989; Bov Municipality 1989; Enviroplan A/S 1983; Eriksen 1985; Gregersen and Poulsen 1990; National Agency of Environmental Protection 1977; Tønning 1987; ØKOconsult aps 1989). The percentage answering that source separation is harder varied from 1 percent to 52 percent. The least additional work is felt in programs where households are equipped with a bin or rack for the storage of recyclables which are then collected from the premises. The most extra work is felt when bring-by systems are used (e.g., bottle banks, drop-off centers).

In a voluntary test program (Eriksen 1985) for source separation of food waste in Tarup, a suburb of Odense, both participants and nonparticipants were asked about their perception of extra work and hygiene problems.[6] While 33 percent of nonparticipants believed that source separation would mean more work, only 9 percent of participants shared this belief (see Table 3.1). The two groups also differed substantially with regard to perceptions of hygiene problems: Only 8 percent of participants experienced hygiene problems, while 37 percent of nonparticipants expected hygiene problems if they were to source separate.

The two groups were asked whether they were interested in participating in a permanent program for the source separation of food waste. Seventy-seven percent of participants in the test program would have liked to participate in a permanent program, while only 12 percent of nonparticipants were interested. The results indicate that willingness to participate in a source separation program is related to beliefs about behavioral costs. For some people, the (expected) additional effort and nuisance can be too taxing. However, it also indicates that people become more positive toward participating when they gain experience.[7] If this is true, the most important (and difficult) thing is to convince people that they should start to source separate (and not give it up too easily).

Experience may make participants more positive for two reasons. First, some people may overestimate the trouble and nuisance of source separation beforehand. As one acquires personal experience with the source separation program, prejudice and skepticism are replaced by knowledge; beliefs about the consequences of source separation are adjusted; and attitudes toward source separation change.[8] (This path is illustrated by the feedback arrow from behavior to beliefs in Figure 3.2.) Second, source separation becomes less troublesome when it has been practiced for a while because one acquires new habits and hence is able to perform the task with little deliberation. The experience thus produces a decrease in the costs of source separation and hence a more positive attitude toward the activity. (This relationship is illustrated in Figure 3.2 by the feedback arrow from behavior to ability.) I will return later to the discussion of habits. Now I turn to the benefits experienced from source separation.

Public Benefits

In a number of evaluations, the participants in source separation programs were asked to choose between alternative reasons for participating (Enviroplan A/S 1983, 1988; Eriksen 1985; Jysk Teknologisk Institut 1985a; Tønning 1987). The answer choices could be classified as public benefits (conservation, pollution prevention, employment, saving foreign currency, supporting Boy Scouts), personal benefits (easy disposability, more room in refuse bin), and compliance with demands from authorities (the municipality, the sanitation department). A majority in every evaluation pointed at public benefits (especially conservation) as their main reason for participating, while few seemed to experience noticeable personal benefits or to be compliant only.

Of course, reliability is threatened when such results are obtained by presenting respondents with reasons they may never have thought of themselves. However, the results from two evaluations that used free response questions point in the same direction (Vilstrup 1989; Søndergaard and Jensen 1990).

Summary

The crucial benefits of source separation—as with other ecological behaviors (cf., e.g., Verhallen and Pieters 1984; Pieters 1989a)—are shared with society at large, while the behavioral costs can be shared only within the family. In this section it has been revealed that the public benefits (a cleaner environment, conservation) can be a strong motivating force, creating high participation rates in source separation programs even though participation incurs personal costs (financial and other costs).

Further, it has been indicated that consumers who are inexperienced with source separation sometimes have exaggerated expectations about personal costs. There may be a general need to focus on prejudice and skepticism when motivation campaigns for new source separation programs are designed.

Now we turn to the two other main determinants of behavior in our model. Lack of abilities or insufficient opportunities may explain discrepancies between environmental attitudes and observed behavior.

Unfolding Ability

In the model outlined in Figure 3.1, two dimensions of the consumer's ability to source separate in accordance with the rules were included: habits and task knowledge. First, even if a person begins to source separate, in accordance with a conscious intention to do so, it is unlikely that from then on the throwing away of every apple core or empty package will be a thoroughly considered act. By definition, "waste" is any item that has ceased to be of value to the possessor. In the current mass-consumption societies of the West, we—as consumers—need to get rid of waste so often that it would take up far too much of our limited time if we had to concentrate our problem-solving attention on it every time. Instead, we learn routines or habits that make us capable of performing the task in a nearly automatic fashion, employing a minimum of conscious effort. Until the habits of source separation are well ingrained, there is an increased risk that distraction leads to failure.

Second, the person's knowledge about how to reach the goal he or she aims at (e.g., how to correctly separate waste) may be failing (Verhallen and Pieters 1984). This deficiency may be the result of insufficient information, an inability to understand the message, forgetfulness, or a combination. As a result of deficient task knowledge, nonrecyclable materials may be placed in containers for recyclables, or recyclable materials in containers for garbage.

These variables and their influence on behavior are not well documented in the reviewed evaluations. However, data from some evaluations confirm that capability problems should indeed be foreseen when designing source separation programs. In Figure 3.3 the relationships dealt with in this section are illustrated.

Habits

In order for consumers to participate in a source separation program, old waste handling habits have to be terminated and new ones built. This process takes time. As new habits are learned, we expect participants in source separation programs to experience fewer problems, and accordingly, the quantity and quality of source separation to improve.

Presumably, it is more difficult to break with habits the more ingrained they are, that is, the longer the habitual activity has been practiced. This was confirmed in an evaluation of a pilot program in Aalborg two months after its start

Figure 3.3. **Personal Abilities and the Execution of Intentions**

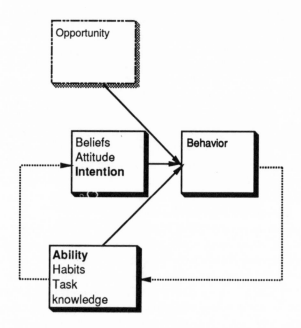

(Gregersen and Poulsen 1990). Here it was found that the proportion of respondents who claimed, without reservation, that source separation was "not more troublesome" than the old, single-stream way of handling waste, decreased with age and thus with the duration of the old habit (see Table 3.2). Table 3.2 contains the results of a second evaluation, four months later, when the proportion of the respondents who expressed that source separation was "not more troublesome" had increased from 63 percent to 75 percent (with the oldest age groups contributing most to the increase).[9] This change in participants' perceptions of problems as they got used to the source separation system was also found in the repeated evaluations of Søndersø's green waste system, two months and one year after the start (Tønning 1987). The percentage experiencing "noticeable extra work" from source separation decreased from 33 percent to 29 percent between the two evaluations.[10]

Some evaluations have tracked the development of collection effectiveness.[11] The results with regard to the influence of habits are mixed. In a program in one of Copenhagen's suburbs, Albertslund, collection effectiveness increased significantly during the test period (Albertslund Municipality 1989).[12] The result was seen as an indication that participants had gradually got into the habit of source separation. However, in two other programs—in Søndersø and Farum—the expected increase in collection effectiveness was *not* found (Tønning 1987; En-

Table 3.2

The Percentage of Participants Experiencing "No Trouble" from Source Separation of Food Waste in Aalborg, Denmark, by Age

	% of Age Groups							% of total
	<19 y.	20–29	30–39	40–49	50–59	60–69	>70 y	
After 2 months	100	80	76	68	61	60	50	63
After 6 months	100	80	77	79	70	79	71	75

Sources: M. Gregersen and C. S. Poulsen, *Markedsundersøgelse for renovationsvæsenet* (Market analysis for the sanitation department) (Vårst, Denmark: Jysk Analyseinstitut, 1990); M. Gregersen and C. S. Poulsen, *Markedsunderøgelse for renovationsvæsenet* (Market analysis for the sanitation department) (Vårst: Jysk Analyseinstitut, 1991).

viroplan A/S 1983). In fact, in Farum a minor *decrease* in collection effectiveness was noted during the first year. Additionally, the purity of the collected materials (paper) declined.

The latter results indicate that other forces act counter to habit building. For a while, enthusiasm may make people concentrate a lot of mental energy on a (recurrent) task such as source separating waste, but as the newness of the endeavor diminishes, so does the mental energy that the average person is willing to invest in it. Apparently, in some cases enthusiasm fades faster than new habits are built.

Task Knowledge

The theoretical aspect of the source separation education concerns the understanding of the sorting rule and mainly the following questions: What should be kept separate for recycling? Which exceptions of the general rule exist? Often, problems in a source separation program can be traced back to a lack of understanding of the answers to these questions.

Most evaluations have found that a smaller or larger share of participants are sometimes uncertain about the sorting rule (Albertslund Municipality 1989; Christiansen et al. 1989; Gregersen and Poulsen 1990; Tønning 1987; Vilstrup 1989). They do not perceive the rule as sufficiently unambiguous and precise (e.g., because of many exceptions from the general rule), and they do not understand the premises of the rule.

In a test program for source separation of dry batteries on the island of Bornholm, people were asked to sort the batteries in four different types when bringing them to collection points (shops selling batteries). In an evaluation of the program, only 30 percent of the sample believed that they knew the relevant differences between the four types (Christiansen et al. 1989). Additionally, more than a third of these respondents mentioned wrong or dubious criteria when asked which sorting rules they used. Over the whole test period, the boxes for the four types contained, respectively, 3.6, 17.4, 20.5, and 96.6 percent erroneously sorted batteries.

A full understanding of the sorting rule for the batteries demands a knowledge of physics and chemistry that is available to only a minor fraction of the population. Most people have to manage with some "rule of thumb." The same is true concerning most other items in the "hazardous waste" group (which is source separated not for recycling purposes but in order to reduce the environmental hazards of such waste).

However, difficulties understanding the rules create problems with more "ordinary" materials, too. For instance, chinaware is often found in bottle banks (see, e.g., Enviroplan A/S 1983, 1988). Also, source separation of the organic fraction for composting is subject to problems of misunderstanding, leading to sorting failures and impure quality of the materials.[13]

Summary

It takes time to acquire new waste handling habits, and the tasks of source separation are difficult to understand, at least for some. Old, ingrained habits and deficient knowledge unwittingly influence behavior and produce discrepancies between stated intentions and actual behavior in source separation programs. If people are motivated to start and continue source separating, the problems related to old habits will gradually disappear. However, problems of deficient task knowledge demand intervention in the form of information and maybe adjustments of the sorting rules.

Unfolding Opportunities

Besides depending on personal abilities, the execution of intended behavior depends on conditions external to the actor that facilitate or hamper the activity. Here, I focus on conditions controlled by the sanitation department. The importance of the proper management of time-and-place utility in increased recycling is not unlike its importance in selling convenience goods. In Figure 3.4 the impact of this variable is demonstrated. The opportunities (or conditions) factor is a broad one and difficult to operationalize. Overall conditions may be of an absolute nature (e.g., the presence or absence of a recycling system for aluminum cans), but generally they are better conceived of as relative (e.g., the distance to the nearest bottle bank). This means that individual consumers may perceive the (same) conditions very differently. In his behavioral model, Triandis (1977, 1980) terms this variable *facilitating conditions*. However, I prefer the neutral term *overall conditions*.

Figure 3.4. **Conditions for the Execution of Intentions**

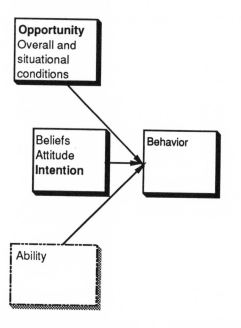

The structural conditions created by a municipal source separation program may—depending on the chosen service level—be more or less facilitating for carrying out intentions of source separation. The fewer the delays, diversions, and obstacles that crop up between the formation of an intention and the performance of the specific act and the more immediately available the tools for its performance, the more facilitating are the conditions. Further, the less facilitating the program design in this respect, the more vulnerable is the source separation program to events and situational circumstances that may make people act against their conscious intentions (see, e.g., Belk 1975; Cote, McCullough, and Reilly 1985).

The evaluation of the test program in Farum illustrates this point (Enviroplan A/S 1983). In this test an experimental design was used, varying the level of service provided (time-and-place utility) while all other conditions (payment, information, etc.) were shared by all participants. Three different systems of collecting source-separated glass and paper from households were tested. In all three systems, the materials were collected from the backyards of single-family houses. The systems differed with regard to time dependence and demands on indoor storage space for the recyclable materials, as described in Table 3.3. In the "high service" area, 91 percent of the recyclable glass and paper was collected, while in the "low" and "lowest service" areas, only between 46 and 61 percent was collected. This substantial difference in behavioral outcomes is not

Table 3.3

Extra Work and Collection Effectiveness in Farum, Denmark

	% Experiencing Extra Work		% Collection Effectiveness	
	From Glass	From Paper	Glass	Paper
High Service[a]	5	1	91	91
Low Service[b]	5	4	61	48
Lowest Service[c]	7	30	53	46

[a]A specially designed rack containing boxes for glass and paper placed next to the garbage bin.

[b]Two small bins, for glass and paper, to be kept in the house and placed next to the garbage bin on collection day.

[c]A small bin for glass only and instructions to bundle paper and put it next to the garbage bin on collection day, together with the glass bin.

Source: Enviroplan A/S, *Kombiner et indsamling af aviser, glas og gagrenovation i Farum kommune* (Combined collection of newspapers, glass, and refuse in Farum municipality). Environment Report No. 54/1983 (Copenhagen: National Agency of Environmental Protection, 1983).

explained by the differences in beliefs that were found in the evaluation. With regard to glass there was no significant difference between the three systems in the experience of additional work, and with regard to paper, only the requirement to bundle it produced a significantly higher perceived amount of extra work.

In the "low" and "lowest service" areas, demands on the individual concerning storing and transporting recyclable materials and complying with timetables lowered the effectiveness of collection to a larger extent than it influenced attitudes. The additional demands in these systems made conditions for source separation and recycling less facilitating and the system more vulnerable to unforeseen events.

Consumers are probably more sensitive to demanding conditions when source separation is a "new" activity. When the habits of source separation become well ingrained, consumers may no longer consider the garbage bin for disposing recyclables. However, facilitating conditions are decisive in building new habits.

Summary and Conclusions

In this chapter, data from evaluations of Danish source separation programs for household waste have been used to illuminate the consumer's motives for, and other determinants of, careful handling of refuse. It was assumed from the outset that an observed behavior can be understood in a frame of reference that considers personal abilities and external opportunities in addition to motivation. The data allow for a partial analysis and an incomplete picture only, but the evidence at hand confirms that source separation behavior is influenced by variations in these three broad variables.

A number of evaluations conclude that nearly everybody has a positive attitude toward source separation and recycling. Few people attribute their positive attitude to beliefs about personal benefits. A large majority base their attitude on the belief that source separation/recycling leads to public benefits— mainly conservation and protection of the environment. Hence, it may be concluded that with regard to waste handling, people not only are concerned with maximizing personal pleasure but also can be motivated to source separate their waste for altruistic reasons.[14] In fact, it seems that even an increased waste assessment as a result of establishing a source separation program does not ruin positive attitudes.[15]

On the other hand, data on behavioral outcomes indicate that the degree of personal convenience afforded by the waste handling program also contributes to waste handling behavior. In spite of positive attitudes toward source separation, effectiveness and quality are reduced if the program is too taxing on efforts and knowledge. Hence, behavior is codetermined, not only by several causes but among these by at least two distinct motives that all people, or at least a large majority, share.

Before we proceed, a few remarks are needed about the divergence between attitudes and behavior that was found in some of the evaluations. How do we explain that outcomes often fall short of the promises expressed in attitude surveys? Surveys show how respondents see themselves, how they would like to see themselves, or how they would like to be seen, rather than how they actually are in some objective sense. Hence, survey data are better suited to describe the shared values in a social system than what people actually do.

In this chapter, both survey data (on attitudes, beliefs, and knowledge) and observational data (on behavioral outcomes) that describe the same behavior are reported. When the data are compared, some divergence is revealed. However, the most important fact to note is not the divergence between the measures, but their broad consistency. After all, the observational data show that in most cases people covered by a program source separate *in spite of* the negative balance between personal costs and benefits and in spite of the absence of any control of the behavior by the authorities or peers. This becomes understandable only in the light of survey data that show that people value the benefits that result for society at large and for the environment and see it as their moral duty to help create these benefits.

The kind of person that materializes in this study has several—in some cases conflicting—goals, some of which have to do with personal pleasure and some with moral values, and all of which function as motives for behavior. Hence, the present analysis lends support to the I-and-we paradigm, the behavioral assumptions of socioeconomics (Etzioni 1988).

This chapter has *not* considered the sensitivity of Danes' waste handling behavior to economic incentives, as none of the reviewed programs used differentiated assessments. Undoubtedly, a change in the waste assessment system so as to establish a more perceptible relationship between the behavior and the size of the bill will affect some people's source separation behavior. However, this coin has another side: If personal gain becomes an incentive for source separation, for some people the gain will become the prime objective. Hence, the system's vulnerability to fraud becomes crucial. A source separation program based on economic incentives requires control systems that are unnecessary in a program based on active support by the participants.

Maybe the most important message to environment policy from this study is that neither carrots nor sticks are necessary for changing consumer behavior in this field. The reported results indicate that information campaigns can change behavior—through working on people's perceptions of the waste problem and hence on their attitudes.

In the basic Fishbein model, given in Figure 3.2, one's behavior is ultimately explained by the information one has about the world.[16] The consequence of this thinking is a strong confidence in information as a means to change behavior.[17] In the framework of my model also, information becomes an important instrument, but only for creating motivation (and relevant task knowledge). When the goal is to change consumer *behavior,* management of physical conditions is as important as management of information.

Research on time expenditures has revealed that the present-day Danish household lives under tighter time pressures than ever before, leaving little room for new time- and attention-demanding activities (see, e.g., Mogensen 1990). In this situation the creation of positive attitudes is not sufficient to guarantee effective and high-quality source separation. But it is not fair to blame the consumer. When source separation is introduced, the consumer is requested to deliver unpaid work to society. In return, society should show due consideration for the personal needs and interests of the consumer when designing source separation systems. The experience of Danish test programs shows that when society does that, it may be rewarded with collection rates above 90 percent of target recyclables.

Of course, volume is not the only goal in a source separation program. The high-value market for secondary resources (as recyclables are now increasingly called) demands high-quality separation. The Danish experience shows that even well-motivated citizens often lack the knowledge to appropriately carry out source separation tasks. Hence, the information campaign that accompanies the implementation of a source separation program should be aimed not only at motivating citizens but also at educating them.

Notes

1. However, industry is by far the largest waste producer in OECD countries. In the late 1980s, OECD countries produced 3.4 times as much industrial waste as municipal waste (OECD 1991).

2. Even if this judgment is based on a large number of cases, it may still be biased due to the fact that the evaluations cover early programs only. In Denmark, as everywhere else, there has been a tendency to start with "easy" quarters (middle-class, single-family houses), where willingness to cooperate is expected to be high.

3. If energy and waste water treatment plants are not included, actual (in 1985) recycling amounts to approximately 20 percent of refuse (National Agency of Environmental Protection et al. 1990).

4. This conclusion is restricted to cases where the waste assessment is a modest share of the household's disposable income and the increase is moderate in absolute terms.

5. In Denmark the waste bill is paid together with the rent (in rented premises) or the property tax (in owned houses). In 1990, payments for the collection of waste from private households in Aarhus amounted, on average, to approximately 1.5 percent of total housing costs (Fogsgaard 1990).

6. Participation in the test was voluntary. About two-thirds of the households that were asked to source separate food waste participated actively in the test program. One-third refused to participate, most of them from the start. All households in the area received a questionnaire at the end of the test period. The response rates for participants/nonparticipants were 62 percent/27 percent, respectively (Eriksen 1985), which means that data on nonparticipants should be interpreted with caution.

7. Of course, one cannot know for sure that the large differences in opinion displayed in Table 3.1 are related to user status (experienced/nonexperienced with source separation of food waste). However, a control survey was made in an area of Tarup that was not covered by the test program. Here, only 29 percent of the respondents were interested in participating in a permanent program (Eriksen 1985). The response rate from this group was only 29 percent, but as it is reasonable to expect a positive bias, it still gives reliable support for my point.

8. That prejudice is in fact present in this area is evidenced by evaluations wherein respondents were asked whether they would like to change their equipment to an alternative design, which they knew from description but had not tried (Enviroplan A/S 1983; Hvidovre Municipality 1989; Jysk Teknologisk Institut 1985a). Regardless of which equipment they had from the outset, few people wanted to change. When, for example, participants in Hvidovre's (a suburb of Copenhagen) test program, using two different types of equipment for collecting paper and glass from the premises of participants, were asked whether they would prefer the equipment used by "the other" group, 1.5 percent of households equipped with a "luxury system" (similar to the "high-service system" used in Farum, see Table 3.3) wanted to change to the "discount system" (two bags for paper and glass to be placed next to the refuse bin on collection day). More surprisingly, only 19 percent of households equipped with the "discount system" wanted to change (Hvidovre Municipality 1989).

9. Every household participating in the pilot program was contacted in the two evaluations. Only 3 percent and 1 percent, respectively, refused to be interviewed (Gregersen and Poulsen 1990, 1991).

10. In Søndersø the major source of extra work was that the collection point was moved from the backyard to curbside.

11. The measure "collection effectiveness" (or just "effectiveness") is the volume of a target material collected relative to the potential estimated from nationwide garbage analyses. Because of variations in potential between regions and local areas, and over time, uncertainties exist about the reliability of this measure.

12. Collection effectiveness for paper and cardboard increased from 51 percent in the period October–December 1987 to 93 percent in the period July–November 1988. For

glass it increased from 64 percent in the period January–June 1988 to 93 percent in the period July–November 1988 (Albertslund Municipality 1989).

13. See, for example, a verbal presentation by Ib Larsen of the Environment Control Department of the City of Copenhagen at the DAKOFA seminar "Organic waste—Collection and biological treatment possibilities," on February 27, 1990, in Copenhagen. Because of these problems, Copenhagen chose to collect only food waste for composting even if it meant that bulky, organic matter, like diapers, that could in principle be recycled as compost would go to the landfill instead.

14. This is not a specific *Danish* phenomenon. Analyses in the Netherlands (Pieters and Verhallen 1986; Pieters 1989a), Germany (Mellen and Scheffold 1985), Austria (Scheithauser and Vogel 1976), the United States (de Young 1985, 1985–86, 1986), Sweden (Berg 1985), and the United Kingdom (Coggins, Cooper, and Brown 1991) reach similar conclusions.

15. Also in the United States, "numerous surveys reveal that an economic reward or a reduction in costs has only a moderate bearing on the propensity to reclaim waste" (Anonymous 1982, p. 6).

16. "Since a person's beliefs represent the information (be it correct or incorrect) he has about his world, it follows that a person's behavior is ultimately determined by this information" (Ajzen and Fishbein 1980, p. 79).

17. Ajzen and Fishbein (1980) thus believe that "in order to influence behavior, we have to expose people to information which will produce changes in their beliefs."

References

Ajzen, I., and M. Fishbein. 1977. "Attitude-behavior relations: A theoretical analysis and review of empirical research." *Psychological Bulletin* 84, May, 888–918.
———. 1980 *Understanding attitudes and predicting social behavior*. Englewood Cliffs, NJ: Prentice-Hall.
Albertslund Municipality. 1989. Kildesorteringsforsøg på Damgårdsarealets 1. byggeafsnit (Source separation test in the first section of the Damgaard area). Søborg: I. Krüger.
Anonymous. 1982. "The public's opinion of recycling." *Resource Recycling* (May/June) 6–7.
Belk, R. W. 1975. "Situational variables and consumer behavior." *Journal of Marketing Research* 2: 157–64.
Berg, P. O. 1985. "Source grouping technology: An introduction to a household waste recycling technology. Dissertation, Chalmers Tekniska Högskola, Göteborg.
Bov Municipality. 1989. Rapport vedr. forsøg med indsamling og sortering af kildesorteret grønt affald i Bov Kommune—perioden 1.9.1987–31.12.1988 (Report concerning test of collection and sorting of source-separated green waste in Bov Municipality—the period September 1, 1987–December 12, 1988). Bov Municipality.
Christiansen, B., C. Jensen, H. Jensen, L. Madsen, M. Grell, M. Vest, and T. Larsen. 1987. Kildesortering af husholdningsaffald (Source separation of household waste). Report from the common environment course of the institutes of higher education. Copenhagen.
Christiansen, K., P. Petersen, O. Michaelsen, J. Stenberg, and B. Andersen. 1989. Indsamling af batterier på Bornholm (Collection of batteries at Bornholm). Working Report No. 13/1989. Copenhagen: National Agency of Environmental Protection.
Coggins, C., D. Cooper, and R. Brown. 1991. "Curbside and drop-off recycling schemes: Some comparisons between the UK and USA." *European Environment* 1 (Part 2): April 21–26.

Cote, J. A., J. McCullough, and M. Reilly. 1985 "Effects of unexpected situations on behaviour-intention differences: A garbology analysis." *Journal of Consumer Research* 12: 188–94.

de Young, R. 1985. "Satisfaction from conservation activities in North America." *Environmental Conservation* 12(3): 259–60.

————. 1985–86. "Encouraging environmentally appropriate behavior: The role of intrinsic motivation." *Journal of Environmental Systems* 15(4): 281–92.

————. 1986. "Some psychological aspects of recycling. The structure of conservation satisfaction." *Environment and Behavior* 18(4): 435–49.

Dholakia, R. R., N. Dholakia, and A. F. Firat. 1983. "From social psychology to political economy: A model of energy use behavior." *Journal of Economic Psychology* 3: 231–47.

Enviroplan A/S. 1983. Kombineret indsamling af aviser, glas og dagrenovation i Farum kommune (Combined collection of newspapers, glass, and refuse in Farum municipality). Environment Report No. 54/1983. Copenhagen: National Agency of Environmental Protection.

————. 1988. Genbrugsforsøg. Indsamling af aviser og glasemballage sammen med stroskrald og haveaffald i Møn Kommune (Recycling test: Collection of newspaper and glass packaging together with bulky waste and garden waste in Møn Municipality). FASAN, Næstved.

Eriksen, R. 1985. Spørgeskemaundersøgelse: Genbrug i Tarup 1984–85 (Questionnaire analysis: Recycling in Tarup 1984–85). Danish Data Archive, Odense University.

Etzioni, A. 1988. *The moral dimension: Toward a new economics.* New York: Free Press.

Fishbein, M., and I. Ajzen. 1975. *Beliefs, attitudes, intention and behavior.* Reading, MA: Addision-Wesley.

Fogsgaard, K. 1990. Krav til systemer og emballage. økonomiske begrænsninger for nuværende renovationsordning og fremtidige renevationsafgifter (Demands on systems and packaging: Economic limitations for current refuse system and future refuse charges). Proceedings of DAKOFA seminar titled "Waste collection—Methods and equipment," September 3, 1990, Copenhagen.

Fowler, F. J. 1991. *Survey research methods.* Beverly Hills: Sage.

Gendan. 1983. Kommunale indsamlinger af glas og papir. Spørgeskemaundersøgelse i Frederiksborg Amt (Municipal collections of glass and paper: Questionnaire analysis in Frederiksborg County). Gendan, Copenhagen.

————. 1985. Kommunale indsamlinger af glas og papir. Statusnotat Frederiksværk Kommune (Municipality collections of glass and paper: Status report Frederiksværk Municipality). Gendan, Copenhagen.

Gendan, Teknologisk Institut, Bioteknik, and VIAK A/S. 1990. Det grønne affaldssystem i AFAV. Bilagsrapport (The green waste system in AFAV: Appendix report). Working Report No. 12/1990. Copenhagen: National Agency of Environmental Protection.

Glenn, J. 1988. "Containers at curbside: Boost to participation." *BioCycle* 29: 26–28.

Gregersen, M., and C. S. Poulsen. 1990. Markedsundersøgelse for renovationsvæsenet (Market analysis for the sanitation department). Jysk Analyseinstitut, Vårst.

————. 1991. Markedsundersøgelse for renovationsvæsenet (Market analysis for the sanitation department). Jysk Analyseinstitut, Vårst.

Grenaa Municipality. 1989. Resumé af indkomne bemærkninger til "Forslag til affaldsplan." Notat (Summary of received comments on "Waste plan proposal": Notes). Grenaa Municipality, Technical Department.

Gruder-Adams, S. 1990. "Recycling participation assessment." *BioCycle* 31: 38–43.

Hvidovre Municipality. 1989. Resultat af spørgeskemaundersøgelse vedr. genbrugsforsøg i Risbjergårds Villaby og i grundejerforeningen Nymarken (Results from a questionnaire analysis concerning recycling tests in Risbjergårds Villaby and in the homeowners' association Nymarken). Hvidovre Municipality, Technical Department.

Jysk Teknologisk Institut. 1985a. Afrapportering af genbrugsforsøgene i Tarup og Vollsmose m.v. Oktober 1984–September 1985 (Report from the recycling tests in Tarup and Vollsmose etc., October 1984–September 1985). Aarhus: Jysk Teknologisk Institut.

———. 1985b. Genanvendelse. Forsøg med indsamling af papir og glas fra private husstande i Århus Amt. Notat vedr. status og udvikling i Århus Kommune, december 1985 (Recycling: Test concerning the collection of paper and glass from households in Aarhus County, notes concerning status and development in Aarhus Municipality, December 1985). Aarhus: Jysk Teknologisk Institut.

Kaysen, O. 1988. "Public attitudes to recycling." In *ISWA 88,* ed. L. Andersen and J. Møller. Proceedings of the 5th International Solid Wastes Conference, Vol. 1, Copenhagen. London: Academic Press.

Mellen, J., and K. Scheffold. 1985. Erfahrungen mit der getrennten Sammlung in Ostrhauderfern-Landkreis Leer. (Experience with source separation in Osthaudfern, Leer County). Müllund Abfall, 1985/1, 5–8.

Ministry of the Environment. 1989. Handlingsplan for øget genanvendelse 1990–92 (Action plan for increased recycling 1990–92). Copenhagen: Ministry of the Environment.

Mogensen, G. V. 1990. *Time and consumption: Time use and consumption in Denmark in recent decades.* Copenhagen: Denmarks Statistik.

National Agency of Environmental Protection. 1977. Genanvendelsesforsøg i Birkerød Kommune fra 1 September 1974 til 31 December 1976 (Recycling test in Birkerød Municipality September 1, 1974 to December 31, 1976). Environment Report No. 5. Copenhagen: National Agency of Environmental Protection.

National Agency of Environmental Protection, National Agency of Forest and Native, and Denmark's Statistic. 1990. Tal on natur og miljø. (Numbers about nature and environment). Copenhagen: Denmarks Statistik.

Organization for Economic Cooperation and Development (OECD). 1991. *Environmental indicators.* Paris: OECD.

Peter, J. P., and J. C. Olson. 1990 Consumer behavior and marketing strategy. Homewood, IL: Irwin.

Pieters, R. G. M. 1988. "Attitude—behavior relationships." In *Handbook of economic psychology,* ed. W. F. van Raaij, G. M. van Veldhoven, and K. E. Wärneryd. Dordrecht, The Netherlands: Kluwer Academic Publishers.

———. 1989a. Attitudes and behavior in a source separation program: A garbology approach. Delft, The Netherlands: Euburon.

———. 1989b. Measurement effects and nonresponse bias in longitudinal research: A garbology approach. Proceedings of the Conference of the European Marketing Academy, Athens.

Pieters, R. G. M., and T. M. M. Verhallen. 1986. "Participation in source separation projects: Design characteristics and perceived costs and benefits." *Resources and Conservation* 12: 95–111.

Pieters, R. G. M., and B. Verplanken. 1991. Changing our mind about behavior. In *The consumption of time and the timing of consumption: Toward a new behavioral and socio-economics,* ed. G. Antonides, W. A. Arts, and W. F. v. Raaij. Nieuwe Reeks: Koninklijke Nederlandse Akademie van Wetenschappen.

Rambøll and Hannemann, Inc. 1990. Det grønne affaldssystem i Høng (The green waste system in Høng). Environment Report No. 144. Copenhagen: National Agency of Environmental Protection.

Scheithauer, A., and G. Vogel. 1976. Die Bereitschaft zur Altstoffsammlung in Österreich. Schriftenreihe Verpackungsforshung, des Österreicher Institutes für Verpackungswesen an der Wirtschaftsuniversität Wien, Heft 5 The Packaging Research series No. 5. Vienna: Austrian Institute for Packaging at Vienna's Business University.

Søndergaard, H., and J. Jensen. 1990. Forbrugernes holdninger til grønne systemer. Resultatet af spørgeskemaundersøgelse blandt 1.600 husstande i København, Odense, Vejle og Frederikssund vedrørende disses affaldssorteringssystemer (The consumers' attitudes toward green systems: Results from a questionnaire analysis of 1,600 households in Copenhagen, Odense, Vejle, and Frederikssund concerning their waste sorting systems). Working Report No. 18/1990. Copenhagen: National Agency of Environmental Protection.

Triandis, H. C. 1977. *Interpersonal behavior.* Monterey, CA: Brooks/Cole.

————. 1980. Values, attitudes, and interpersonal behavior. In *Nebraska symposium on motivation, 1979* ed. M. M. Page. Proceedings of a symposium on motivation, 1979, University of Nebraska. Lincoln, NE: University of Nebraska Press.

Tønning, K. 1987. Det grønne affaldssystem i Søndersø (The green waste system in Søndersø). Aarhus: Jysk Teknologisk Institut.

Verhallen, T. M. M., and R. G. M. Pieters. 1984. "Attitude theory and behavioral costs." *Journal of Economic Psychology* 5: 223–49.

Vilstrup K. S. 1989. Brugerbedømmelse af kildesortering af husholdningsaffald i forsøgsområdet på Amagerbro: Tabelrapport (User evaluation of source separation of household waste in the test area at Amagerbro: Table report). Vanløse.

ØKOconsult aps. 1989. Papirindsamling via specialcontainere og genbrugsstation. Indsamling fra private husstande i Birkerød og Gladsaxe kommuner (Paper collection using special containers and drop-off centers: Collection from private households in Birkerød and Gladsaxe Municipalities). Environment Report No. 114. Copenhagen: National Agency of Environmental Protection.

Part II
Bioeconomics

4

SYLVIE FAUCHEUX

New Approaches in Ecological Economics: Energy Analysis and the Socioeconomic Elements of Environmental Economics

Introduction

The relationship between economics and the biosphere can no longer be ignored because of the current proliferation of environmental problems such as the degradation of natural resources and the emergence of global forms of pollution (depletion of the ozone layer and intensification of the greenhouse effect) (Faucheux and Noël 1990).

It seems necessary to adopt a multidimensional approach to the economy (Daly 1987) concerning the economic sphere (production, consumption, trade, and so on). The marketplace or prices are supposed to be autoregulation mechanisms. The broader social sphere that comprises such elements as politics, religion, and the state interfaces not only with the economy but also with the biosphere, without which there could be no life, let alone any society or economy. These three spheres are not linked merely by a simple relationship of enclosure. Constant interchanges take place between them, and they have their own regulating mechanisms. Each, if subjected to imbalances, can disturb the others (Passet 1979).

In the 1980s this multidimensional approach to economics governed the thinking of all environment-oriented economic currents concerned with sustainable development. This concept stems from the idea that the continuity of economic development depends on the reproduction of both the economy and the natural environment. However, though this concept enjoys general support, there is considerable divergence as to the conceptual and operational content of the form (Turner 1993).

One school of thought, redolent of neoclassical thinking, takes account of the sustainability in the weak sense of the term. It holds that the cause of un-sustainability arose from free access to the goods and services supplied by the biosphere, since the market price for these is either weak or nonexistent. According to this approach, one means of attaining sustainability would be the use of economic instruments such as taxation, which would tend to raise the price. This is tantamount to solving the problem by internalizing external effects and, in the final analysis, using prices as the tool for regulating sustainability.

Systematic analysis demonstrates that the evaluative criteria valid within one of the major subsystems (economy, social sphere, or biosphere) retain their validity for the subsystems contained in the latter but do not do so for those in which this subsystem is itself contained. This means that, while money is the measure of value in the economic sphere, it is not necessarily the yardstick for the social sphere or, even less, for the biosphere. In the case of the latter there are too many nonmarket elements for recourse to prices—even shadow prices—to make any sense.

In a multidimensional economy of the kind postulated for sustainable development, what is needed is a means of measurement common to both the economic and the natural spheres. This can be only physical in character for the natural sphere. The physical units, when applied to the economic sphere, can relate only to the economic real dimensions and not to its monetary dimension (Faucheux 1990, 1994). Such reasoning is behind another current approach to sustainable development, which advocates energy as a possible common physical unit.

It seems that this energy-based approach is especially worthy of economists' attention, as a veritable school of economic thought founded on energy evaluation is currently being evolved after some perilous vacillation in the 1970s. Disregard for this approach gives rise to two risks: The first risk is that of discarding a working tool relevant to environmental economics at a time when this discipline is confronted by unprecedented challenges. The second is that of encouraging a reductionism in energy terms that is even more impoverished than monetary reductionism. The term *energy reductionism* signifies the systematic replacement of all monetary valuations by energy-based valuations with the consequent transformation of economics into a branch of thermodynamics (Faucheux and Pillet 1994).

As far as the biosphere itself is concerned, the monetary dimension does not exist. There is merely a physical dimension, which is called ecological reality. This organizational level concerns the economist only to the extent that it im-pinges on the economic sphere. Energy evaluation, if it actually does provide a common medium of expression between economic and ecological realities, has therefore an important part to play. While a number of elements of the biosphere are linked to the economic sphere, they are too few to make possible efficient management not only of pollution but also of exhaustible or renewable natural resources on the basis of analyses rest only on monetary valuation. That is why, if energy is indeed a common denominator for the whole range of natural phenomena, it can fill in the gaps left by monetary valuation.

The more long term the view that is taken, the greater is the importance attached to real phenomena. That is why, as Judson (1989) explained, analyses based on energy valuation are particularly important in that they apply to decisions taken in the long run that may have irreversible effects on a large scale (Toman 1992). So long as we look at time from an economic angle (the short, medium, or long term), monetary considerations can predominate. Nonetheless, as soon as time measured in terms of the biosphere enters the economic analysis—an intergenerational period having no link whatsoever with the long term in the economic sense—energy valuation has an important role to play. This chapter is in two parts. The first part concerns the limits of the traditional environmental economic analysis which cannot take into consideration the natural sphere and its specifications. The second part concerns ecoenergetic analysis and its ability to take account of multidimensional consideration necessary to environmental management.

The Means of Integrating the Environment into Economic Analysis and the Relevant Limitations

The predominating economic theory relating to the environment breaks down into a theory of natural resources and a theory of internalization. The only natural resources taken into account by economic analysis are those that impinge on the market, that is to say, those that have an equivalent monetary value and therefore form part of economic reality. By contrast, all contributions made by "free" natural resources to the production of economic goods and services are ignored, since they possess no price by which they could be measured. Resource theory is therefore unable to assess neither the contribution made by the environment to the economy nor, in the terminology used here, the contribution of ecological to economic reality.

For their part, the advocates of internalization theory claim that they can measure in monetary terms, on the basis of individual utility, all the effects on the environment of the waste produced by the economic system. Voices are being raised against the limitations of such a method, especially since the emergence of global forms of pollution, too many elements of which fall outside the economic domain and the scope of individual calculations.

Exclusion of the Specificity of Natural Resources

In the context of contemporary economic analysis, the issue of exhaustible natural resources can be approached in three ways.

Backstop technology theory. The first, which rests on Hotelling's (1931) exhaustible resources theory, dispenses with any attribution of specificity to natural resources. It should be remembered that in this approach the aim is not to maximize the period separating us from the exhaustion of a stock of fossil fuel or some other form of exhaustible resource, but rather to maximize the monetary value of these resources within a finite period. The approaches, both microeconomic and macroeconomic, that stem from this analysis are direct descendants of neoclassical growth theory, in which capital and labor are the sole production factors.

The backstop technology theory advanced by Nordhaus (1973) stresses the regulatory role of price in the management of exhaustible resources. It pursues Hotelling's analysis and, in particular, takes up the idea that over time the price of a resource rises as it is consumed, so leading to the introduction of substitutes. This is, of course, possible only by an increase in the capital stock underpinning technical progress. Backstop technology is capable of producing energy, admittedly at a higher cost than traditional methods, but at a constant cost and on an inexhaustible basis. It can be brought into operation as soon as the market prices of other, traditional sources of energy rise sufficiently to cover its development costs. It becomes competitive, and, since it now calls not on exhaustible resources but on renewable flows, the market price ceases to rise. Production is able to free itself of its dependence on exhaustible energy sources, and, after backstop technology has taken the place of the whole range of fossil fuels, there is a return to the traditional production function in which capital and labor are the only factors.

A theory of this kind entirely dispenses with the possibility that growth or development could be impeded by an absolute scarcity of a source of fossil fuel. The very existence of a possible energy problem or of a problem involving the exhaustion of any other form of natural resources is negated, as a backstop technology exists for all other forms of resources. Neoclassical growth theory is thereby reaffirmed. The competitive forces of the market ensure that suitable substitution takes place automatically, so disposing of any worries about absolute scarcity. It is enough to allow the market to operate freely, to encourage competition, and to safeguard the security of private property.

The macroeconomic KLEM models (called in the literature macroenergetic models), which incorporate energy and materials as full-fledged factors of production and entail the use of substitutable-factor production functions, also conform to this line of thought. This applies to the Cobb-Douglas and CES cases, which are the most customary functions. Because they conform to the tradition of backstop technology theory, most macroenergetic models lead to the conclusion that energy or materials can be substituted for capital as factors of production. The most important factor is always capital, making it unnecessary to move away from the reference macroeconomic model, that is, the standard growth model. Furthermore, in conformity with the neoclassical model, these functions treat the various factors of production on an equal footing without regard for the specificity of natural resources, that is, materials and energy. However, these resources obey the laws of conservation dictated by physics. Matter is subject to Lavoisier's law of conservation ("nothing is lost, nothing is gained"), excluding any movement that is pursued indefinitely. The increasing efficiencies of scale cannot continue without limit.

Energy, for its part, obeys the laws of thermodynamics. The first of these lays down the conservation of energy and the equivalence of the various forms of energy. What is involved is the transposition of energy according to Lavoisier's formula. According to the second law, energy is not lost and but is downgraded into heat, thus increasing the entropy of the universe. The second law describes a transformation. It states that, when heat is converted into energy, only a part of the heat is used, while the remainder evades utilization. While the quantity of energy remains constant, there is an unavoidable decline in quality. It follows that efficiency, which is defined as the ratio between the minimum amount of work required for a given task and the work represented by the energy actually expended in performing the task, is always less than unity (except in the case of heat generation). This reduction in the energy available for performing work is measured by an abstract quantity known as *entropy*.

Entropy imparts properties of concavity to production functions. However, this problem is usually hidden, as is evidenced by the work of Dasgupta and Heal (1974), who analyze production with the intervention of natural resources as a factor of production but who do not concern themselves with the implications for the convexity features of the production facilities under consideration. It follows that for production processes that use such factors as energy, which obey the conservation laws of physics, there certainly exists an absolute maximum output figure. Thus, the mean productivities of natural resources such as materials or energy must be subject to an absolute majorant. A production process that uses given quantities of the energy factor is therefore subject to constraint in terms of absolute maximum output.

As Lesourd (1984) has demonstrated, these properties are therefore incompatible with the existence of a convex production function, and hence of functions of the type exhibiting an exponential growth, and are incompatible with the Cobb-Douglas and CES production functions, for which the mean productivity of the factors is not subject to an upper limit. The most common macroeconomic analyses of exhaustible resources have consequently led first to a denial that growth could be inhibited by energy constraints and second to a disregard for the specificity of these resources by appealing to functions that are incompatible with the laws of thermodynamics.

The problem of expectations. A second type of approach to the issue of exhaustible natural resources, initiated by Solow (1974), has sought to draw attention to the specificity of exhaustible resources. This microeconomic approach also relies on Hotelling's (1931) work. According to Solow, the stability of the equilibrium that is the fundamental principle of the exhaustible-resource economy is not necessarily ensured. He shows that Hotelling and the advocates of backstop technology have forgotten to incorporate the problem of expectations into their analysis.

Having pointed out that the condition for balanced flow is that the net price should increase in line with compound interest at the current rate, Solow considers the case where producers expect that net prices will grow too slowly. Deposits of natural resources then prove to be an inefficient way of holding wealth, and the owners prefer to step up production to convert the resources into cash. The prevailing price drops, with the result that pessimistic forecasts of net prices lead to increased pressure on current prices. There is no return to a state of balance. On the contrary, the effect that caused the imbalance is cumulative. It follows that, as soon as expectations are taken into account, the price of the energy resource may no longer be in step with the resource's degree of scarcity. Solow also shows that the market may experience dysfunctions that prevent prices from reflecting the scarcity of the resource. For instance, it is sufficient for the supply to be dominated by a monopoly or an oligopoly for the setting of prices to become a function of policy and not of the scarcity of the products, or for price to be essentially determined by the tax system prevalent in the producer countries, as happens with energy resources.

Solow further explains that intertemporal optimal allocation by the market is not necessarily ensured when it comes to natural resources. The rate at which the market anticipates future profits does not always coincide with the rate at which society as a whole wishes to allow for the future well-being of the planet's inhabitants (Benhaïm 1993). The hypothesis by which the competitive balance is optimal in the sense proposed by Pareto may be placed in question by the introduction of an exhaustible resource. The market interest rate is usually higher than the social rate of temporal preference, notably because individual temporal preference does not seem to provide a good basis for intertemporal options. Individuals, either through lack of imagination or because they are conscious of the brevity of their lives, may opt for the present enjoyment of future goods and services, but society is not in a position to do likewise. There is, in fact, no argument justifying inequality of treatment between generations.

Solow thus takes up a position midway between the foregoing two extremes: that of the Club of Rome and of many authors of the stationary-state school, who predict the inevitable end of growth as a result of the absolute scarcity of exhaustible energy resources, and that of backstop technology theory, for which there exists only relative scarcity. Solow demonstrates that technological progress combined with the substitution of capital can counteract, though only in part, the inadequacy of exhaustible resources. Furthermore, he acknowledges that the laws of thermodynamics place constraints on economic growth that cannot always be disposed of simply by substituting capital for energy resources.

In Solow's analysis, exhaustible natural resources acquire the status of specific capital. Unlike capital in the strict sense, the stock of which grows in step with investment, natural resources are at best preserved at their original level and usually decline as a function of consumption. The stock of such resources suffers disinvestment, and an increase in the stock of capital in the strict sense is unable to provide complete compensation.

All the same, the specificity of energy is not genuinely incorporated into the economic calculation. This lack of integration is such that, in a later analysis, Solow abandons all contributions made by this work. He passes from the notion of intergenerational equity in the use of exhaustible resources to that of intergenerational equity as regards total resources, that is, an inclusive concept of capital in the strict sense, natural resources, and human capital. He adduces Hartwick's (1978) rule, according to which investment in reproducible capital must be equal to the earnings derived from the use of exhaustible resources, and he shows that the reduction of inputs in exhaustible resources can be offset by an increase in reproducible capital. Intergenerational equity can be maintained by a recomposition within the stock of global resources (Solow 1986). This assumes, of course, that the possibility of substitution between capital and exhaustible resources is virtually unlimited. This therefore brings us back to a model close to that of backstop technology. It is unfortunately this second analysis by Solow (1986) that has been taken up and is being pursued in many current studies on sustainable growth (Mäler 1992; Nordhaus 1992).

Translog functions and their limitations. An effort to integrate the specificities of energy and other commercial exhaustible natural resources—that is, materials—has recently been undertaken by macroeconomic analysis. For this purpose, use has been made of KLEM models that employ new production functions and flexible functional forms that can easily take account of more than two factors and that are, above all, characterized by variable elasticities of substitution. Most of these functions take the form of linear expressions capable of approximating a wide range of real production functions. This capability applies especially to the translog production function, which, as a generalization of the Cobb-Douglas production function, defines input and output variables in quadratic logarithmic form. The translog function marks a considerable advance in encompassing the substitutability of factors at the production level, as it allows elasticities of substitution that may a priori be of any nature. It therefore enables questions to be asked concerning the substitutable or complementary character of the relationships between energy or materials and other factors.

What is more, the translog function is able to meet the conditions imposed by the physical laws of conservation, that is, the second law of thermodynamics, which, as has been shown, manifests itself in the economic context by setting a limit to mean productivities. In the case of a homogeneous translog function of the first degree, the mean efficiency of the factors will admit a majorant. Therefore, by using the translog function to analyze the concavity of the fit of the output on logarithmic coordinates of any production system, it is possible to see whether or not the mean productivity of the energy is subject to an upper limit and thereby to determine whether or not there exists a minimum quantity of energy to obtain a given added value P. In other words, it is possible to ascertain whether or not energy is a limiting factor for the growth of the activity concerned.

However, although translog functions meet all the conditions for integrating the specificity of exhaustible resources into the economic analysis, a number of application-related problems render such integration theoretical rather than practical (Faucheux 1993). It should be mentioned, for instance, that its scope with regard to the analysis of substitutability seems to be limited in practice. The results of such analysis carried out on different models reveal appreciable divergences, even when specificities of equivalent form are used (Amable 1987). Similarly, the information conveyed by the concavity is also severely limited by the fact that, to facilitate modeling, use is made of monetary (not physical) indicators, the stability and reliability of which are very much open to question.

This analysis, like those considered previously, has difficulty in breaking away from the neoclassical model. The fact is that all these analyses rest, to a varying extent, on the following two basic hypotheses:

1. the substitutability of exhaustible energy resources and capital, thanks to technological progress, which renders the scarcity of resources at worst relative, but never absolute, and
2. the regulatory role of the market, which, by means of changes in relative prices, provides a suitable guide for the optimal allocation of resources.

These hypotheses are at the root of the limitations of the predominant economic analysis of exhaustible resources. Such an analysis is not able to provide working tools for the management of these resources. It can no longer evaluate either the impacts on the production process of their scarcity or an increase in their price.

The Limits of Economic Analysis with Regard to
Pollution Management

Any form of pollution directly affects the well-being of the consumer. The value of the pollution—or more correctly, its cost—is in these circumstances based on the principle of individual preferences. Thus, pollution problems have provided yet another field for the application of neoclassical economic theory.

The economic concept involved here is that of negative externality. Only by the internalization of this concept is it possible to restore the optimum. Many authors have shown that there is no reason that the optimum so defined should correspond to a situation of zero production or zero pollution, since it represents only the application of economic rationality by the emitter and the victim to the solution of a problem not resolved by the market (Faucheux, Froger, and Noël 1993).

Even though it presents a number of problems, a management tool of this kind has found applicability to localized pollution. The difficulties started to emerge with cases of transboundary pollution such as acid rain. Even here, the induced ecological problems are relatively limited and are, above all, not liable to jeopardize the balance of the biosphere. If the market is able to cope with localized forms of pollution, it can no longer apply in cases of global pollution.

Irreversibility: An important characteristic of global pollution. Global pollution combines irreversibility and biological impacts. In one sense all actions are irreversible inasmuch as it is always impossible to move back through time. However, the consequences of most actions are reversible provided that adequate means of reversal are used. This is true of pollutions of the traditional type, which can usually be cleared up. By contrast, for pollutions on a global scale, such as the depletion of the ozone layer and the intensification of the greenhouse effect, time is the only possible remedy. Because of the prolonged period between emissions of a gas and its ultimate effect on the ozone layer and on the climatic balance, it might take decades or hundreds of years to eliminate the pollution. Furthermore, in contrast to cases of traditional pollution, it is not possible at present to wait until the effects of global pollution are detected, as it is then liable to be too late to take corrective measures. It follows that the term *irreversible* means simultaneously that a given action places a constraint on future options and that its consequences are permanent (at least on the human scale) (Froger, Zyla 1994). Other types of environmental problems possess this irreversible character—for instance, the flooding of a valley by damming to store water for hydroelectric power generation. Other kinds of pollution, and especially toxic pollution due to cadmium, mercury, PCBs, and so on, have biological repercussions. However, until now no occurrence of pollution has simultaneously exhibited these two characteristics on a scale encompassing the entire planet as well as strong uncertainty (Vercelli 1994).

It should be noted that the methods and means of internalization, which are numerous (and will not be recounted here), all assume inter alia the identification of the emitter and recipient of the externality. In particular, the character of partial microeconomic equilibrium of the suggested solutions tends to link the solutions to a universe comprising two agents or, at best, to a classical competitive market scenario. As soon as the problem is confronted by numerous or unknown agents, this instrument becomes difficult to use. But the fact is that the depletion of the ozone layer—and to an even greater extent, the intensification of the greenhouse effect—involves a multitude of actors on both sides.

Cost-benefit analysis and antipollution policy. Parallel to these attempted solutions based on the internalization of externalities, we have witnessed the development of the technique of cost-benefit analysis as a guide to rational decision making on antipollution policy. Cost-benefit analysis assigns a monetary value to the benefits of policies—that is, to the costs of the pollutions they avoid—and compares the benefits with the costs of the policies themselves. Monetary valuation of the benefits enables the decision maker to make a choice guided, once more, exclusively by verification of the economic rationale of the investments dedicated to the fight against pollution. All that has to be done is to select those policies where the marginal benefit exceeds, or is equal to, the marginal cost. As far as ozone is concerned, the resources demanded by the various alternative policies for controlling the ozone-depleting gases may still be regarded as limited, since only one area of industry is implicated and is therefore not considered strategically important.

Cost-benefit analysis, as a decision-making tool, requires a knowledge of the costs of pollution (which enables the advantages of antipollution policies, interpreted as avoided losses, to be established) and of the costs of the battle against pollution. It also assumes that both sets of costs can be evaluated in monetary terms and are comparable.

In order to calculate the economic benefits of a policy for controlling the gases blamed for the diminution of the ozone layer or for the intensification of the greenhouse effect, we first have to establish the dose/response ratio between emissions and the various effects they generate. The purely economic impacts occur at the end of a causation chain composed of many levels of order. By way of illustration, the first level, in the case of the greenhouse effect, relates to climatic change (alteration of the precipitation pattern, greater range of temperature variations, etc.). The second level relates to the primary effects of climatic changes (effects on plant production, on freshwater ecosystems, etc.), which are physical and therefore extraeconomic in nature. The socioeconomic impacts start to appear only at the third level of order. The various socioeconomic activities affected by the impacts of the two preceding levels (agriculture, fishing, tourism, industry, etc.) and their cost are observable at the microeconomic level (farm, enterprise, etc.), then at the macroeconomic level (sectors and countries) and at world level, corresponding respectively to the fourth and fifth levels of order.

Part of the scientific controversy relates to the dose/response ratios between emitted quantities of CO_2 and CFCs, to mention only these, and to the ways they affect first the atmosphere and thereafter the biosphere. The difficulty is aggravated by the fact that we can no longer argue from the ideal position postulated by traditional economic theory, in which there is a linear relationship between emission and damage, a position that corresponds fairly well to pollution of the traditional kind. Unidirectional linearity has been exchanged for interaction and complexity. Under these circumstances the dose/response ratio loses much of its significance.

Even assuming that such a ratio could be established, the monetary valuation of these effects poses a second problem. It is apparent that the purely commercial impacts produced at the end of the chain account for only a part of the negative effects of these forms of pollution. Thus, they alone lend themselves to direct monetary valuation, since they affect commercial activities. For the others we have to call on a method of shadow pricing. It has already been stated that individual preferences provide the basis for measuring the costs of the impacts of pollution, or, in other words, for gauging the benefits to be expected from an antipollution policy that enables such effects to be eliminated. It is assumed that the net preference for a thing is reflected in its willingness to pay. The sum of individual willingness to pay (which may vary with the individuals questioned) is an indicator of what is socially desirable. In the absence of an existing market or of a substitution market for the benefits, economic theory recommends, for establishing willingness to pay, the creation of a notional market by asking individuals what they are prepared to pay to continue enjoying the benefits. If, confronted with localized pollution, we tentatively allow the cost of such pollution, to be calculated by reference to the sum the users are ready to pay, what is to be said when the pollution is global in character?

The widening of the field covered by value (option value, bequest value, existence value, etc.) (Pearce and Turner 1990) does not free us from the limitations inherent in any method of evaluation that rests solely on willingness to pay. In the context of global pollution, too many elements lie outside the domain of the economy and individual calculations for any monetary valuation of the benefits of a control policy to retain any sense whatsoever or for any pertinent role in the selection of the optimal standard to be adopted.

Finally, in the context of traditional pollution, the linkage of costs and benefits (in terms of avoided losses) is made possible by their chronological proximity, the occurrence of pollution, and the costs arising from the remedial measures that are perceptible in the short—or, at most, medium—term. What is more, the consequences and their costs are already apparent when a remedial policy is instituted. With global environmental problems, in which the stakes include the biological integrity of living species, the policies necessarily have to be adopted before the totality of the effects is felt. The result is large-scale staggering over time of the impacts of the various costs arising from global environmental problems.

The costs of global pollution will begin to be truly felt only from 2050 onward, that is, beyond the range of economic predictions, which, even in the case of ultra-long-term forecasts, never exceeds thirty years (Faucheux and Noël 1990). The costs of policies, be they adaptive or preventive in nature, are incurred as soon as the initial measures are taken, with the sole difference that, for adaptive policies, costs are limited to the short term, whereas costs continue into the medium and long term for preventive policies. Similarly, the effects of adaptive policies are virtually immediate—without, however, putting a final stop to the cost of pollution. By contrast, the effects of preventive policies materialize only beyond the economic horizon, owing to the slowness of the great biogeochemical cycles whose balance they are designed to restore. There exists an intuitive link between these considerations and the precautionary principle. Such a principle implies the current safeguard of environmental resources against the potentially catastrophic outcomes of economic activities (Perrings 1991).

Assuming that the costs of global forms of pollution can be evaluated in monetary terms, there is an additional reason that prevents them from being compared to the costs of the various antipollution policies. Such a procedure would necessitate the use of a discount rate, and the action of discounting, by depreciating the future in relation to the present, results in a further contraction of the period of economic calculation, which is already incommensurable with the time span over which the impacts make themselves felt. The benefits to be expected from control policies would consequently be systematically underval-ued in relation to their costs, and this might lead to a wait-and-see decision or to inadequate regulations, with the results that have already been pointed out. The use of a discount rate lower than that applied to ordinary projects would not alter the essential problem because, for impacts whose cost may be very high but that will occur only after fifty or one hundred years, the discounted value—even at a very low rate—would amount to mere background noise (Benhaïm 1993).

The observation may be made here that Pearce demonstrated in 1976: that cost-benefit analysis raises problems when an attempt is made to apply it to dynamic pollution processes characterized by an uninterrupted growth of ecolog-ical instability. In this situation, the optimal solution invariably demands an emission level lower than that dictated by consideration of a cost-benefit analysis alone. It should be noted that global pollution processes do, indeed, exhibit this dynamic characteristic. Pearce went further, considering this tool unsuitable, or even dangerous, in the case of pollutions where the biological effects are not tempered by any assimilative capacity of the surroundings. Beyond a certain threshold, global pollution, which is our present concern, and toxic pollution processes fall into this category. The gases blamed for the depletion of the ozone layer accumulate in the atmosphere by virtue of their life span, which may in some cases be as much as a hundred years. As far as CO_2 is concerned, if possibilities of assimilation exist (vegetable biomass, oceans, etc.), the question of these gases' possible saturation arises.

All in all, the use of cost-benefit analysis poses additional problems since, if the benefit represented by the avoided cost of the pollution cannot be reasonably evaluated in monetary terms, no reliable technique exists that would enable us to compare costs and benefits on an equal footing. Thus, because the biosphere is involved as a result of global pollution processes, traditional methods of manag-ing global pollution based on the internalization of external effects can no longer be used as sole decision-making aids when it comes to establishing the standards and policies to be adopted.

The Treatment of the Environment in the Light of Ecoenergy Analysis

From what has been said above it seems that, for the management of the major types of contemporary environmental problems, economic theory can no longer acquiesce in an economic treatment of ecological reality, that is, in the broader internalization of external effects. On the contrary, what is needed is exterioriza-tion, that is, a linkage between the economy and the biosphere. To this end it is necessary to devise a means of relating economic reality to ecological reality, notably a common means of measuring value.

It will be possible to postpone the exhaustion of resources—that is, finitude (Daly 1987a)—only if economic theory acquires a tool for assessing all the effects on the economy of environmental goods and services. This would provide the means for improved arbitration between the use of ecological natural resources and natural resources passed through the market. Similarly, the postponement of the threat posed by global pollution processes—that is, the deferment of a state of entropy (Daly 1987a)—would be conditioned by a better knowledge of all the effects of the economy on the environment.

These management problems relating to the economy/biosphere interface cannot be resolved merely by the traditional methods described above, since these all have recourse to the monetary measurement of values. This form of measurement cannot ensure the commensurability of economic and ecological reality, as it refers only to the contained subsystem—the economy—and has no significance in relation to the biosphere. One therefore proposes to direct research toward ecoenergy analysis in order to avoid limits of the monetary approach.

Ecoenergy Analysis as a Tool for the Management of Finitude

Toward a breaking amount of noncommercial natural input services. With regard to the involvement of elements of the biosphere in the production process, the conventional economic approach, as we have seen, assigns importance only to those commercial exhaustible natural resources that have acquired the status of factor of production. Economic theory has interested itself only in natural inputs with an equivalent monetary value, that is, in those elements of ecological reality that also belong to economic reality. The contribution of all free natural resources is ignored.

The vitality of a national economy depends not only on the labor of the population, the efforts of machines, and the work of nature, chiefly paid for in the form of rent, but also on many natural processes external to the mechanisms of the market. Ecological reality therefore participates in national production; hence, the economy is closely linked to the ecological dimension represented by the biosphere. It is therefore important not only to distinguish between the services for final consumption and the productive services rendered by the environment but also to differentiate the latter services. Natural productive services must no longer be identified exclusively with the inputs that figure in the national accounts, that is, with only commercial natural resources. The concept must be widened to include the contribution made by nonmarket resources. This effort must be made to encompass both commercial and noncommercial natural input services. The contribution of noncommercial natural input services should be included in economic theory, since it is by this means that finitude can be deferred.

It seems essential to know exactly for what purpose (and to what extent) a natural resource is used in production before it becomes scarce—and thereby oversteps the threshold of economic consideration by acquiring a price—or simply disappears by virtue of its uniqueness. In order to avoid mistaken choices affecting the use of these resources and to achieve an efficient allocation, it is now desirable to establish their precise contribution to the various production processes in which they play a part and the possibilities of substitution that exist between them and other natural resources or perhaps between them and labor and/or capital.

With regard to commercial natural input services, it is also found that these are physical objects that are sought for themselves and not for their physical, chemical, or other properties supplying specific services. The point is that very often the same type of function can be fulfilled by noncommercial natural input services, although this fact is not known, because the latter have not been evaluated. In view of the now-emerging threat of the scarcity or prohibited use of some commercial natural input services, it is important that the potential of all commercial and noncommercial natural input services be evaluated. This is the effort needed to derive full benefit from the fact that there is not always a one-to-one relationship between supplied services and natural resources, since more than one such resource can provide identical services. Moreover, the possibilities of substitution between commercial and noncommercial natural input services would, among other things, provide a means of evaluating the contribution made by the latter to production processes.

Judgment is possible as soon as knowledge is obtained of the real and potential contributions of natural resources that pertain solely to ecological reality and of those that simultaneously form part of economic reality. But there is a measure of value common to both the ecological and economic realities, and that is energy. Thus, the present purpose is to put forward an energy evaluation procedure applicable to noncommercial natural input services.

Toward an ecoenergy analysis of the production function. To the extent that the methods proposed by economic theory tend to assign zero value to the contribution made by noncommercial natural input services to productive activity, care has to be exercised in the selection of the valuation procedure when we come to consider ecoenergy analysis.

The methods that make use of an energy scale based on the first law of thermodynamics alone should not be adopted in the present case. To compute indifferently in kilocalories all the inputs from the environment and those passing through the medium of the market is tantamount to considering as equivalent all the forms of energy that they represent. It means depriving oneself at the outset of the possibility of establishing a hierarchy of energy qualities, which is just what is needed here in order to determine the true contribution to economic output of each energy input. All energy flows, whether they originate from commercial or noncommercial natural input services or from human effort, do not possess the same utility in particular because they do not have the same capacity to perform "work." Attempts at an ecoenergy analysis that embraces the economic system and the biosphere are often prevented from carrying much conviction in every case by a lack of awareness of this problem and the failure to provide a measuring tool that takes into account the various forms of energy.

The exergetic approach, which is founded on the first and second laws of thermodynamics (about which we have spoken elsewhere) provides a means, in

Borel's (1984) words, "of evaluating quantitatively what is referred to qualitatively as energy degradation, i.e. of calculating accurately the consequences of the various thermodynamically irreversible processes and so quantifying the thermodynamic losses of a system" (p. 10). It serves to measure the efficiency of thermodynamic systems with the accent on their ability to perform mechanical work.

Exergy is defined as the maximum amount of work that can be extracted from a thermodynamic system and provides a definition of the thermodynamic quality of energy in terms of a quantitative characterization of entropic losses. It therefore serves to establish a kind of qualitative hierarchy of the various forms of energy as a function of their ability to perform work. However, exergy refers to work only in the mechanical sense of the term. But, contrary to received belief, the greater or lesser capacity of any form of energy for performing mechanical work cannot by itself define its work potential or, more accurately, its utility. The notion of work is far broader than the restricted sense assigned to it by the exergetic scale. That is to say, the useful work that a form of energy is able to supply includes, but is not limited to, mechanical work. It follows that, while the qualitative exergy hierarchy based on the energetic evaluation procedure has, indeed, a great deal to tell us, it is not sufficient to encompass and arrange in hierarchical order all the forms of energy operating at the interface of the economic sphere and the biosphere.

The valuation procedure to be applied is that based on a scale capable of ranking forms of energy as a function of work in the broad sense assigned to the term by Odum: "Useful works are transformations that feed back materials and services" (Odum 1983, p. 100). Besides encompassing the first and second laws of thermodynamics, an approach of this kind involves the principle of maximum power inherent in systems that operate far from equilibrium, namely, open or living systems. This principle, introduced in 1922 by Lotka, asserts that systems in competition tend to maximize energy flow in unit time and that the systems prevailing are those that develop forms that maximize the flow of useful energy. In other words, those systems are capable of responding in such a way as to maximize the inflow of energy in order to increase their efficiency. This principle encompasses the cumulative action of energies acting in a chain. The approach is a global one, since it embraces the conversions that take place in the whole range of chains and energy circuits. In other words, it covers the overall organization of an ecoenergy system.

Odum (1988) has put forward an evaluation procedure incorporating this principle. The term first applied to it was *embodied energy,* then *emergy* (Pillet and Odum 1987), which signified contained energy and was defined as a means of measuring the cumulative action of energies operating in a chain. Analyses that make use of the emergetic method for studying systems interfacing the environment and the economy really got under way on a large scale with the work done for IIASA by the Odum and Odum (1983). Their work has since been pursued in collaboration with Pillet (1990).

The Odums' purpose is to describe in its entirety the energy network of a productive system, or a national economy, in which all inputs are interpreted as energy flows so as to identify the system's commercial and noncommercial contributions to output. The analytical idea underlying this method is that, at each level of an energy chain, the bulk of the energy is lost in the transformation process and only a small quantity is converted into higher-quality energy. Within the overall framework of the maximum power principle underlying the preceding observations, any form of energy, regardless of whether or not it passes through the medium of economic reality, is always the result of a process in which source (for example, solar) energy is transformed. At the various transformation stages the effective energy is quantitatively reduced, but increased in concentration and therefore in quality. The greater the distance from the initial energy source (the sun), the greater is the degree to which the energy obtained is processed, concentrated, and rendered recoverable. Thus, the overall efficiency of the system is optimized. In accordance with the second law of thermodynamics, any creation of higher-quality energy is paid for by a sacrifice of lower-level energy.

Consequently, the ratio of the quantity of solar energy required to generate a unit of another form of energy by transformation can serve as a measure of energy efficiency. Odum (1988) applies the term *transformity* to this ratio, which is designated by the abbreviation *Tr*. Transformity defines the degree of concentration, and hence the quality, in energy terms of the form of energy at a given point in the system under consideration. Reference is then made to the solar transformity of energy expressed in solar emjoules[1] per effective joule.[2] The solar transformity of a form of energy indicates the number of joules of solar energy incorporated in a unit in this form. It should be pointed out with regard to this procedure that the economist can rely on the work carried out by ecologists, who have determined the solar transformities of many forms of energy.

Once the transformity of any form of energy has been determined, its quality can be obtained, still in accordance with Odum (1988), by multiplying its transformity by its quantity of effective energy. The emergy quantity of this form indicates the quantity of solar energy needed for its generation. So, the emergy of a quantity of any form of energy corresponds to the solar energy required to produce it. For greater clarity, the procedure for evaluating the emergy of any form of energy i in an ecoenergy system can be described as follows:

$$C_i(p) \ emJ = E_i(p) \ J \cdot Tr_i(p) \ emJ/J \qquad (4.1)$$

where $C_i(p) =$ the quantity of emergy of the form of energy i at a
point p of the ecoenergy system
$E_i(p) =$ the quantity of effective energy of form i at point p

$Tr_i(p) =$ the solar transformity of form i at point p

The emergy of a form of energy determines the available energy of any transformation within an ecosystem of a system linking the environment and the economy. This measurement enables each stage of such a system to be evaluated and expressed on a common basis. It also provides us with the means of arranging the various forms of energy into a hierarchy. The magnitude of the transformity of any form of energy, whether it originates from the economic system or from nature, will indicate its degree of concentration and therefore its capacity for enhanced recovery and for the control or performance of work that would otherwise not have been possible.

The emergy approach also enables us to dispose of Punti's (1987) criticism concerning the inability of energy analyses to distinguish between natural resources (including both commercial and noncommercial natural input services) according to their degree of renewability. This bears energy from consideration as an efficient resource management tool. What does degree of renewability mean? It is believed that even exhaustible resources, such as primary forms of energy, are renewable on a very longtime scale—the geologic time scale—which bears no relation to the economic time scale.

Punti's objection does, indeed, appear sound when it refers to energy analyses based on an assessment associated with the first law of thermodynamics or to those using an exergy evaluation. In the former case, all forms of energy are expressed in the same way in calories without distinction as to their capacity to perform work or, of course, their respective renewal periods. In the latter case, we have to content ourselves with measuring thermodynamic efficiencies, classifying energy inputs merely according to their ability to perform mechanical work. While no information can therefore be deduced from these two energy-related approaches regarding the renewable character (in the sense usually given to the term) of the various forms of energy representing each commercial or noncommercial natural input service, the same does not apply to the emergy evaluation procedure.

As has just been shown, solar transformity reflects the concentration or dispersion in which each form of energy occurs. For instance, it reflects the fact that oil is two thousand times more concentrated than solar energy, forty times more concentrated than wind energy, and twenty times more concentrated than the energy of photosynthesis. This concentration is linked to the time factor, which means that the time required for the reconstitution of any form of energy is inherent in its solar transformity, which, let it not be forgotten, is always calculated in situ. It follows that, if we know the solar transformity of any form of energy, we are then able to determine the time needed for the reconstitution of a joule in this form. Taking the effective quantity consumed during a period of time t, we are able, by multiplying the unit reconstitution period established above, to ascertain the time required for the renewal of this consumed quantity. Since we know that, as the transformity of a form of energy becomes greater, so its renewability diminishes, we can infer that the emergy approach assigns a value to accumulated time and is therefore able to compare, two by two, the various forms of energy on the basis of their degree of renewability.

It follows that the emergy evaluation procedure provides us with a means of arranging all forms of energy into a hierarchy not only according to their utility within a natural system or a system comprising the environment/economy interface but also according to their greater or lesser renewability. We should add, in conclusion, that in this context such evaluation can only complement a monetary assessment (Faucheux and Pillet 1994).

A tool of this kind covers the whole range of inputs used by the economic system by means of the common denominator energy, so as to convey a picture of the share in economic output of noncommercial natural input services. This means that consideration is given to the entire spectrum of energy flows, extending from those with little structure to the higher—that is, very concentrated—forms of energy. The approach therefore encompasses all the commercial and noncommercial contributions made by the natural environment to economic activities, as well as those originating solely from the economic sphere, on the basis of the same work-performing capacity.

A Genuine Tool for Managing Finitude

The notion of finitude relates chiefly to the exhaustible resources that are for the most part considered a factor of production. Energy accountancy—and energy calculation—play the roles of decision-making aids complementary to economic calculation in the management of these commercial resources (Faucheux 1994). Moreover, it is essentially the exergy approach that enables the wastages caused by production processes that consume fossil fuels or raw materials to be identified and remedied. This finitude-management tool depends on technological progress. It provides a means of cutting down the consumption of noncommercial natural input services by improvements in the thermodynamic efficiency of productive systems. However, its effectiveness at a given time t is not limited merely by the state of the art t; it also encounters an absolute limit rooted in the second law of thermodynamics. The emergy approach analysis can complement the exergy tool appropriate to energy calculation, as it is able to bring about savings of exhaustible resources by substituting renewable resources. As has been shown, many noncommercial natural input services possess features in common with renewable resources. Ecoenergy analysis and its emergy valuation procedure are able to quantify the physical contribution of each of these resource types to real economic production. It is therefore possible to identify all the commercial and noncommercial renewable resources capable of performing the same work as an exhaustible resource and to carry out their substitution, always provided that this is technically feasible. The potential for deferring finitude is therefore greatly increased by using the emergy tool to complement the exergy approach. ·

It must also not be forgotten that good management of finitude must take into account what we may refer to as the paradox of natural resources. Every natural resource is both renewable (on the geologic time scale) and exhaustible (when the renewal thresholds or natural cycles are broken). What is needed, therefore, is a unit of measurement that makes it possible to evaluate the rate at which each natural resource is reconstituted, so that this reconstitution rate can be brought into line with the relevant consumption rate. This approach would enable the effects of an economic process on resources, and hence on the stability of the natural system, to be established. We have seen that it is possible, by using the transformity of each resource, to determine its ecological cost, that is, the time needed for its reproduction. The choice of natural input services can then be made in the light of their renewal time or degree. An energy valuation that utilizes these various scales or valuation procedures can provide a means of measuring both energy efficiencies and the impacts of economic systems on the available forms of energy.

The increase of the overall emergy value of the natural input services used by a production process over time may have two causes: either an increase in total quantities of energy at their effective value or an increase in total solar transformities.[3] Recourse to energy valuation will not merely enable this trend to be halted but will also provide the means for finding a remedy. In the event of the first cause, wastage has taken place and one or more forms of energy are being used in greater proportions than in the past for producing identical quantities of the same goods. This then poses an efficiency problem that can be identified by an energy calculation using the exergy scale in accordance with the methodology. If the second cause obtains, it can be inferred that highly concentrated, and therefore the most exhaustible, forms of energy, such as fossil fuels, have been more heavily consumed over a period of time. In these circumstances light can be shed on the situation by analyzing the consumed quantities of each input against its solar transformity. Hence, the complementary application of the exergy and emergy approaches enables us to determine the counterpart, in terms of products supplied by ecological reality, of the growth in purely economic goods (which they allow). Finally, the emergy approach helps to determine the standard that must be respected with regard to the maximum consumption level of natural resources in order to avoid their exhaustion.

Consider the following equation, which can be formulated in the manner stated by Punti (1987):

$$Rp(1 + S) = Rc \qquad (4.2)$$

where Rp = the resources produced by nature during the period of time considered, measured in units of ecological cost (i.e., renewal time)

       Rc = the resources consumed over the same period, also measured in units of ecological cost

       S = the stability indicator

Every time a production process is characterized by $S > 0$, then over time t, the process consumes more resources than nature is able to reproduce during the same period. A resource-exhaustion phase is initiated. If $S = 0$, the process absorbs over time t all that the biosphere produces during the same period, and equilibrium is maintained. Lastly, if $S < 0$, the process consumes only a part of what nature produces, and there is a surplus. Although for a long time the third case prevailed, the situation today fits the first. Both commercial natural input services and many noncommercial services are being overexploited in a way that can ultimately lead only to their exhaustion. Consequently, $S = 0$ marks the limit that must not be overstepped.

Ecoenergy analysis can contribute to establish the standard that the economic system must respect with regard to the consumption of natural resources geared to their renewal time. It results in an allocation of resources that ensures the viability and stability of the two systems—biosphere and economic sphere—thus forming a very-long-term interface and possibly warding off absolute finitude. Once this constraint is in place, the economic calculation of profit maximization regains its full pertinence. This is the reason why it is necessary to stress so forcefully the complementarity of energy calculation, ecoenergy analysis, and the traditional approach to resource management.

The Ecoenergy Approach as a Tool for Entropy Management

Sooner or later, the misuse of natural ecosystems by overexploitation or pollution upsets energy flows. It should be remembered that organisms, chemical cycles, water, air, human beings, and even machines are linked by energy flows. With the help of an ecoenergetic diagram, it is possible to track and even anticipate the implications in ecological and economic terms of the introduction of a pollutant into the ecosystem. It is, indeed, possible to describe and evaluate the implications of the resulting changes for the energy flows circulating not only in natural systems but also in the systems operating at the biosphere/economy interface and to do so at different levels ranging from a microsystem to the entire planet. However, when it comes to evaluating the ultimate services rendered by the environment (or the losses caused by the disappearance of such services in the wake of pollution, which amounts to the same thing), ecoenergy analysis is an imperfect tool. It provides no means of evaluating the subjective ultimate services, such as recreational services, afforded by natural systems.

As has been said, as far as these services are concerned, the internalization of external effects and the use of shadow pricing are, generally speaking, fairly appropriate in the case of traditional pollution. Similarly, ecoenergy analysis is unable to identify the genetic, or even biological, effects of pollution. However, despite its imperfections, it often enables us to predict ecological imbalances prior to final breakdown. Even if it focuses on only one aspect of environmental processes, ecoenergy analysis can often help to set pollution standards inasmuch as it provides one of the best methods of describing and analyzing ecosystems. It can act as a preliminary biological filter (Daly 1987b) before moving on to classical economic calculation. Without setting a sufficient standard, ecoenergy analysis has the merit of setting a necessary one and therefore of ruling out a number of possible courses in the area of environmental decision making.

However, several difficulties stand in the way of using ecoenergy analysis for global forms of pollution. The measurement in energy terms of the damage suffered by the natural system due to pollution involves measuring the reduction in the energy flows passing through the ecosystem. The depletion of the ozone layer manifests itself in an increase in the flows of solar energy entering the biosphere, while the intensification of the greenhouse effect prevents the necessary re-exit of a part of these flows. The result in both cases is a surplus of solar energy. It must be pointed out here that not every energy flow is beneficial to the receiver and, more especially, that the quantity of energy entering and leaving the biosphere constitutes a limiting factor for its reproduction and is subject to an optimum from which it is dangerous to stray in either the positive or the negative direction. The whole problem here centers on the fact that, to date, ecoenergy analysis has focused on the impacts due to insufficient rather than excessive energy. Its application in the latter case could give rise to serious mistakes.

It would be possible to approach the problem differently and to apply ecoenergy analysis to all the impacts due to the intensification of the greenhouse effect and/or the depletion of the ozone layer. However, here again we encounter a problem inasmuch as this analysis, just like the shadow-pricing method of evaluation, presupposes that we know the dose/response ratio, that is, that we possess a perfect knowledge of all the impacts and all the mechanisms created by these forms of pollution. As stated earlier, the controversy and the scientific uncertainties relate essentially to these effects, of which there are many. It should be added that the traditional emissions → effects sequence is complicated by an additional element. In the case of ozone, that element is the depletion of the ozone layer, and in that of the intensification of the greenhouse effect, that element is climatic change.

It follows that the acceptable pollution threshold can be fixed neither by traditional economic theory nor by the ecoenergy approach. These difficulties probably stem from the fact that posing the problem of the optimal pollution standard fails to raise the right question, especially when preventive measures are at issue. The point is that preventive measures relating to entropy involve the management not of entropy itself but of everything that lies upstream of the economic system; it entails inter alia improved management of finitude. The standard within this new perspective may be provided in view of the basket of existing technologies, by the ecoenergy approach.

Managing entropy. If one holds to the genuine prevention principle, which appears to be the proper strategy in the fight against global pollution, the standard must be set by reference not to the pollutant emissions of a production process but to the quality of its inputs, that is, to their entropic potential. In this connection, Kümmel (1989) speaks of "clean growth," where the aim is to manage entropy upstream of the economic system by a judicious choice of inputs. It is here that the energy approach can, once again, be of great service.

Let us remember that not only the intensification of the greenhouse effect but also acid rain and many other forms of more traditional atmospheric, and even aquatic, pollution originate wholly or in part from the use of fossil fuels. One preventive measure would, of course, be to reduce its consumption. Pollution management today joins hands with the management of finitude. With this end in view, energy analysis provides us with a whole range of indicators that enable us to set not a pollution standard but an energy consumption standard.

It seems essential to act on the energy supply. This entails the substitution of nonfossil fuels for fossil fuels. It is immediately apparent that ecoenergy analysis and its emergy valuation procedure are particularly effective decision-making aids in this context. As explained above, they make it possible to opt between various commercial and noncommercial forms of energy according to their respective utility. So, if two forms of energy are capable of performing similar work and one is derived from a fossil fuel while the other is not, the decision should be in favor of the latter. Nevertheless, alterations of this kind cannot be immediate, given the inertia affecting changes in the energy supply. Nor is it the intention to rush into the blind imposition of energy solutions that, while admittedly reflecting the emergy approach, are geared only to the basket of currently existing technologies. The ideal would therefore be to find a means of acquiring an apprenticeship period during which major research and R & D programs could be evolved steering toward the right energy solution while at the same time cutting down the consumption of fossil fuels. This means can be attained through the control of energy consumption, the techniques of which are supported by energy calculation.

Action is focused this time on energy demand, and it brings back into the foreground the question of energy savings, which had tended to be neglected following the decline in fossil fuel prices at the start of the 1980s. It has been shown that energy calculation, especially when the exergy approach is used, is able to provide the indicators essential to the setting up of a genuine energy-saving policy. What is really needed is a tool of broader scope for the purposes of identification and valuation—a tool that would measure the pollutant potential of the inputs used by a production process. Thanks to its recent developments, ecoenergy analysis is able to provide such a tool.

On the one hand, many cases of atmospheric pollution or of the contamination of water resources and the oceans are due to toxic heavy metals and to compounds of petrochemical products. These elements are usually obtained from energy-producing materials or base stock of high solar transformity. Consequently, this value indicates not merely the time required to create a resource, as has been shown, but also its pollution potential. It should therefore enable options to be calculated with due regard for both the finitude and the entropy constraints.

On the other hand, a school made up of economists such as Murota and Tamanoï, energy specialists, and ecologists was formed in Japan in September 1983 under the name Society for Studies on Entropy (Pillet and Murota 1987). Otherwise, some authors belonging to the neo-Austrian school (Faber et al. 1990; Kümmel 1989) were also among the pioneers of what is since called the entropy valuation procedure (Schembri 1993). Their purpose is to measure the quality of inputs in terms of the impurities they contain or, more precisely, in terms of what they call the entropy mix of the substances in question. The sources used stem from the theoretical analysis of entropy introduced by Georgescu-Roegen (1970) and from the input/output type of analysis applied to the environment by Daly (1971), the limitations of which, as in the case of material balances, are partly linked to the absence of homogeneous measurement.

The aim is to produce entropy balances for production processes. The issue is not the increase of entropy as such but the quest for a means of minimizing the generation of entropy. This approach leads to a definition of the theoretical entropy quality of production processes, to which technology could then be subordinated. Like the emergy approach, entropy production rests on an ecoenergy valuation procedure. In this instance, the concern is not the aggregation of different sorts of entropy but the measurement of the generation of entropy in the biosphere, the lithosphere, the atmosphere, and the hydrosphere. As stated by Kümmel (1989), who interprets entropy production as a true pollution index which he seeks to incorporate in a model of environmental constraint on industrial growth, the entropy of a production process is defined as follows:

$$S = k \ln \Omega \qquad (4.3)$$

where k is the Boltzman constant and Ω is the number of states available to the molecules of the system in a multidimensional space. This space is characterized by the position of the coordinates and the movements of all the molecules traversing it. If it is assumed that there are in the biosphere system n different types of molecules and the number of states available to molecules of type i is designated as Oi, then each different combination of states of the molecular subsystems i, j, represents a different state of the total system. The total number of states available to the molecules of the biosphere is given by the product P of the states of the subsystems Ω i in such a way that

$$\Omega = \Pi \, \Omega_i \qquad (4.4)$$

By combining equations (4.3) and (4.4), we obtain the entropy of the biosphere at a given instant such that

$$S = k \ln \Pi \Omega i = k \, \Sigma \ln \Omega_i \qquad (4.5)$$

This concept can be used as a pollution indicator insofar as the pollution is partly characterized by the diffusion of all sorts of molecules in the biosphere. If we take the derivative ds/dt of equation (4.5) and divide by the space R of the biosphere, we obtain a measurement of the density of entropy production U in the biosphere:

$$U = R^{-1} \, dS/dt = (k/R) \sum d \ln \Omega \, i/dt = \sum U_i \qquad (4.6)$$

The entropy approach to pollution analysis therefore consists in identifying the density of entropy production in the subsystem of i molecules

$$Ui = (k/R) \, d \ln \Omega_i/dt \qquad (4.7)$$

with the pollution of chemical and/or radioactive and/or thermal nature associated with these i molecules. U in equation (4.6) would represent the total pollution. In sum, entropy production provides us with an instrument for measuring pollutants. As an indicator, entropy production allows us to compare, on a unified scale, the pollution potential of different substances used in production processes.

The entropy approach is an aid, if not to the fixing of an emission standard, at least to the setting of a standard for the inputs consumed by productive systems. This standard could be established in the following way: For an identical production process, an inventory would be compiled of the various possible combinations of raw materials allowed by the state of the art, together with their respective entropy indices. The standard would then specify the combination with the lowest entropy production. A system of economic entropy-regulating mechanisms could then be instituted to enable this standard to be achieved at minimum cost. This new tool would also lend itself to the efficient management of many other types of pollution besides those of a global character. The energy approach therefore provides us with decision-making aids in the battle against both finitude and entropy, that is, against unsustainable development. This is the reason that ecoenergy analysis and energy calculation are now seen as methods of refining the economic calculations rooted in the theory of traditional environmental economics.

The emergence of global environmental problems has given birth to the idea that the economy must be able to manage development while safeguarding the reproduction of the environment which provides its inputs and receives its waste. The recent concept of sustainable development stresses that this reproduction of the natural sphere depends on that of the economic sphere. In these circumstances, sustainable development demands respect for the mechanisms and rules of the biosphere. This calls for a reexamination both of economic development theories as a whole and of the predominating theories of environmental economics. The former exclude from their field of analysis all concerns relating to finitude and entropy. The latter have difficulties envisage developments associated with the long term, and with reproduction and mutations, and they exhibit limited capacity for coping with large-scale environmental problems. Probably the core of the problem lies in the fact that both areas are seen as specific, not to say minor, aspects of economic theory, as is expressed in the following comment by Passet (1989) on environmental economics:

> In scientific terms, the idea that there might exist an *environmental economy,* conceived as an appendage to a *general economy* not concerning itself with this issue, makes no sense. In fact, there is a science of economics which, without forgoing its concern with the phenomena pertaining to its traditional domain, relates, or fails to relate, to the biosphere. (p. 15)

Similarly, any desire to devise general economics independently of development economics, that is, independently of any analysis as to how the phenomena relating to this domain evolve in the long term, is meaningless. To implement a sustainable development, it seems that we can proceed beyond this division and avail ourselves of the support provided by a number of new indicators offered by ecoenergy analysis (Faucheux 1994; Faucheux, Froger, and Noël 1993).

Notes

1. The introduction of the emjoulem was suggested by Scienceman (1987) to distinguish emergy from other approaches.
2. The calorie can very well be used in place of the joule. This is, indeed, what Odum has done in most of his work. However, the statutory unit of work, energy, or heat is today the joule (J). One joule = 0.239 calories.
3. The reader is reminded at this point that the emergy of a quantity of any resource is the product of these two quantities.

References

Amable, B. 1987. *Portées et limites des fonctions de production avec facteur énergie.* (Ranges and limits of production functions using the energy factor). Paris: Maison des Sciences de l'Homme (April).
Artus, P., and C. Peyroux. 1981. Fonctions de production avec facteur énergie: Estimations pour les grands pays de l'OCDE (Production functions using the energy factor: Estimations for the major countries of the OECD). *Annales de l'INSEE* 44: 3–38.
Ashford, N. A., and R. F. Stone. 1988. *Cost-benefit analysis in environmental decision-making: Theoretical considerations and applications to protection of stratospheric ozone.* Report for the U.S. Environmental Protection Agency, April. Washington, DC.
Benhaïm, J. 1993. "Taux d'actualisation social et économie de environnement ." *Revue française d'économie* 8 (3): 111–48.
Berthelemy, J. C., and J. G. Devezeaux de Lavergne. 1987. Le modèle MELODIE: Un modèle énergétique de long terme pour l'économie française (The MELODIE model: A long-term energy model for the French economy). *Revue d'Economique Politique*, vol. 5.
Boiteux, M. 1985. Mérites et limites de l'analyse énergétique (Merits and Limits of energy analysis). Revue de l'Energie 376 (September): 98–107.
Bonny, S. 1986. *L'énergie et sa crise de 1974 à 1984 dans l'agriculture française.*

Approche économique (Energy and the energy crisis of 1974 to 1984 in French agriculture: An economics approach). Doctoral thesis, May. Paris: Institut National de la Rocherche Agronomique.

Borel, L. 1984. *Thermodynamique et énergétique* (Thermodynamics and power). Lausanne: PPR.

Christensen, L. R., D. W. Jorgenson, and J. R. Lau. 1973. "Transcendental logarithmic productions frontiers." *Review of Economics and Statistics* 53: 28–45.

Clarck, W. C., and R. E. Munn, eds. 1986. *Sustainable development of the biosphere.* IIASA, Laxenburg. Cambridge: Cambridge University Press.

Collard, D., D. W. Pearce, and D. Ulph, eds. 1988. *Economics growth and sustainable environments.* Essays in memory of Richard Lecomber. London: Macmillan Press.

Costanza, R., S. C. Fraber, and J. Maxwell. 1989. "Valuation and management of wetlands ecosystems." *Ecological Economics* 1 (4): 350–51.

Daly, H. E. 1987a. "The economic growth debate: What some economists have learned but many have not." *Journal of Environmental Economics and Management* 14: 323–336.

———. 1987b "Filters against folly in environmental economics: The impossible, the undesirable and the uneconomic." In *Environmental economics,* ed. G. Pillet and T. Murota, 1–10.

Dasgupta, P., and G. Heal. 1974. "The optimal depletion of exhaustible resources." *Review of Economic Studies,* Symposium on the Economics of Exhaustible Resources, 3–28.

Faber, M., and J. L. R. Proops. 1985. *Interdisciplinary research between economists and physical scientists: Retrospect and Prospect.* Discussion paper No. 48, University of Keele (February).

Faber, M., J. L. R. Proops, M. Ruth, and D. Michaelis. 1990. "Economy-environment interactions in the long run: A neo-Austrian approach." *Ecological Economics* 2 (1): 27–55.

Faubry, F., J. E . Montcomble, O. Vidal de la Blache, and P. Zagame. 1989. Le modèle Hermès-France (The Hermès-France model). *Economie et Prévision* 66: 74–90.

Faucheux, S. 1990. *L'articulation des évaluations monétaire et énergétique en économie* (Articulating monetary and power valuations in the economy). Doctoral thesis, Université Paris I, Panthéon-Sorbonne (July).

———. 1993. "The role of energy in production functions." *Global Energy Issues* 5 (1): 44–55.

———. 1994. "Energy analysis and sustainable development." In *Valuing the environment: Methodological and measurement issues,* ed. R. Pethig. New York: Kluwer.

Faucheux, S., and J. F. Noël. 1990. *Les menaces globales sur l'environnement* (Global threats to the environment). Paris: La Découverte.

Faucheux, S., G. Froger, and J. F. Noël. 1993. *Quelle hypothese de rationalite pour le developpnent soutenable* (A rational hypothesis for sustainable development). *Economie Appliquée,* (December)4.

Faucheux, S., and G. Pillet. 1994. "Alternative ecological economic valuation procedures." In *Valuing the environment: Methodological and measurement issues,* ed. R. Pethig. New York: Kluwer.

Fericelli, J., and J. B. Lesourd, eds. 1985. *Energie: Modélisation et économétrie* (Energy: Modeling and econometrics). Paris: Economica.

Foltke, C. 1986a. "Energy economy of salmon aquaculture in the Baltic Sea." Report for National Swedish Board of Fisheries. Drottningholm: Institute on Freshwater Research.

———. 1986. "The Baltic salmon: Ecological and economic evaluation of a natural resource." Report for National Swedish Board of Fisheries. Drottningholm: Institute on Freshwater Research.

Froger, G., and E. Zyla. 1994. Decision making for sustainable development: Orthodox of system dynamics models, presented for the international symposium: Models of sustainable development. Exclusive or complementary approaches of sustainability, Paris, March 16–18.

Georgescu-Roegen, N. 1970. *The entropy law and the economic process.* Cambridge, MA: Harvard University Press.

————. 1986. "The entropy law and the economic process in restrospect." *Eastern Economic Journal* 12: 3–25.

Godard, O., and J.M. Salles. 1989. *Entre nature et société: Jeux et enjeux des irréversibilités dans le champ de l'environnement* (Between nature and society: Gambling and the stakes of irreversibility in the field of the environment). Paper presented at the international conference: Irréversibilités dans les modes de croissance, institutions, technique et économique, Paris, June 21–23.

Hartwick, J. 1978 "Substitution among exhautible resources and intergenerational equity." *Review of Economic Studies* 45 (2): 347–54.

Henry, C. 1989a. "Investment projects and natural resources: Economic rationality in Janus' role." *Ecological Economics* 1 (2): 117–35.

————. 1989b. "Sustainability, prices and institutional backing." Seminar on the Economics of Environmental Issues, Paper No 2. OECD, October 2–3. Paris.

Hotelling, H. 1931. "The economics of exhaustible resources." *Journal of Political Economics* 39: 137–75.

Judson, D. H. 1989. "The convergence of neo-Ricardian and embodied energy theories of value and prices." *Ecological Economics* 1 (3): 261–83.

Kalaydjian, R. 1988. *Calcul économique et concept de politique énergétique* (Economic calculation and the concept of energy politics). Doctoral thesis, Ecole des Hautes Etudes en Sciences Sociales, Paris.

King, J. 1987. *Beyond economic choice: The application of a resource accounting method to long term development planning in the context of population, resources and the environment.* Paris: UNESCO.

Kümmel, R. 1989. "Energy as a factor of production and entropy as a pollution indicator in macroeconomic modeling." *Ecological Economics* 1 (2): 161–81.

Le Goff, P., ed. 1979. *Energétique industrielle* (Industrial energy), vols. 1–3. Paris: Editions Technique et Documentation.

Lesourd, J. B. 1984. *Energie et substitution entre facteurs de production* (Energy and substitution between production factors). Grenoble: Presses Universitaires de Grenoble.

Lotka, A. J. 1922. "Contribution to the energetics of evolution and natural selection as a physical principle." *Proceedings of the National Academy of Sciences* 8 (6): 147–54.

Mäler, K. J. 1992. "Economic growth and the environment." Paper for International Economic Association, Varena, October.

Nordhaus, W.D. 1973. "The allocation of energy resources." Brookings Papers on Economic Activity. No. 3, pp. 529–76.

————. 1992. "Is growth sustainable: Reflections of the concept of sustainable economic growth." Paper for International Economic Association, Varena, October.

Norgaard, R.B. 1989. "Three dilemmas of environmental accounting." *Ecological Economics* 1 (4): 303–15.

Odum, H. T. 1983. *Systems ecology: An introduction.* New York: John Wiley and Sons.

————. 1988. "Energy, environment and public policy: A guide to the analysis of systems." UNEP Regional Seas Reports and Studies 95. Nairobi (Kenya): UNEP.

Odum, H .T., and E. C. Odum. 1981. *Energy basis for man and nature.* New York: McGraw-Hill.

————1983. *Energy analysis overview of nations.* Working paper, IIASA, Laxenburg (Austria).

Passet, R. 1979. *L'économique et le vivant* (The economy and living). Paris: Payot.

————. 1989. L'économie de l'environnement naturel et de la biosphère (The economy of the natural environment and the biosphere). *Cahiers du C3E* 84 (December).

Pearce, D. W. 1976. "The limits of cost analysis as a guide to environmental policy." *Kyklos*, 97–112.

Pearce, D. W., and D. Ulph, eds. 1988. *Economics growth and sustainable environments.* London: Macmillan.

Pearce, D. W., and K. Turner. 1990. Economics of natural resources and the environment. Hemel Hempstead, England: Harvester Wheatsheaf.

Perrings, C. 1987. *Economy and environment.* Cambridge: Cambridge University Press.

————. 1991. "Reserved rationality and the precautionary principle, technological change: Time and uncertainty in environmental decision-making. In *Ecological economics: The science and management of sustainability,* in Costanza R. (ed.) Ecological Economics: The Science and Management of Sustainability. New York: Columbia University Press.

Pillet, G. 1988. "Shadow-pricing environmental goods and services, using the emergy method." *Environmental Conservation* 15(3).

————. 1990. *Analyse du rôle de l'environnement dans les processus macroéconomiques* (Analysis of the role of the environment in the macroeconomic process). Report FN 1.378–0.86. University of Geneva, Center of Human Ecology and Environmental Science, January. Geneva.

Pillet, G. and H. T. Odum. 1984. Energy, externality and the economy of Switzerland. *Schweiz. Zeitschrift für Volkswirtschaft und Statistik* (120)3: 409–35.

————. 1987. *E 3, energie, ecologie, economie* (E3: Energy, Ecology, Economy). Geneva: Georg Editeur.

Pillet, G., and T. Murota, eds. 1987. *Environmental economics: The analysis of a major interface.* Geneva: Roland Leimgruber.

Pimentel, D. 1987. Ecological resource management for a productive sustainable agriculture. In *Food and natural resources,* ed. D. Pimentel and C. W. Hall. New York: Academic Press.

Pimentel, D., and M. Giampetro. 1987. "Food energy security for society: The cost of a rapidly growing world population." Communication to Second Vienna Center Conference on Economics and Ecology. Barcelona, September 26–29.

Punti, A. 1987. "Some limits of the energy value in natural resources accountancy." Communication to Second Vienna Center Conference on Economics and Ecology. Barcelona, September 26–29.

Schembri, P. 1993. L'approche entropique dans le prolongement de la théorie néo-autrichienne du capial (The entropy approach in continuing the neo-Austrian theory of capital). *Cahiers du C3F,* 93–115.

Scienceman, D. M. 1987. "Energy and emergy." In *Environmental economics: The analysis of a major interface,* ed. G. Pillet, and T. Murota (pp. 277–90). Geneva: Leimgruber.

Slesser, M. 1985. *Carrying capacity assessment with a pilot study of Kenya. A resource accounting methodology for assessing the sustainability of national economies in the context of population, resources, environment and development.* Report for the Food and Agriculture Organization of the United Nations. Rome.

————. 1987. *The use of resource accounting in development planning, validation of the ECCO model using United Kingdom data from 1974 to 1984 and potential for application.* Edinburgh: Resource Use Institute and Centre for Human Ecology, Edinburgh University.

Solow, R.M. 1974. "The economics of resources or the resources of economics." *American Economic Review* (May): 1–14.

————. 1986. "On the intergenerational allocation of natural resources." *Scandinavian Journal of Economics* 88: 127–44.

Toman. J. "Economics and sustainability: Balancing tradeoffs and imperatives." Resources for the Future, Washington, D.C., Doc ENR 91-OS Rev.

Turner, K. 1993. *Sustainable environmental economics and management principles and practice*. London and New York: Belhauer Press.

Vercelli, A. 1994. Hard uncertainty and environment in sustainable growth and uncertainty. Fondazione F. Mattei, Milan, January 10–11.

5

EBERHARD K. SEIFERT

Economic-Ethical and Bioeconomic Elements of "Practical" Economics

Introduction

The general principles of bioeconomics as originally developed by Georgescu-Roegen[1] are on the research agenda of the European Association for Bioeconomic Studies (EABS).[2] The agenda concerns the proper thermodynamic- and entropy-related arguments of these principles and their corresponding new epistemology: the differentiation between arithmomorphic concepts (as used mostly in neoclassical mainstream economics) and a new, non-Hegelian, form of dialectic concepts. This approach can be characterized as the recent and perhaps best elaborated alternative in the history of economics to the (neoclassical) approach of "economics as physics"—Mirowski's (1991) concise criticism of a false conception of theoretical economics).[3]

Against this still dominant conception of theoretical economics,[4] this contribution tries to reconstruct in "desperate brevity" the antiterm *practical* (as opposed to *theoretical*) along some main lines in the history of economic thought. This approach leads in some way to the idea of anamnesis, that is, the efforts of a physician to uncover the entire history of an acute crisis. It discusses five theses on the history and present-day relevance of an alternative to the dominant engineering approach to economics.

To begin with the fact, one must note that there is today a discourse on ethics and economics; at least in the United States and German-speaking region, but with rising interest all over Europe and other countries too, including Japan. This trend is documented quite well by new journals and institutions in this interdisciplinary field, as well as a growing number of publications and conferences.

Whatever the quite different claims made in this recent debate may be, we have, as economists, first to remind ourselves that the strained relationship between ethics and economics is not new. As Sen (1988) recalled in his Royer lectures—"On Ethics and Economics"—economics has had rather different origins from those of ethics. While the origins of both are related to politics, economics is concerned respectively with ethics on the one hand and with what may be called engineering[5] on the other. The ethics-related tradition goes back at least to Aristotle.[6] Concerning these traditions, the four sections that follow thus recall some prominent positions in the history of economic thought to remind us not only of the problems and questions we are faced with in our discipline but also of what it really means to recombine ethics and economics with respect to the state of the art of economics as a science.

In the light of this historical sketch and with the support of the last and fifth section, which focuses again on the bioeconomic paradigm but mainly on its epistemological impact, it becomes clear at least to some degree what is meant in this context by the unusual and perhaps even misleading term in economics, namely, *practical*. Although *practical* implies also the real practice of intervention in the economic process,[7] in the following context, this term has primarily an epistemological connotation.

The Historical-Ethical Dimension

In the present economic-ethical discourse, even in German-speaking regions,[8] insufficient consideration is paid to the fact that exactly such a discourse already existed about a hundred years ago, just a century after the establishment of economics as a science by Adam Smith. The so-called historical school, which considered itself more precisely "historical-*ethical*"[9] within German *Nationalökonomie* or *Staatswirtschaftslehre*,[10] combined its sociopolitical efforts toward social reform with an explicit critique of the basic methodological assumptions of classical English economics.

Gustav von Schmoller—to mention him as *pars pro toto*—the head of the new school of ethical economics (or younger historical school), is significant not only for his later famous discussion on methodology, the *Methodenstreit*, with Carl Menger (induction versus deduction). He also pointed out in his earlier works of the 1970s and 1980s, which deal with the question of justice in economics (Seifert 1989b), that the classical economists based their thinking on a false "technical"[11] (if for their time understandable) comprehension of the proper subject of economics. The kind of reasoning and arguments typical of that period are best illustrated briefly by translating one of Schmoller's main arguments in his famous dispute with the conservative historian Treitschke (Small 1924–25; Seifert 1989b):

> To summarize that which I have tried to develop: every national economic organization is dominated by two series of causes which are relatively independent from each other. On the one hand are the natural-technical causes, which exclusively formed the central focus of older national economies; on the

other hand are those causes arising from the psychological and moral norms of nations, which had been from time to time acknowledged but not investigated regarding their relevance to the national economy. A science of national economy, by strictest definition, shall only exist when not only the first series of causes but also the second series of causes is researched. The first series form a natural substructure, the foundation of the national economy; those causes arising from the second source assume the form of a far more flexible intermediate structure resting upon this foundation; only both series together give rise to a definite result; a national economy structure can only be erected upon both series. A large portion of the research conducted in the area of the national economy up to this point has suffered from one major error, by deriving economic conditions exclusively from the ranks of the first series of causes. Researchers either forgot about or did not see the entire intermediate structure and thus heaped one false conclusion upon another. This research suffered from the compulsion to explain that which lies beyond technology via technical and natural means; they maintained that an absolutely necessary and given way of life and legal constitution resulted from certain technical facts although history has shown that both can be quite heteromorphic. They failed to recognise the nature of social norms and the power of moral sentiments and cultural ideas which dominate the national economy. Herein lies the difference! Making a difference between the national economic congress and our position, the point is not that we enthusiastically seek an extensive state authority but rather lies in the fact that we—in addition to natural and technical causes—also draw near to psychological and ethical causes and assume a total development process of national economic organisational forms based on these causes; that we believe in the kind of process which those thinkers repudiate or are forced to leave unexplained who see only natural laws operative in economics. The science of economics arrived at the above mentioned incorrect conclusions at a time which believed—for the period probably correctly—to have recognised law as a simple constant and which in its rejection of all traditional morality as monstrous and depraved, viewed the centre of the individual as existing in an eternally constant natural force, a time which exults like a little child over the licentious, arbitrary and freakish nature of the natural force. It was the period of "Sturm und Drang" of the absolution to every evil; this was the slogan and the error of Rousseau and Adam Smith. (1774/75, p. 57 f.)

Economics as a Moral Science

Nevertheless, this much-criticized classical understanding of the fundamental methodological questions in economics was once more summarized by J. N. Keynes (with partial consideration of the German discussion) in his well-known 1890 publication "The Scope and Method of Political Economy," which itself became the classical and influential treatment of this topic in the Anglo-Saxon world. This John Neville Keynes (father of the more famous John Maynard) separated scientific-theoretical economics from the specific German ambition to treat economics as essentially a moral science. (It is worthy to note that his son would later emphasize—against the ambitious econometric approaches of the

1930s—that economics is indeed "essentially a moral science," without, however, offering any further *explicit* explanation of this methodological position. For more on his moral understanding, see his 1930 essay "Economic Possibilities for Our Grandchildren.")

A very short summary of J. N. Keynes's arguments in favor of five distinct essentials concerning the Senior-Mill-Cairnes tradition of methodology in economics in contrast to the historical school could be helpful and memorable, since it demonstrates the still-valid Anglo-Saxon manner of thinking that also influenced German development after World War II. Following Blaug's (1988) summary without any further commentary, readers may compare this view with the foregoing statement of Schmoller and form their own opinion on the question of whether Keynes gave a fair interpretation of the scientific and social reform–oriented aims of this practical economics.[12] According to Blaug, Keynes claimed

> (1) that it is possible to distinguish between a positive science and a normative art of political economy; (2) that economic events can be isolated at least to some extent from other social phenomena; (3) that the direct induction of concrete facts, or the method of a posteriori, is inappropriate as a starting point in economics; (4) that the right procedure is the a priori method of starting from "a few and indispensable facts of human nature . . . taken in connexion with the physiological properties of the soil, and man's physiological constitution"; and (5) that economic man is an abstraction and hence that "political economy is a science of tendencies only, not a matter of facts." . . . His summary of the historical school as holding an "ethical, realistic, and inductive" view of economics is equally succinct: the historical school denies each of the five Senior-Mill-Cairnes theses and, in addition, has a favourable rather than a negative attitude to government intervention in economic affairs. (p. 83)

Ethics and the Enlightenment

The old battle on methodology provoked by the German historical school[13] is a good example that the current renewed economic-ethical questioning of theoretical economics is not merely the latest in a traditional series of ups and downs in stressing the ethical aspects of modern economics. This questioning also refers back to the fact that the very establishment of modern political economy as a science by the moral philosopher Adam Smith was itself only the presupposed outcome of a certain and lengthy process of the differentiation of economics out of the traditional trivium of ethics, politics, and economics (Seifert 1987).

This theoretical decision and the reconstruction of the decisive, possibly deficient, arguments involved in it have only recently come under serious investigation. MacIntyre's moral-philosophical analysis (1984–88) of the "Scottish Enlightenment," which culminates in Smith, appears as a consistent but equally unsuccessful attempt within the generally doomed "Project of Enlightenment" to find a rational justification for ethics. This thesis surely deserves a whole discussion of its own. However, based both on some new research on Smith in general, especially induced by his bicentennial in 1991, and on some of my own investigations into the problems in question (Seifert 1991), I would like to focus on the following two points: first, Smith, in his so-called "natural system of freedom and justice" of civil (i.e., commercial) society, did not avoid the problems of both decline and decay of capitalism in a strict market economy. This has been shown by Robert Heilbroner (1975), who elaborated some arguments of his teacher Adolph Lowe. In the end Smith (1978) was compelled to admit:

> So it may be very justly said that the people who clothe the whole world are in rags themselves. . . . These are the disadvantages of a commercial spirit. The minds of men are contracted and rendered incapable of elevation, education is despised, or at least neglected, and heroic spirit is almost utterly extinguished. . . . To remedy these defects [of a pure market economy, the author] *would* be an object worthy of serious attention. (p. 541)

"Would"—but that would require some ethics and the power to impose serious attention on sheer market forces—a problem the German ethical economists clearly saw and tried to realize with their "practical" economics.

Second, this inherent and even self-conscious deficit within Smithian economics leads to yet another problem. The question of the possible contradictions between his economic theory, *The Wealth of Nations* (1776), on the one hand, and his earlier essay on ethics, "Theory of Moral Sentiments" (1759), on the other, was already discussed in the last century. This persistent "old Adam Smith problem" is complicated nowadays by another problem: Why is there no "politics" in his system of moral philosophy?

Shortly before his death—as we now know, based on notes of students and some other findings—Smith destroyed a large number of unpublished manuscripts, including, it is suspected, all his written efforts for such a book on politics. Did he perhaps become aware, at the end, that there is such a systematic deficit and theoretical mistake in the intellectual construct of a pure economics (that does not combine ethics *and* politics) for a civil or commercial (in this context, stateless) society?

Thus, the following questions are strongly to be claimed: at the very beginning, was modern economics[14] as a science "disembedded" (Polaniy 1944)—that is, separated from the traditional and inseparable (Aristotelian) corpus of practical philosophy?[15] Was there already a systematic defect in its construct? In other words, did an ethics- and politics-free—that is, value-free and physics-oriented—economic theory concern itself only with the basic laws of the functioning of the proper economic system or the rational, only self-interested, economic behavior of people?

The Practical Philosophy of Aristotle

The theory influencing Western thinking from which the Enlightenment attempted to distance itself in various phases[16] was Aristotle's philosophy (although scholastically reworked) in general and his practical philosophy—including economics as well as ethics and politics—in particular. For systematic and epistemological reasons, the science of human behavior, which includes the art of economizing, was not given the same status (that of laws) as the realm of physics, the science of physis.[17] Economics was not considered a science of particular laws governing economic conditions and behavior, but the art of proper housekeeping which was to be ethically justified and guided. This kind of housekeeping is based on the fundamental differentiation and discrimination between an unnatural and a natural means of chrematistics, the art of getting things (*chremata*) needed within the house: the *oikos* for the ethical good life.

The right chrematistics—as developed in Book I of Aristotle's *Politics* (1986)—is "natural" because it aims toward a final and limited means (the ethical good life), whereas unnatural chrematistics is wrong because this kind of acquisition lacks any built-in final aim, but is the endless means in itself.[18]

The Consequences of the Industrial-Economic Treatment of Nature

To return abruptly to present times and especially to the rising ecological problems, the founder of the bioeconomic approach, Georgescu-Roegen, remembered in his address to the First International Conference of the EABS (1991):[19]

> One particular sin ... should not ... be overlooked, especially in advanced economies [where] it is a widespread practice. It is the sin of ignoring the original meaning of economizing as found in Aristotle's ... *Oeconomia*. According to that meaning, we should economize by ceasing to overheat, overcool, overspread, and many other such overdos. No environmental policy should possibly ignore an ethical issue that pertains to the fate of the future human generations. (p. 10)

Georgescu-Roegen's statement reflects industrial experience. At least in the highly industrialized West, economic growth[20] and social reform have to a large extent pacified the social question that dominated the nineteenth century. (One forgets too easily that this fact of political and institutional reform alone implies an obstruction of pure economic theory.) This has, however, apparently caused a much graver problem: the ecological consequences of our industrial-economic treatment of nature. Here again the old question arises that bioeconomist Georgescu-Roegen rhetorically raised and developed toward a new epistemology: "Why is economics not a *theoretical* science?" (1971, p. 322).

His own specific attempt to elaborate on this problem first describes the fundamental differences between arithmomorphic (theoretical) and dialectical concepts (which lack distinct characteristics but which are the only adequate ones for social sciences and economics in favor of historical and institutional investigations [1979–81, 1987]). Second, it points out that the basic assumptions of the dominant standard economics are still in the grip of mechanistic philosophy,[21] preventing the discipline from accepting the fundamental insight that human-industrial production cannot change the laws of nature (as expressed by thermodynamics and the entropy law). We cannot create or destroy matter or energy, but our industrial mode of production increases entropic, irreversible degradation in unprecedented dimensions.

Thus, we bite the hand that feeds us, consuming nature for our enjoyment of life. On the contrary, economizing in accordance with biophysical conditions has to consider the bioeconomic impact of low-entropy production; in accordance with the bioeconomic paradigm, the idea of an independent system of economic laws (independent from ethics and politics, that is, from value judgments) is rejected. Therefore, the growing insight into the fundamental impact of production processes on energy and matter (transformation from available to less available states) should do more to afford an economic rethinking in favor of a far-reaching reduction in our entropy-increasing consumption of nature.

Conclusion

The present, mainly ecological, problems imply a new, practical form of housekeeping,[22] in accordance with ethical and bioeconomical[23] issues, and not primarily purely economic ones, so that even (corrected) prices[24] would tell the ecological truth.[25] If humanity wishes to take to heart the evolutionary command to preserve the species of *Homo sapiens*, instead of embracing the maximizing principle of modern (neoclassical) economics, which maximizes the utilities of each living generation, then for the sake of future generations the guiding bioeconomic principle practically would suggest minimizing future regrets."[26]

Notes

1. See Georgescu-Roegen's still most comprehensive exposure of his new paradigm in *The Entropy Law and the Economic Process* (1971). The term *bioeconomics* was suggested to him by J. Zeman; see Georgescu-Roegen 1975.

2. The EABS was founded in 1990 and had its first international conference on "Entropy and Bioeconomics" in Rome in November 1991. The proceedings as well as the *EABS Newsletter* can be ordered from the EABS office (I–20122 Milano, 11 via Larga).

3. The first and best general introduction to both main aspects, which fortunately also stresses extensively the epistemological questions, is offered by Dragan/Demetrescu (1986/1991); it contains information about Georgescu-Roegen's work and his complete publication list. Some additional information I gave especially with respect to the German discussion in addition to the first publication of Georgescu-Roegen's 1986 "retrospect" article.

4. See, for example, the symposia in the new journal *Methodus* (1991) on such themes as "Has formalization in economics gone too far?" and "How scientific is economics?"

5. This "approach is characterized by being concerned with primarily logistic issues rather than with ultimate ends and such questions as what may foster *the good man* or *how should one live*. . . . The engineering approach to economics has come from several different directions including . . . being developed by some actual engineers such as Leon Walras" (p. 4).

6. He argues, "that the importance of the ethical approach has rather substantially weakened as modern economics has evolved. The methodology of so-called 'positive economics' has not only shunned normative analysis in economics, [but] it has also had the effect of ignoring a variety of complex ethical considerations which affect actual human behaviour and which, from the point of view of the economists studying such behaviour, are primarily matters of fact rather than of normative judgement. If one examines the balance of emphases in the publications in modern economics, it is hard not to notice the eschewal of deep normative analysis, and the neglect of the influence of ethical considerations in the characterization of actual human behaviour" (p. 7).

7. See, for example, the reconstruction of different kinds of theoretical legitimization of "intervention" by two of the most prominent *Kathedersozialisten* and social reform economists in nineteenth-century Germany, G. Schmoller and A. Wagner (Seifert 1990a).

8. See, for example, in Germany the publications of the working group of the *Verein für Socialpolitik* (Enderle 1985; Hesse 1988). Furthermore, the series *St. Galler Beiträge zur Wirtschaftsehtik*, edited by the holder of the first chair in that field in the German-speaking regions, includes as No. 3 the conference volume I edited on new approaches between economics, ethics, and environment (1989).

9. P. Mirowski (1991) complained that there "is not yet any synoptic survey of the German Historicist school in English" (p. 148), although early American economists like Veblen et al. seemed to be quite familiar with the German literature, and in some respect influenced by this ethical-historical approach to economics. German in those days was a language scientists often were able to understand. Even in Germany after World War II, enforced by the overwhelming Americanization of economics, this school was forgotten; only in recent years have there been some efforts to reconstruct this strong and unique tradition, fortunately with the participation of American scholars. (See, for example, N.A. Balabkins, *Not by Theory Alone. . . . The Economics of Gustav von Schmoller and its Legacy to America* (1988) or J. C. O'Brien, ed., "Gustav von Schmoller: Social Economist," the special issue of the *International Journal of Social Economics* 16/1989.

10. On the foregoing development of this *staatswirtschaftliche* tradition in Germany, different in many respects from the Western one, see Maier (1980), or recently, Tribe (1988).

11. Compare this critique to the above-mentioned Royer lectures of Sen and his term *engineering approach*.

12. Nevertheless, in stressing the cultural dimensions of socioeconomic development, there has been a specific bias of the historical school against nature (Seifert 1989b).

13. The older *Methodenstreit* between Schmoller and Karl Menger was followed by the inner-German controversy within the *Verein für Socialpolitik*, initiated by the members of the so-called youngest historical school, especially Max Weber and Werner Sombart. Hennis (1987) recently offered a lucid reconstruction of *Max Weber's Fragestellung* toward what he (Weber) then first called programmatically *socio-economics*, bringing the specific social aspects of life together with economics. This term survived not only in the prominent oeuvre of J. A. Schumpeter, as above all Swedberg has the merit to rediscover (1991). In some, but not all, respects, it seems to me that the new scientific and social movement in the United States—the communitarians, with Amitai Etzioni as leading figure and programmatical herald of a new socioeconomics—is reinventing (although under the specific conditions and problems of the United States today and in keeping with its special traditions) some of these original German arguments against a pure and not social as well as practically oriented economics. Concerning the late W. Sombart and his unique approach to a new epistemology of economics, the *Verstehende Nationalökonomie* as first laid down in *Die Drei Nationalökonomien* (1930), I showed in a paper presented to the 1991 conference on Sombart (at the yearly international Heilbronn meetings organized

ELEMENTS OF "PRACTICAL" ECONOMICS 115

by Professor Backhaus/Maastricht in honor of famous German social scientists) that he criticized in some later publications of the 1930s the pure (i.e., physics-oriented) kind of economics. For the future of a *late-capitalism* (undermining the lawlike structures of a self-regulating market economy by its own development), he favors a new kind of practical art of economics, not a pure, natural science–oriented epistemology (Seifert 1991).

14. Although his *Wealth* obviously was a real intellectual breakthrough, it was not really the beginning of classical political economy, but a certain and very successful amalgam of former efforts (Seifert 1987).

15. This classical trivium contained the hierarchy of ethics, politics, and economics (as an art).

16. It is the special merit of MacIntyre's analysis (1984–88) to reconstruct the different attempts of modernity toward a rational ethics as successive stages of failure.

17. At the very beginning of his *Ethics,* Aristotle (1986a) states that the science that studies the supreme Good for man is part of politics in general and that "our account of this science will be adequate if it achieves such clarity as the subject-matter allows, for the same degree of precision is not to be expected in all discussions, any more than in all the products of handicraft" (p. 1094b11 ff.).

18. A brief exposition of this Aristotelian approach stressing the ethical dimension was delivered to the conference of the Greek Philosophical Society in Athens in 1987 (Seifert 1989a). For a very rich and systematic reconstruction of Greek economic thinking, see the magnum opus by Lowry (1987).

19. This address, with the title "Looking Back," is in one way something of a legacy.

20. Together with the specific relations of the First World to the Third World, with all the advantages of the former.

21. Besides Georgescu-Roegen's own work, see also Mirowski (1984, 1986, 1988).

22. This would profit from an explicit reconstruction of the tradition of practical philosophy, maintained for special historical reasons not in the Anglo-Saxon sphere, but only within specific German-speaking regions (Seifert 1989a, 1990a).

23. Compare the "Minimal Bioeconomic Program" (Georgescu-Roegen 1976, pp. 30–35).

24. This would mean the end of the idea of pure market prices, as an outcome of the mechanics of the utility maximization of each living generation.

25. This idea is favored and programmatically institutionalized by its president, E. U. v. Weizsäcker (1990) into the main tasks of the new Wuppertal Institute on climate, energy, and environment.

26. Very interesting for the current debate on sustainability is the reconstruction of the logic of subsistence economies by historian Dieter Groh (1986, 1988) with essentially three strategical categories: "underproductivity, risk minimizing, leisure preference."

References

Aristotle. 1986a. *Ethics.* The Nicamachean Ethics. Hammonsworth Penguin Books.
———. 1986b. *Politics.* Middlesex: Penguin Books.
Balabkins, N. W. 1988. *Not by theory alone . . . The economics of Gustav von Schmoller and its legacy to America.* Berlin.
Blaug, M. 1988. *The methodology of economics, or how economists explain.* Cambridge: Cambridge University Press.
Dragan/Demetrescu. 1986. *Entropy and bioeconomics: The new paradigm of N. Georgescu-Roegen.* Milan (2d ed., 1991, Rome).
Enderle, G., ed. 1985. *Ethik und Wirtschaftswissenschaft* (Ethics and Economic Theory). Berlin: Duncher & Humblot.

116 ECONOMY, ENVIRONMENT, AND TECHNOLOGY

848444444

Georgescu-Roegen, N. 1971. *The entropy law and the economic process.* Cambridge: Cambridge University Press.

———. 1975. "Bio-economic aspects of entropy." In *Entropy and information in science and philosophy,* ed. J. Zeman. Amsterdam.

———. 1976. "Energy and economic myths." In *Georgescu-Roegen: Energy and economic myths, institutional and analytical economic essays.* New York: Pergamon Press.

———. 1979–81. "Methods in economic science." In *Journal of Economic Issues,* June 1979 (317–27); March 1981 (188–93).

———. 1987. "The entropy law and the economic process in retrospect." Deutsche Erstübersetzung mit Geleitwort von E. K. Seifert (German trans. with an introduction by E.K. Seifert), IÖW-Schriften (Institut für ökologische Wirtschaftsforschung), May 1987. Berlin No. 5.

———. 1988. "Interplay between institutional and material factors: The problem and its status." In *Barriers to full employment,* ed. J. A. Kregel, E. Matzner, and A. Roncaglia. London: Macmillan Press.

———. 1991. "Looking back." In *Address for the First International Conference of the European Association for Bioeconomic Studies,* ed. E. K. Seifert and J. M. Alier. Rome, November 1991. Nagard.

Groh, D. 1986. "How subsistence economies work." *Development* 3: 23–30.

———. 1988. Strategien, Zeit und Ressourcen. Risikominimierung, Unterproduktivität und Mußepräferenz—die zentralen Kategorien von Subsistenzökonomien (Strategies, time and resources. Risk descrimination and imposed preferences of the most important categories of the economy of substitution). In *Ökonomie und Zeit,* ed. E. K. Seifert. Frankfurt: Haagt Herchen.

Heilbroner, R. 1975. An inquiry into the human prospect. London: Calder & Boyars.

Hennis, W. 1987. *Max Weber's Fragestellung: Studien zur Biographie des Werkes* (Max Weber's Question: Studies related to the work bibliography). Tübingen: Mohr.

Hesse, H., ed. 1988. *Wirtschaftswissenschaft und Ethik.* Berlin.

Keynes, J. M. 1930. *Economic possibilities for our grandchildren.*

Keynes, J. N. 1891. *The scope and method of political economy.* London: Macmillan. (Reprint 1986.)

Lowry, T. S. 1987. *The archaelogy of economic ideas.* Durham: MacIntyre.

Maier, H. 1980. *Die ältere deutsche Staats—und Verwaltungslehre* (The old German treaty of State and Administration.) 2d ed. Munich: C.H. Beck 'che Verlagsbuch hamdelung.

Methodus, 1991. *Bulletin of the International Network for Economic Method* 3 (June).

Mirowski, P. 1984. "Physics and the 'marginalist revolution.'" *Journal of Economics* 8: 361–79.

———. ed. 1986. *The reconstruction of economic theory.* Boston: Kluwer-Nijoff.

———. 1988. *Against mechanism.* Totowa, NJ.

———. 1989. "The when, the how and the why of mathematical expression in the history of economic analysis." *Journal of Economic Perspectives* 5(1): 145–57.

———. 1991. *More heat than light: Economics as social physics, physics as nature's economics.* New York: Cambridge University Press.

O'Brien, J. E., ed. 1989. "Gustav von Schmoller: Social economist." Special issue, *International Journal of Social Economics* 16(9–11).

Polaniy, K. 1980. *The great transformation.* New York: Octagon.

Schmoller, G. v. 1874–75. *Über einige Grundfragen der Socialpolitik und der Volkswirtschaftslehre* (About Some Essential Questions of Social Policy and the Economic Theory). Leipzig (1898).

Seifert, E.K. 1987a. *Wirtschaftsethik in ökologischer Absicht.* IÖW-Schrift Nr. 9. Berlin.

————. 1987b. "Politische Ökonomie"—Genese und Bedeutungswandel eines beladenen Begriffs (Political Economy—Genesis and Change in Meaning of a over emphasized term). In *Politische Ökonomie—Heute,* ed. W. Vogt. Regensburg.

————. 1988. "Schmoller on justice—Today." In *International Journal of Social Economics* 16: 69–92.

————. 1989a. "Aristotelian justice in modern economics." In *On justice: Plato's and Aristotle's conception of justice in relation to modern and contemporary theories of justice,* ed. K. Boudouris. Philosophical Conference of the Greek Philosophical Society, Third International, Athens, May 1987.

————. 1989b. "Kultur versus Natur? Anmerkungen zu einer Grundfrage der Wirtschaftsethik. Ein Jahrhundert nach Schmoller. (Culture vs. Nature, remarks on an essential question in economic ethics)." In *Gustav Schmoller Heute: Die Entwicklung der Sozialwissenschaften in Deutschland und Italien,* ed. M. Bock, H. Homann, and P. Schiera (pp. 223–49). Berlin/Bologna.

————. 1990a. Theoretische und normative Grundlagen "kathedersozialistischer" Interventionsmuster in der "socialen Frage" des 19 (Theoretical and normative issues in academic inspired socialism on State Intervention about Social Affairs in the Nineteenth Century). Jahrhunderts. In *Interventionismus. Theoriegeschichtliche und aktuelle Dimension,* ed. H. Stadtmüller and K. G. Zinn Hgs, (pp. 46–70). Aachen.

————. 1990b. "Von der staatswissenschaftlichen zur ökologischen Kritik des Ökonomismus." In *Ökonomie und Ethik. Moral des Marktes oder Kritik der reinen ökonomischen Vernunft,* ed. C. Mattissen. From the political to the ecological critics of the economy. Freiburg: (pp. 61–96).

————. 1991. "Das Fortschrittsparadox bei Adam Smith—sein unvollendetes System einer Moralphilosphie in ökonomischer Absicht." In *Der andere Smith. Beiträge zur Neubestimmung von Ökonomie als Politischer Ökonomie,* ed. A. Meyer-Faje and P. Ulrich (pp. 55–96). Bern/Stuttgart P. Haupt: Paradox of Progress in Adam Smith's writings: his incomplete system, his moral philosophy in an economic perspective.

————. 1992. Sombart's new outline of scope and method of economics: *Methodologie oder Verfahrenslehre der Neuen Nationalökonomie* facing the transition of the *Wirtschaftssystem* to late-capitalism since World War I. In Proceedings of the International Conference "W. Sombart—Social Economist," ed. J. Backhaus. Heilbronn. Forthcoming.

Seifert, E. K., and R. Pfriem, eds. 1989. *Wirtschaftsethik und ökologische Wirtschaftsforschung.* Bern/Stuttgart: Panl Haupt: (Economic Ethics and Ecological Research in Economics).

Sen, A. 1988. *On ethics and economics: The Royer lectures.* Oxford: Oxford University Press.

Small, A. W. 1924–25. "The Schmoller-Treitschke controversy." *American Journal of Sociology* 30: 48 ff.

Smith, A. 1759. "Theory of moral sentiments." London: A. Millar.

————. 1776. *An Inquiry into the Nature and Causes of the Wealth of Nations.*

————. 1978. *Lectures on jurisprudence.* Glasgow: London.

Sombart, W. 1930. *Die Drei Nationalökonomien. Geschichte und System der Lehre von der Wirtschaft* (The Three Economic Theories, the History of the Evolution of Economic Systems). München/Leipzig.

Tribe, K. 1988. *Governing economy: The reformation of German economic discourse, 1750–1840.* Cambridge: Cambridge University Press.

Weizsäcker, E. U. v. 1990. *Erdpolitik. Ökologische Realpolitik an der Schwelle zum Jahrhundert der Umwelt* (Earth politics, ecological and pragmatic politics at the beginning of the century of the environment). Darmstadt: Akademische Bugesellschaft.

Part III
Sustainable Development

$$6$$

PAUL EKINS

Sustainable Development and the Economic Growth Debate

Introduction

In relation to the 1992 Earth Summit—the UN Conference on Environment and Development (UNCED) in Brazil—it is perhaps worth reflecting on what is perhaps the major change in approach over the twenty years since the 1972 UN Conference on the Environment in Stockholm. Today the key phrase is sustainable development. Then, it was limits to growth. The purpose of this chapter is to examine and relate these two concepts, to see whether they are compatible and on what terms, and to judge which provides a more realistic approach to the environmental economic problems of the present time.

The Economic Growth Debate

In order to shed light on the arguments for and against limits to growth that raged so heatedly in the 1970s, not just among economists but in society at large, it is necessary to unpack the concept, in particular by asking, What sort of limits? and Limits to what kind of growth? At the outset it should be observed that the limits in question can be either ecological or social, while the kind of growth in question can be that of the throughput of physical resources, GNP, or welfare.

The term *limits to growth* itself was the title of a book by Donella and Dennis Meadows and a team from Massachusetts Institute of Technology (MIT) (Meadows et al., 1972), which was the principal fuel for the subsequent debate. For the Meadows team the limits were ecological limits. The limits applied to economic growth, understood as growth in production as measured by GNP, which the Meadows team assumed implied a similar increase in the consumption of resources. Their oft-quoted conclusion left no doubt as to how serious they thought these limits were:

> If the present growth trends in world population, industrialization, pollution, food production and resource depletion continue unchanged, the limits to growth on this planet will be reached sometime within the next one hundred years. The most probable result will be a rather sudden and uncontrollable decline in both population and industrial capacity. (p. 23)

Although the Meadows team used a (for those times) relatively sophisticated computer model to derive their results, in fact these were fully deducible from their assumptions concerning the five initial parameters of their system: population, industrial capital, food, nonrenewable resources, and pollution. They assumed that population and industrial capital would grow exponentially, leading to a similar growth in demand for food and nonrenewables and in pollution. The supply of food and nonrenewable resources was, however, taken to be absolutely finite. Not surprisingly, exponential growth within finite limits resulted in systematic breakdown; the expansive nature of compounded growth also meant that the finite limits could be raised by a factor of four without significantly affecting the results.

While the limits-to-growth thesis struck a chord with the general public, economists and other scientists were quick to seek to discredit it. One of the most comprehensive rebuttals came from a team at Sussex University's Science Policy Research Unit (Cole et al., 1973). They criticized the relationships in the Meadows model, the assumptions on which the model was based, and its emphasis on purely physical parameters: "The major limitation of Meadows' approach is that they have chosen to be unconcerned with politics, unconcerned with social structure, unconcerned with human needs and wants" (p. 212).

On the basis of its critique, the Cole team reran the Meadows model with different assumptions and produced quite different results. This was also not surprising a priori because the key assumption they replaced was that of absolute limits, by introducing ongoing exponential increases in available resources (through discovery and recycling) and the ability to control pollution. "To postpone collapse indefinitely these rates of improvement must obviously be competitive with growth rates of population and consumption so that even if the overall growth is rapid, it is also 'balanced.' In this case some kind of stable but dynamic equilibrium is obtained." The authors also claim that, at 1 and 2 percent, "the actual numerical values used as improvement rates for the various technologies in the exercises are not significant except that they are fairly small and not improbable in the real world" (p. 119). The probability of the last sentence is derived from a historical survey, which showed that such improvement rates had in fact occurred in the past. The Cole team saw no reason to believe that they would not continue in the future.

Beneath the difference between the Cole team's optimism and the Meadows team's pessimism lies a different perception as to how serious the environmental problems were at the time. The Cole position is coolly stated: "The world does face a problem of energy production and consumption, some areas of the planet do suffer from pollution, the green revolution does create many problems even as it solves others" (Cole et al. 1973, p. 211). The Meadows position is frankly apocalyptic: "Taking no action to solve these problems is equivalent to taking strong action. Every day of continued exponential growth brings the world system closer to the ultimate limits of that growth. A decision to do nothing is a decision to increase the risk of collapse" (Meadows et al. 1972, p. 183). It is this difference in basic perspective that seems to permit reputable scientists to make such different assumptions on the basis of the same historical evidence and arrive at such contradictory conclusions.

Lecomber (1975) admirably expresses the difference between resource optimists and pessimists. He identifies the three key effects that can reduce depletion or pollution: changes in composition of output, substitution between factor inputs, and technical progress (more efficient use of the same input). If these three effects add up to a shift away from the limiting resource or pollutant equal to or greater than the rate of growth, then the limits to growth are forestalled indefinitely. But, Lecomber warns, this "establishes the logical conceivability, not the certainty, probability or even the possibility in practice, of growth continuing indefinitely. Everything hinges on the rate of technical progress and possibilities of substitution. This is perhaps the main issue that separates resource optimists and resource pessimists. The optimist believes in the power of human inventiveness to solve whatever problems are thrown in its way, as apparently it has done in the past. The pessimist questions the success of these past technological solutions and fears that future problems may be more intractable" (p. 42). Lecomber looks for evidence in an effort to judge between these two positions, but without success. "The central feature of technical advance is indeed its uncertainty" (p. 45). This conclusion is of relevance to the contemporary situation with sustainable development, as will be seen.

Many of the same points as those of the Cole team are made, and the same beliefs about the efficiency of future technical change are held, by Beckerman (1974) in his defense of economic growth. However, Beckerman also introduces several other arguments not related to technology. First, Beckerman stresses: "It is essential not to confuse the issue of how consumption should be spread over time, which is the growth issue, with that of how resources should be used at any moment of time. The fact that resources are misallocated at any moment of time on account of failure to correct for externalities does not necessarily mean that the growth rate is wrong" (pp. 18–20). Beckerman's point is that insofar as environmental degradation is caused by externalities, or spillover effects, which are failures of resource allocation, they cannot be solved by tinkering with rates of economic growth. This is true as far as it goes, but misses the important point that, if these externalities persist to any given extent, their absolute effect in a large economy will be greater than in a small one. This point can be illustrated by considering the pollution from vehicle exhaust, a classic spillover effect as far as nearby pedestrians or cyclists are concerned. In a low-GNP economy with few vehicles, the effect may be unimportant. In a high-GNP economy, with many vehicles and consequent congestion, the effect may cause considerable discomfort. Yet the emissions per vehicle may be unchanged, as may the overall proportion of such emissions to GNP. But failure to remedy the externality at the low-GNP level has brought about, with economic growth, a major nuisance. Given that such failures to remedy externalities are common, due not least of all to the opposition of the vested interests that are causing them, opposition to the economic growth that amplifies them would seem a not irrational position on the part of those adversely affected.

The other point Beckerman misses about rectifying resource misallocations is that per se it may reduce GNP growth. Lecomber (1975) says, "It is misleading to regard environmental policies of this sort as *alternatives* to reducing economic growth since this would be their incidental effect. Benefits which are not included in GNP would be traded for other (smaller) benefits which are. GNP would fall and, during the period of transition to such policies, growth would fall, probably substantially" (p. 59). Of course, there is no certainty that correcting resource misallocations reduces growth, but two facts point to the likelihood of this. The first is that advocates of growth often believe that it does, and environmental protection measures and agencies are often attacked on the grounds that they reduce growth. The second is that if misallocations could be corrected at zero cost, which is what *no reduction in growth* implies, then there was no economic rationale for them in the first place. While such singular misallocations may exist, it is highly unlikely that, and would represent a major breakdown of economic theory if, the enormous externalities reflected in current environmental degradation were of this sort.

Whatever the potential of technological change, there are certain physical constraints, defined by the laws of thermodynamics, that cannot be circumvented. The second law—that all activity and transformation of energy or materials leads to an increase of entropy—has been most extensively related to economics by Georgescu-Roegen (1971). In this analysis it is the increase of entropy that is the ultimate limit to growth. Economic activity increases entropy by depleting resources and producing waste. Entropy on earth can be decreased only by importing low-entropy resources (solar energy) from outside the earth. This energy can renew resources and neutralize and recycle waste. To the extent that the human economy is powered by solar energy, it is limited only by the flow of that energy. However, the use of fossil fuels has led to great increase of entropy both in itself and by enabling a physical throughput of resources and creation of waste well beyond solar energy's capacity of regeneration. The increased entropy is apparent in the now-familiar litany of environmental problems, including greenhouse effect, ozone depletion, acid rain, deforestation, desertification, toxic pollution, water depletion, and species extinction.

Growth in physical production and throughput that is not based on solar energy must increase entropy and make these problems worse, implying an eventual limit to such growth. Growth in physical production based on solar energy is limited by the quantity and concentration of that energy. GNP can free itself from these limits only to the extent that it decouples itself from growth in physical production—what Daly (1977, p. 118) calls angelized GNP. As will be seen later, such decoupling has occurred to some extent, but the entropy law decrees that it can never be complete. As Daly puts it: "It would be necessary for us to become angels in order to subsist on angelized GNP" (p. 119).

The second new argument, or whole new dimension, that Beckerman (1974) introduces is explicit ethical judgment. Although he considers that "society's relative valuation of present as compared with future consumption" is "a subjective matter and is not one on which economists have any special claim to pontificate" (p. 17), on another subjective matter, that of the intrinsic worth of nonhuman life forms, he has no hesitation in pontificating on behalf of economists very strongly indeed. In a section titled "Man as the Measure of All Things," he writes, "Thus we are not interested in animal or vegetable life for its own sake, but only in so far as it provides benefits to humans" (p. 108). This is an extreme anthropocentric position comparable to pre-Copernican astronomy, which placed the earth, and the people on it, at the center of the universe. It is perfectly possible to feel that living things have value irrespective of human benefit, indeed, even to believe that life had value before the evolution of the human species. Pearce, Markandya, and Barbier (1989) refer to such values as existence values, which include "concern for, sympathy with and respect for the rights or welfare of non-human beings" (p. 61). Beckerman's position is a classic example of a common failing in so-called positive economics, whereby a questionable ethical judgment is presented as a statement of fact.

The third Beckerman (1974) position that is presented as fact is the overall benefit of economic growth, still understood as growth in GNP: "A failure to maintain economic growth means continued poverty, deprivation, disease, squalor, degradation and slavery to soul-degrading toil for countless millions of the world's population" (p. 9). Beckerman also states, "This book is chiefly about why economic growth is still an important source of increased welfare and why it can safely be pursued without fear of environmental catastrophe" (p. 35). In believing that GNP is designed to measure changes in economic welfare (rather than production or income), Beckerman differs from some economists, but he concedes that it may not be a very good measure of such changes (p. 77). However, he considers that there are significant positive as well as negative omissions from GNP and cites Nordhaus and Tobin's (1973) figures as showing that "the absolute rise in the 'good' items that are normally excluded from GNP has exceeded the absolute rise in the 'bad' items (both those that are included in and those that are excluded from GNP) . . . the adjustment for disamenities such as the costs of urban congestion turn out, according to the Nordhaus and Tobin estimates, to have been relatively small compared to the enormous rise in the value of the increase in leisure and non-market activities" (Beckerman 1974, p. 86).

Beckerman's argument is therefore twofold: Poor countries need economic growth to pull them out of poverty; rich countries pursue economic growth because of the net benefits it brings. With regard to the first of these arguments, there is now some doubt, rather more than when Beckerman was writing, whether economic growth per se is what poor people in poor countries need to improve their life prospects; access to resources for subsistence, which would not show up as economic growth, may be even more important. The second argument is a view that is diametrically opposed to the views of Mishan (1967, 1977).

In the works so far surveyed, the emphasis has been on the feasibility of economic growth. Its desirability has been either a moot point or, as with Beckerman, strongly asserted. It was the institutionalist economist Kapp (1950) who made the first thoroughgoing exploration of the social costs of the growth process, but it was Mishan who first brought these costs to widespread public notice. He identified them thus:

> The uglification of once handsome cities the world over continues unabated. Noise levels and gas levels are still rising and, despite the erection of concrete freeways over city centers, unending processions of motorized traffic lurch through its main thoroughfares. Areas of outstanding natural beauty are still being sacrificed to the tourist trade and traditional communities to the exigencies of "development." Pollution of air, soil and oceans spreads over the globe. ... The upward movement in the indicators of social disintegration—divorce, suicide, delinquency, petty theft, drug taking, sexual deviance, crime and violence—has never faltered over the last two decades. (Mishan 1977, p. 10)

It is Mishan's thesis that these and other ill effects are the result of economic growth and far outweigh its benefits. Mishan sees the pursuit of such growth as leading Western civilization to its nemesis. As long as these effects remain important, as they undoubtedly still do, Mishan's thesis stands unfalsified. Whether he will be proved right is of course a different matter.

The concern of ecologists was with the physical limits to economic growth. Mishan's focus was on the limits to social welfare that can be derived from growth. Hirsch (1976) adds to the picture by postulating social limits to growth, distancing himself from the ecologists' critique with the words: "The concern with the limits to growth that has been voiced by and through the Club of Rome (Meadows et al. 1972) is strikingly misplaced. It focuses on distant and uncertain physical limits and overlooks the immediate if less apocalyptic presence of social limits to growth" (p. 4).

Hirsch's social limits derive from two causes: the increasing importance of positional goods and the breakdown of individual morality, in an affluent, growing economy. The positional economy "relates to all aspects of goods, services, work positions, and other social relationships that are either 1) scarce in some absolute or socially imposed sense or 2) subject to congestion or crowding through more extensive use" (p. 27). As incomes rise, the demand for positional goods increases; with a fixed or very inelastic supply, the goods are rationed through either price (e.g., desirable resort properties) or criteria of eligibility (e.g., more stringent examinations), or their quality is degraded through over-crowding (e.g., roads). The effect is to reduce either growth or the welfare to be derived from it, or both.

On the subject of morality, Hirsch writes, "The point is that conventional, mutual standards of honesty and trust are public goods that are necessary inputs for much of economic output. . . . Truth, trust acceptance, restraint, obligation, these are among the social virtues which are also now seen to play a central role in the functioning of an individualistic contractual economy" (p. 141). Yet, Hirsch asserts, these are precisely the virtues that are undermined by the selfsame individualism. "Economic growth undermines its social founda-tions" (p. 175).

Daly (1977) brings the argument full circle by indicting "growthmania" for errors in both the ecological and moral spheres: "Economics has overlooked ecological and moral facts of life that have now come home to haunt us in the form of increasing ecological scarcity and increasing existential scarcity . . . ultimate means have been treated as if they were limitless, and the Ultimate End as if it were unreal" (pp. 170, 176).

Daly's solution to growthmania is the steady-state economy, "an economy with constant stocks of people and artifacts, maintained at some desired, suffi-cient levels by low rates of maintenance 'throughput'" (p. 17). The throughput is limited by strict quotas, auctioned by the government, on depletion of resources. The population is limited by the equal per capita issue of transferable birth licenses. And inequality of income and wealth is limited by the setting of maximum and minimum levels, with redistribution from rich to poor. The dual ecological and social components of Daly's steady state are made ex-plicit in the subtitle of his book: "The Economics of Biophysical Equilibrium and Moral Growth."

The 1970s' limits to growth critiques, both physical and social, failed to dent the social consensus in favor of economic growth. The new governments of Margaret Thatcher and Ronald Reagan at the end of the decade moved strongly to stimulate growth by attacking perceived constraints in the form of labor orga-nizations in the United Kingdom and environmental regulations in the United States. Limits-to-growth arguments withered in this thrusting, pro-growth atmo-sphere, so that by the time the Brundtland Commission produced its report, *Our Common Future* (WCED 1987), on environment and development, the emphasis was placed on a perceived complementarity between growth and environment. In her introduction to the report, Brundtland calls for "a new era of economic growth—growth that is forceful and at the same time socially and environmentally sustainable" (p. xii). Later the report defines this position further: "The concept of sustainable development does imply limits—not absolute limits but limitations imposed by the present state of technology and social organizations on environmental resources and by the ability of the biosphere to absorb the effects of human activities. But technology and social organization can be both managed and improved to make way for a new era of economic growth" (p. 8).

This bullish attitude was justified by statistics that showed that during the period 1972–86, the relationship between energy use and economic growth in industrial countries had undergone a significant change from the broadly proportional relationship that had existed before. In the United States, energy intensity (the amount of energy used per unit of GDP) from 1973 to 1986 diminished by 25 percent. Over the OECD as a whole it fell by 20 percent from 1973 to 1985. In the same period for countries belonging to the International Energy Agency, GDP grew by nearly 32 percent, but energy use only by 5 percent (WRI 1990, p. 146). A decoupling of economic growth from energy consumption was proclaimed.

A major difference in the environmental debate since the publication of the Brundtland Report has been the positive engagement of business, which in the 1970s was still broadly unconvinced that there was a problem. This situation has changed dramatically and many businesses are now engaged in environmental management programs that go well beyond legal requirements (Business International 1990). Two significant international business initiatives have been launched: the Business Charter for Sustainable Development of the International Chamber of Commerce (ICC) and the Business Council for Sustainable Development (BCSD), established to give advice from a business perspective to the 1992 UN Conference on Environment and Development. Both of these initiatives believe environmental sustainability to be compatible with growth: "Economic growth provides the conditions in which protection of the environment can best be achieved, and environmental protection, in balance with other human goals, is necessary to achieve growth that is sustainable" (ICC 1990). At the BCSD launch in 1991, its chairman, Stephan Schmidheiny, stated bluntly: "Sustainable development combines two key objectives—environmental protection and growth" (BCSD 1991). In an earlier interview with the newspaper *Neue Zürcher Zeitung* (Schmidheiny 1990), however, Schmidheiny himself had confused this message by admitting, in response to the question, "Isn't this combination [of growth and environmental protection] just a dream, because it means bringing together things that don't match?" that "For the time being that's true."

The alleged compatibility between growth and the environment was given a new twist by Bernstam (1991), who postulated that industrialization under free market conditions exhibits a characteristic relationship between growth and the environment. In Bernstam's view, in the early days there is a negative trade-off at the expense of the environment. This effect diminishes as industrialization proceeds, and, at a certain historical moment, there is a positive relationship between the two. At this point, "economic growth can reduce pollution if it increases the productivity of resources (that is, reduces wastes) faster than both resource output and population growth" (pp. 33, 34).

Bernstam asserts that in industrial market economies this condition is now being met by the operation of what he calls the "invisible environmental hand" (p. 40)." I have subjected this assertion to rigorous criticism elsewhere (Ekins 1992), but most importantly, it remains at the level of pure conjecture. In fact, it is flatly contradicted by trends in energy use since 1986. U.S. energy intensity actually increased (that is, more energy was used per unit of GDP) in 1987 and 1988, as did that of several European countries (WRI 1990, p. 146), and there is no evidence at all that, over a prolonged period, Bernstam's condition for growth to reduce environmental impacts is being met.

Achieving Sustainability

From this review of the economic growth debate it can be seen that there is as yet nothing approaching consensus as to the ultimate relationship between economic growth and either environmental or social sustainability, but the key parameters of these relationships are now clear. First, with regard to the environment, it can be stated that further GNP growth will *not* increase current rates of economically induced environmental destruction *only if* the following factors act in sum to reduce the environmental intensity of GDP (the environmental damage per unit of GDP) by more than the rate of GDP growth: change in composition of GDP, substitution of factor inputs, and increase in resource productivity. Second, with regard to welfare, there can be no presumption that GDP growth, especially if it increases environmental destruction but even if it does not, increases social welfare. Third, with regard to social sustainability, it is quite possible that the type and pace of technological change required to make GDP growth and environmental protection compatible objectives will exacerbate the sort of social problems identified by Mishan (1967, 1977) and Hirsch (1976), with unpredictable results. These three conclusions point to a clear strategy for the achievement of environmental sustainability.

Shifting the Policy Emphasis from Growth to Sustainability

The dominant objective of economic policy must be shifted from GDP growth to environmental sustainability. I have argued this in detail elsewhere (Ekins 1989), but, in the present context, such policy would seek to ensure that possible, environment-benefiting changes in the composition of GNP, factor substitution, and resource productivity were indeed realized. If the technological optimists are right, then GNP growth would also be achieved. If not, at least sustainability would be approached. Maintaining an emphasis on economic growth, with all the pressure that seeks to maintain business as usual, is much less likely to introduce the changes for sustainability that are necessary.

An equation introduced by Ehrlich and Ehrlich (1990, p. 58) indicates the scale of the technological challenge if both sustainability and GNP growth are to be achieved. They relate environmental impact (I) to the product of three variables: population (P), consumption per capita (C), and the environmental intensity of consumption (T). This last variable captures all the changes in technology, factor inputs, and the composition of GNP. Thus: $I = PCT$.

The contemporary concern with sustainable development indicates that current levels of I are unsustainable. With regard to energy consumption and climate change, the Intergovernmental Panel on Climate Change (IPCC) calculates that carbon dioxide emissions will quickly have to fall by a minimum of 60 percent to stabilize atmospheric concentrations of CO_2, and three other greenhouse gases—N_2O, CFC-11, and CFC-12—need cuts of more than 70 percent (Houghton et al. 1990, p. xviii). With regard to other environmental problems, the Dutch National Environmental Policy Plan (MOHPPE 1988) argues for cuts in emissions of 80–90 percent for SO_2, NO_x, NH_3 and waste-dumping; 80 percent for hydrocarbons; and 100 percent for CFCs. Thus with regard to I overall, it seems conservative to suggest that sustainability demands that it should fall by at least 50 percent. With regard to consumption, what is considered a moderate economic growth rate of 2–3 percent results in a quadrupling of output over fifty years. With regard to population, the UN's recent projections indicate a global figure of 10 billion by about 2050 (Sadik 1991, p. 3)—about twice today's level— with 95 percent of that growth in the Third World. Using this assumption and classifications and data from World Bank 1992, the necessary reductions in T (T_R) in order to reduce environmental impacts to 50 percent of the current value by 2050 would be as follows (see Appendix for detailed calculation):

1. No growth in P or C T_{R1} = 50%
2. Growth in P, no growth in C T_{R2} = 65%
3. Growth in P and C in South T_{R3} = 81%
4. Growth in P and C in North T_{R4} = 89%
5. Growth in P and C in North and South T_{R5} = 91%

These figures clearly illustrate some important aspects of the technology/sustainability relations. T_{R5} shows that, with moderate GNP growth in North and South, and projected population growth, the environmental impact of each unit of consumption would need to fall by 91 percent over the next fifty years to meet the rather conservative definition of sustainability that has been adopted. This is a very tall order indeed, and one does not have to be a technological pessimist to entertain serious doubts as to its feasibility.

Comparing T_{R1} and T_{R2}, expected population growth at existing consumption levels increases the required cut in T from one-half to two-thirds. Although 95 percent of the population growth takes place in the South, the detailed calculation shows that the far higher level of consumption in the North means that the growth of population in the North (5 percent of total population growth) accounts for well over one-half of the increase in environmental impact due to population growth as a whole and thus over one-half of the extra required reduction in T due to that growth.

Comparing T_{R4} with T_{R2} (89 percent to 65 percent) shows the extent to which growth in the North makes the achievement of environmental sustainability more technologically demanding. Comparison of T_{R4} with T_{R3} is evidence of the enormously skewed nature of current consumption patterns: the sustainable quadrupling of just the North's consumption per head, from a high base, demands considerably greater technical change than sustainably quadrupling the South's consumption per head for more than double its present population (89 percent as opposed to 81 percent reduction in T). In the latter case, the calculation shows that even after quadrupling the South's per capita consumption, this is still only about one-sixth of current levels in the North. It is also clear that the required technological improvement in the North, even without Northern growth, is substantial if the South is to have ecological space for environmentally sustainable growth. Goodland and Daly (1992, p. 130) also make this point.

In the light of this, it is surprising that sustainable development thinking does not seem to differentiate between the need for and environmental feasibility of growth in the Third World and the quite different situation, on both counts, of the already rich world. In particular, the Brundtland Report (WCED 1987), with its now famous definition of sustainable development as that which "meets the needs of the present without compromising the ability of future generations to meet their own needs" (p. 43), makes no distinction between the vastly different "needs" in the First and Third worlds; nor does it draw attention to the fact that the majority of First World consumption, and presumably an even greater proportion of any growth in that consumption, is far more related to satisfying consumer wants than meeting human needs.

The conclusion is clear: The best chance of achieving sustainable development lies in differentiating between North and South. In the South there must be an emphasis on balanced, sustainable growth through a twin focus on environmental regeneration and careful industrialization using the most environmentally advanced technologies and bearing in mind the difficulties of transferring technologies between different technological and cultural milieus. In the North, the concentration must be on ecologically transforming industrial production and consumption patterns. Any growth in production that this process may bring about will have to be compensated for by even greater decreases in environmental intensity.

Providing More Rigorous Indicators of Welfare and Production

So far in this chapter, economic growth and growth in GNP have been taken to be synonymous, and they are usually so understood. Thence, the positive link with social welfare is also normally taken for granted. As we have seen, a key theme in the limits-to-growth debate was a rejection of this positive link between growth and welfare. More recent developments have been a challenge of the identification of economic growth with growth in GNP and a determined effort to reform GNP so as to take account of environmental impacts.

Hueting (1986; see also Hueting and Leipert 1990) has consistently denied that economic growth means growth in GNP. His argument is that the purpose of the economy, and therefore the proper subject of economics, is the promotion not of production and consumption but of welfare (to which, of course, production and consumption may contribute). Logically, therefore, economic growth should mean an increase in welfare, which could have a variety of components of which Hueting identifies seven: production, environment, employment, leisure, working conditions, income distribution, and safety of the future (Hueting 1986, pp. 243–44). GNP growth at best is an indicator of production growth (but see below); economic growth means that welfare has increased, implying ideally that the contributions of all of the above have been taken into account. It is to make operational such a broader notion of economic growth that various different indicator systems have recently been proposed, including the Human Development Index (UNDP 1990) and Anderson's (1991) Global Report indicators. (For further discussion of these issues and the elaboration of a four-component indicator framework, see Ekins 1990 and Ekins and Max-Neef 1992.)

If the link between GNP growth and welfare is problematic, GNP's status even as an indicator of economic production is increasingly being called into question. GNP is supposed, of course, to measure, as a triple identity, production, expenditure, and income. The problem is that there is an important and growing class of expenditures, called defensive expenditures, which are more in the nature of intermediate costs, although they are often classed as final expenditures. Leipert (1989) classified such expenditures in six areas—the environment, transportation, housing, security, health, and work—and found that in the Federal Republic of Germany such expenditures had increased from an equivalent of 5 percent to an equivalent of 10 percent of GNP between 1970 and 1985. Moreover, if GNP is to be a true figure of income, then not only does the depreciation of physical capital need to be deducted, as occurs in the computation of net national product (NNP), but the depletion of the earth's resources (natural capital) needs also to be subtracted if the (sustainable) income is not to be overstated. Finally, to the extent that the economy has become unsustainable, this represents accumulated costs in the past that should have been deducted from GNP but were not. Hueting Bosch, and de Boer (1991) recommend that across all areas where environmental unsustainability is apparent, sustainability standards should be set and the cost of attaining them be deducted from GNP.

The conclusion on these adjustments to GNP is that, for it to approach an indicator of sustainable income (or production, but not welfare), it should be subject to four subtractions: depreciation of manufactured capital, depletion of natural capital, defensive expenditures, and the cost of reaching sustainability standards. This conclusion is broadly in line with the recommendations in Pearce, Markandya, and Barbier (1989, p. 108). Were these adjustments to be made comprehensively, then much of the context of the limits-to-growth debate would disappear, because the new, adjusted GNP simply would not grow in an economy that was fast depleting natural capital or generating social and environmental externalities. The real issues at stake would then be much clearer: Was natural capital being depleted too quickly? Were the externalities excessive? Was the sustainability gap narrowing? These questions about the ecological impact of economic activity rather than the level of GNP itself have in any case been the substantial concern behind the environmental limits-to-growth debate.

Conclusion

The debate about economic growth has focused attention on three extremely important sets of questions, which remain unanswered and extremely relevant today. Are the current level and likely future increase of human economic activity:

1. globally, having an environmental impact that, at best, reduces economic possibilities in the future and, at worst, is likely to precipitate widespread collapse?
2. in industrial countries, generating a range of negative social and environmental effects that actually outweigh many of the benefits of current affluence and of its nominal increase?
3. in market economies, producing intense competitive and individualistic pressures that not only prevent individuals from enjoying their affluence, as in 2, above, but also undermine the cultural and moral fabric of society on which the economy itself actually depends?

In the twenty years or so since the debate began in earnest, none of these questions have been conclusively answered in the negative. On the contrary, question 1 now commands an almost universal positive response, which has given rise to the concern with sustainable development. However, the facile assumption that such development automatically, as it were, renders compatible economic growth and environmental protection, rather than entails a difficult trade-off between them, is, as we have seen, invalid except under stringent conditions of changing consumption patterns and technological progress. Not only does such an assumption risk intensifying current unsustainability, but it also does not even begin to address the profounder questions 2 and 3. These questions can be addressed only by adjusting GNP as earlier discussed, by placing GNP in an operational formulation of economic welfare that goes well beyond it, and by addressing specifically the moral and cultural issues raised by the predominant emphasis in economic thinking on individual preferences and self-interest. Such approaches provide an opportunity to invest the term *sustainable development* with some deeper human social and institutional significance, which at present it signally lacks.

References

Anderson, V. 1991. *Alternative economic indicators.* London: Routledge.

Beckerman, W. 1974. *In defence of economic growth.* London: Jonathan Cape.

Bernstam, M. 1991. *The wealth of nations and the environment.* London: Institute for Economic Affairs.

Business Council for Sustainable Development (BCSD). 1991. "Top world business leaders support major new initiatives on environment and development." Press release, February 19, 1991. Geneva: BCSD.

Business International. 1990. *Managing the environment: The greening of European business.* London: BI.

Cole, H. S. D., C. Freeman, M. Jahoda, and K. L. R. Pavitt, eds. 1973. *Thinking about the future: A critique of the limits to growth.* London: Chatto & Windus for Sussex University Press.

Daly, H. E. 1977. *Steady-state economics: The economics of biophysical equilibrium and moral growth.* San Francisco: W. H. Freeman.

Ehrlich, P., and A. Ehrlich. 1990. *The population explosion.* London: Hutchinson.

Ekins, P. 1989. "Beyond growth: The real priorities of sustainable development." *Environmental Conservation* 16(1): 5–6, 12 (Foundation for Environmental Conservation, Geneva).

———. 1990. "An indicator framework for economic progress." *Development* 3/4: 64–73 (Society for International Development, Rome).

———. 1991. "The sustainable consumer society: A contradiction in terms?" In *International Environmental Affairs* 3(4): 243–58. Hanover, NH: University Press of New England.

———. 1992. "Review of Bernstam 1991." In *Science and Public Policy,* February. Guildford, UK: Beechtree Publishing. Forthcoming.

Ekins, P., and M. Max-Neef, eds. 1992. *Real-life economics.* London: Routledge.

Georgescu-Roegen, N. 1971. *The entropy law and the economic process.* Cambridge, MA: Harvard University Press.

Goodland, R., and H. Daly. 1992. "Ten reasons why northern income growth is not the solution to southern poverty." In *Population, technology and lifestyle: The transition to sustainability,* ed. R. Goodland, H. Daly, and S. El Serafy. Washington, DC: Island Press.

Hirsch, F. 1976. *Social limits to growth.* Cambridge, MA: Harvard University Press.

Houghton, J., G. Jenkins, and J. Ephraums, eds. 1990. *Climate change: The IPCC scientific assessment.* Oxford: Oxford University Press.

Hueting, R. (1986) "An economic scenario for a conserver economy." In *The living economy: A new economics in the making,* ed. P. Ekins. London: Routledge.

Hueting, R., P. Bosch, and B. de Boer. 1991. *Methodology for the calculation of sustainable national income.* Voorburg: Netherlands Central Bureau of Statistics.

Hueting, R., and C. Leipert. 1990. "Economic growth, national income and the blocked choices for the environment." *The Environmentalist* 10(1): 25–38.

International Chamber of Commerce (ICC). 1990. "The business charter for sustainable development: Principles for environmental management." Paris: ICC.

Kapp, K. W. 1950. *The social costs of private enterprise.* Cambridge, MA: Harvard University Press.

Lecomber, R. 1975. *Economic growth versus the environment.* London: Macmillan.

Leggett, J., ed. 1990. *Global warming: The Greenpeace report.* Oxford/New York: Oxford University Press.

Leipert, C. 1989. "Social costs of the economic process and national accounts: The example of defensive expenditures." *Journal of Interdisciplinary Economics* 3(1): 27–46 (AB Academic Publishers, Berkhamsted, Herts).

Meadows, D. H., D. L. Meadows, J. Randers, and W. Behrens. 1972. *The limits to growth.* New York: Universe Books.

Ministry of Housing, Physical Planning and Environment (MOHPPE). 1988. *To choose or to lose: National environmental policy plan.* The Hague: MOHPPE.

Mishan, E.J. 1967. *The costs of economic growth.* London: Staples Press.

———. 1977. *The economic growth debate: An assessment.* London: George Allen & Unwin.

Nordhaus, W., and J. Tobin. 1973. "Is growth obsolete?" In *The measurement of economic and social performance,* ed. M. Moss. Princeton, NJ: Princeton University Press.

Pearce, D., A. Markandya, and E. Barbier. 1989. *Blueprint for a green economy.* London: Earthscan.

Sadik, N. 1991. *The state of the world population 1991.* New York: UN Fund for Population Activities.

Schmidheiny, S. 1990. Interview by *Neue Zürcher Zeiting,* December 8–9.

United Nations Development Program (UNDP). 1990. *Human development report.* Oxford/New York: Oxford University Press.

World Bank. 1992. *World development report 1992.* Oxford/New York: Oxford University Press.

World Commission on Environment and Development (WCED). 1987. *Our common future* (the Brundtland report). Oxford/New York: Oxford University Press.

World Resources Institute (WRI). 1990. *World resources 1990–91.* Washington, DC: WRI.

Appendix

Calculations of Required Reductions in Environmental Intensity to Achieve Sustainability using the Ehrlich Equation, $I = PCT$

Where subscript 1 indicates the quantity now, subscript 2 indicates the quantity in fifty years' time; superscript 1 indicates high-income countries; superscript 2 low- and middle-income countries (the Third World), according to the World Bank's classification and using data from World Bank 1992; and superscript T indicates the whole world, and using the assumptions for population growth and sustainability, we have:

$$I_1^1 = 2 \times I_2^1, \ I_1^2 = 2 \times I_2^2 \text{ for sustainability}$$

$$P_1^T = P_1^1 + P_1^2$$
$$P_2^T = P_2^1 + P_2^2 = 2 \times P_1^T; \text{ Population growth} = P_1^T$$

$$P_2^1 = P_1^1 + 0.05 \times P_1^T; \ P_1^2 = P_1^2 + 0.95 \times P_1^T$$

$$P_1{}^1 = 816.4 \text{ million}; \quad P_1{}^2 = 4145 \text{ million}; \quad P_1{}^T = 4962 \text{ million}$$
$$\text{(exc. former USSR)}$$

$$P_2{}^1 = 1064 \text{ million}; \quad P_2{}^2 = 8860 \text{ million}; \quad P_2{}^T = 9924 \text{ million}$$

$$C_1{}^1 = \$19{,}590; \quad C_1{}^2 = \$840$$

$$P_1{}^1 C_1{}^1 = \$15.99 \times 10^{12}; \quad P_1{}^2 C_1{}^2 = \$3.48 \times 10^{12}; \quad (P_1 C_1)^T = \$19.47 \times 10^{12}$$

$$I = (PC)^T \cdot T$$

where $(PC)^T = P^1 C^1 + P^2 C^2 =$ Total global consumption.

Using this formulation and the earlier assumptions about population and sustainable environmental impact, the environmental implications of five different development paths can be analyzed.

1. No growth in population or consumption:

T must be reduced by 50 percent

Growth in population, and, with regard to consumption:

2. No growth in consumption: $C_2{}^1 = C_1{}^1, C_2{}^2 = C_1{}^2$

$$P_2{}^1 C_2{}^1 = 1064 \times 19590 \times 10^6 = \$20.8 \times 10^{12}$$
$$P_2{}^2 C_2{}^2 = 8860 \times 840 \times 10^6 = \$7.44 \times 10^{12}$$

$$(P_2 C_2)^T = P_2{}^1 C_2{}^1 + P_2{}^2 C_2{}^2 = \$28.2 \times 10^{12}$$

$$T_2 = 1/2 \times (P_1 C_1)^T / (P_2 C_2)^T \times T_1 = 1/2 \times (19.47) / (28.2) \times T_1$$
$$= 0.35 \times T_1$$

So T must be reduced by 65 percent

3. Growth only in the South: $C_2{}^1 = C_1{}^1, \; C_2{}^2 = 4 \times C_1{}^2$

$$C_2{}^2 = \$3360$$

$$P_2{}^1 C_2{}^1 = 1064 \times 19590 \times 10^6 = \$20.8 \times 10^{12}$$
$$P_2{}^2 C_2{}^2 = 8860 \times 3360 \times 10^6 = \$29.8 \times 10^{12}$$

$$(P_2 C_2)^T = P_2{}^1 C_2{}^1 + P_2{}^2 C_2{}^2 = \$50.7 \times 10^{12}$$

$$T_2 = 1/2 \times (P_1C_1)^T / (P_2C_2)^T \times T_1 = 1/2 \times (19.47) / (50.7) \times T_1$$
$$= 0.19 \times T_1$$

So T must be reduced by 81 percent

4. Growth only in the North: $C_2^1 = 4 \times C_1^1, C_2^2 = C_1^2$

$$C_2^1 = \$78360$$

$$P_2^1C_2^1 = 1064 \times 78360 \times 10^6 = \$83.4 \times 10^{12}$$
$$P_2^2C_2^2 = 8860 \times 840 \times 10^6 = \$7.44 \times 10^{12}$$

$$(P_2C_2)^T = P_2^1C_2^1 + P_2^2C_2^2 = \$90.84 \times 10^{12}$$

$$T_2 = 1/2 \times (P_1C_1)^T / (P_2C_2)^T \times T_1 = 1/2 \times (19.47) / (90.84) \times T_1$$
$$= 0.11 \times T_1$$

So T must be reduced by 89 percent

5. Growth in North and South: $C_2^1 = 4 \times C_1^1, C_2^2 = 4 \times C_1^2$

$$C_2^1 = \$78360$$
$$C_2^2 = \$3360$$

$$P_2^1C_2^1 = 1064 \times 78360 \times 10^6 = \$83.4 \times 10^{12}$$
$$P_2^2C_2^2 = 8860 \times 3360 \times 10^6 = \$29.8 \times 10^{12}$$

$$(P_2C_2)^T = P_2^1C_2^1 + P_2^2C_2^2 = \$113 \times 10^{12}$$

$$T_2 = 1/2 \times (P_1C_1)^T / (P_2C_2)^T \times T_1 = 1/2 \times (19.47) / (113) \times T_1$$
$$= 0.09 \times T_1$$

So T must be reduced by 91 percent

7

Andrea Baranzini and Gonzague Pillet

The Physical and Biological Environment—The Socioeconomy of Sustainable Development

Introduction

Sustainability is now becoming a key word for every policy concerning development, economics, ecology, and social issues. However, we sometimes get the feeling that sustainability is used as a black box with very different meanings. In this chapter we will try to shed some light on this notion. The first section points out some general features that we believe are implicit in the definition of sustainability given in the Brundtland Report (WCED 1987). The second section develops the various relationships that one finds between the economy and the physical and biological environment. There we stress the necessity to guarantee the physical viability of the system before starting any discussion on sustainability. The third section attempts to provide some measurable physical indicators of survivability. The fourth section presents some enlarged neoclassical models of sustainability, but we point out that more short-term available indicators are needed. The fifth, and final, section contains concluding remarks and qualifications.

Some Implications of Sustainable Development

Although the concept of sustainable management has a long history in the management of natural resources (e.g., Clark 1990), it was only after the World Commission on Environment and Development report (WCED 1987) that the

This paper was presented at the Fourth Annual International Conference of the Society For the Advancement of Socio-Economics, Irvine, CA, March 27–29, 1992. We would like to thank Sylvie Faucheux, Hubert Greppin, and Giovanni Farro-Luzzi for useful comments. The usual disclaimer applies.

concept has been broadened and has entered the political agenda. The report argues that "sustainable development is development that meets the needs of the present without compromising the ability of future generations to meet their needs" (p. 43). One of the most important means to attain this objective is economic growth. To quote the report: "What is needed now is a new era of economic growth—growth that is forceful and at the same time socially and environmentally sustainable." WCED argues that the necessity of a five-fold to tenfold increase in world industrial output is required to attain sustainability, because the fruits of growth should be used for income redistribution and to restore the natural environment. As pointed out by Haavelmo and Hansen (1991), such policy statement seems to be based on the belief that there are no limits to material growth. Meanwhile, the WCED is highly concerned with pollution and exhaustion of natural resources, reflecting the belief that there exist some serious limits to growth. The Brundtland Report is therefore sometimes viewed "as a matter of conflicting goals" (cf. Hueting 1990).

Unsustainability of the current path of development originates from at least two (interdependent) factors: The first is economic and the second is ecological. Economic unsustainability arises from the development that has taken place in very different ways around the world, resulting in an increase in disparities and poverty (World Bank 1990), therefore impairing the future of new generations in some regions of the world. Ecological unsustainability occurs because current (over) exploitation and destruction of the world's natural resources and services are global, very often irreversible, and with long-term effects, leading therefore to inevitable unbalanced consequences for the welfare of future people.

While the WCED (1987) report is an important step in the direction of suitable change, the concept of sustainable development still does not have a precise meaning. Since the WCED's definition, an impressive literature on sustainability has flourished; for instance, Pezzey (1989) and Pearce, Markandya, and Barbier (1989) have already found more than twenty different interpretations of this concept in the economic literature. From our point of view, it seems important to point out some key elements that directly follow from the WCED's definition.

First, the aim of development is to answer people's needs and thus increase their welfare. However, welfare has very different components, such as produced goods and services, income and wealth distribution, leisure time, health, freedom, environmental goods and services, and employment security (Hueting 1989). Therefore, development should not only imply a quantitative increase in economic goods and services. Moreover, production growth may be in conflict with other elements that contribute to welfare, for instance because of diminished environmental services (pollution).

Second, the time frame to confront and analyze every action lies in a long-term setting. On the one hand, this means that quantitative increases in produced economic goods that are material- and energy-intensive goods cannot be sustained indefinitely, because our material world is a finite one. In other words, quantitative economic growth should not be confused with development. Development means a qualitative improvement of some potentiality, whereas growth means a quantitative increase in physical scale (cf. Daly 1987a, 1990), which definitely depends on thermodynamic laws.[1] On the other hand, this definition recognizes welfare interdependence between generations. It also suggests an equity norm to solve conflicting problems that would prevent future generations' welfare from being diminished by present-day actions. This equity norm (and therefore sustainability) is Pareto efficient, as development should increase today's welfare without diminishing future welfare (Faucheux and Noël 1990).

Third, the above definition of sustainability seems to be grounded in three criteria, namely, biophysical (or environmental), social (or ethical), and economic. As Daly (1987b) points out, these three criteria define three filters in deciding respectively what is (physically) possible; what is possible and (socially) desirable; and finally, what is possible, desirable, and economically feasible. Dryzek (1989) in his metaphor of the *Titanic* described well the fragmented vision of sustainability that possesses different disciplines. Whereas some ecologists have seen that some icebergs are in the way of the *Titanic*, the great majority of economists are deciding the more efficient arrangement of the couches, while political scientists are discussing the electoral behavior of the people who are sitting on the couches. Clearly, icebergs should receive more attention.

Fourth, to implement and enforce measures that permit attainment of sustainable development, it will probably be necessary to have some important institutional modifications at both the international and the national levels. At the international level it is interesting to note that agreements concerning the reduction of threats to the global community are receiving much more attention than in the past. It is, however, difficult to imagine that all future international agreements will be as successful as the Montreal protocol on the reduction of CFCs (cf., e.g., Faucheux and Noël 1990). Other environmental concerns such as global warming, but also population growth, wealth distribution, and others, are much more difficult to tackle within current institutional barriers. It is also imperative to redefine what role government should play in implementing sustainable development at the national level. In any case, if sustainability is not just another empty box that merely increases the gap between the discourse on environment and the hard facts (Sachs 1988), it appears necessary to imagine possibly new roles for government and international organizations such as the World Bank, International Monetary Fund (IMF), General Agreement on Tariffs and Trade (GATT), and United Nations Organization (UNO). Institutions that combine social controls with a minimal sacrifice of personal freedom are needed to avoid the constraints that current choices impinge on future generations' freedom. It is, however, clear that discussions on institutional changes will split the debate between advocates of state intervention and supporters of free market mechanisms (cf. Anderson and Leal 1991). It is nonetheless important to remember that both the state and the market should be used to ensure sustainability, as both are collective decision-making mechanisms. Sustainable policies should therefore be analyzed at various levels, including the economic, the political, and the administrative spheres (on this topic, cf. Bürgenmeier 1992, 1993).

In what follows we will focus on the relationship between the physical environment and the economy for directing much of our attention toward measurable indicators that can effectively guide us to a sustainable development path. We thus leave aside other subjects related to sustainability.

Environmental Functions and the Issue of Survivability

The physical and biological environment and the economic system are deeply interconnected. Indeed, the former provides useful economic and vital functions to the economy, while the latter, through its economic activities, can greatly modify the environment. In particular, the environment makes three potentially competitive functions available to the economy: resource supplier, waste assimilator, and final services supplier. (For an analysis of environmental functions, compare, for instance, Hueting 1980; de Groot 1986, 1988; Baranzini 1990). Figure 7.1 simplistically presents the interactions between the environment and the economy. The resource box (R) represents the first of these environmental functions and it accounts for renewable and nonrenewable resources. However, the extraction of natural resources from the environment transforms its ability to provide economic functions because of such factors as natural habitat destruction. In the production process (Q in figure 7.1) the economy utilizes natural resources as primary factors which are then transformed into economic products (C), thus contributing to welfare (U). The economic process cannot physically create these natural resources and therefore cannot be viewed as a system completely isolated from its physical basis. In this sense, the economic process is only a physical transformation of energy and matter, and not a source of creation in a physical sense (cf. Georgescu-Roegen 1979). There is, however, creation from the economic perspective based on the new energy forms that evolve from the former physical transformation (Passet 1979; Pillet and Odum 1987). In the physical perspective, it follows that the possibilities of substitution between human labor, man-made capital, and natural resources are bounded by the respective roles of these factors in the production process.2 Energy and matter are raw materials that are transformed, and labor and capital are the factors that transform these raw materials. Substitution between factors that have very different roles in the production process is therefore difficult (Daly 1991a, 1991b). Substitution is easier if the factors have similar roles in the production process (e.g., substitution of capital for human labor; substitution of one natural resource for another). If they have different roles, complementarity is the major characteristic. As already pointed out, capital goods and labor need natural resources for their construction and maintenance, and this further reduces the set of substitution possibilities (cf. Cleveland et al. 1984; Ayres and Nair 1984; Georgescu-Roegen 1971, 1979, 1982). Production of goods is impossible without energy and matter, and capital and labor cannot create these resources and cannot therefore be

Figure 7.1. **Economic Functions of the Environment**

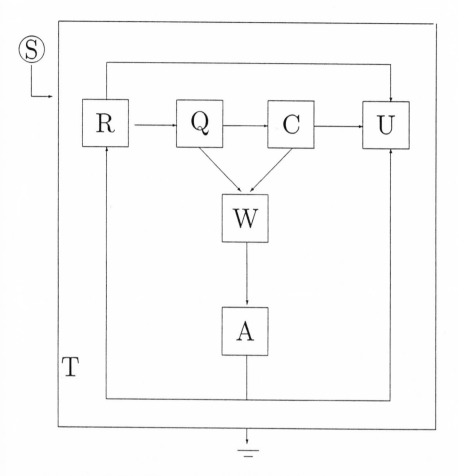

substituted for natural capital in production processes.[3] If there is basic complementarity between natural resources and man-made capital, the fundamental
question that arises is, Which of the two factors is the limiting one? The answer
is related to the scale of the economic system relative to the environmental
system. If the economic system is small relative to the environment which provides natural resources, it is man-made capital which is limiting. However, since
the famous Club of Rome's Limits to Growth (Meadows et al. 1972), the unlimited availability of natural resources relative to the needs of the production
process has been seriously questioned. Clearly, as in the past, technological
progress can overcome future resource constraints, but this is finally a matter of
faith. Following Costanza (1989), we can simplify this issue by separating the
views on technology in two antagonist groups: the technological optimists versus

Table 7.1

Payoff Matrix of Technological Choices

		Future State of the World	
		Optimists are right	Pessimists are right
Current technological policy	Technological optimists' policy	High	Disastrous
	Technological pessimists' policy	Moderate	Tolerable

Source: Adapted from R. Costanza, "What Is Ecological Economics?" *Ecological Economics* 1 (1989: 1–7.

the technological pessimists. The former believe that technological improvements will always eliminate absolute scarcity of natural resources and that a technological solution can always be found for every environmental problem. In contrast, the latter believe that technology will not be able to escape fundamental energy and resource constraints and feel very skeptical about technological solutions. Technological pessimists favor an anticipatory policy, whereas optimists favor a reactive policy by which problems are solved at the time they appear. Table 7.1 summarizes the consequences of following an optimistic/pessimistic policy, depending on what the future state of the world will be.

Table 7.1 shows the fundamental consequences of choosing between different policy alternatives. Because of uncertainty about tomorrow's state of the world, the problem is, What will be the consequences if we choose a policy that is not adapted to what will happen in the future? This payoff matrix indicates that if we are optimists and we are wrong, the consequences will be disastrous, whereas if we are wrong while following the technological pessimists' policy, consequences will be tolerable. The choice of current technological policy will be determined by the attitude toward risk of the collectivity in the presence of catastrophic events, and if there is some form of risk aversion, a "maximin" strategy should be chosen. In this case, the collectivity should follow the technological pessimists policy, because its worst outcome is better than the worst outcome of the optimists' policy. Moreover, if there is ignorance on future consequences resulting from the chosen policy and if the results of these policies lead to irreversible (negative) effects, there are some benefits to implement policies that are reversible. Indeed, this kind of policy will not foreclose opportunities to take advantage of future information.[4]

The second environmental function denoted in Figure 7.1 is the assimilative capacity (A). This is the capacity of the physical and biological environment to absorb and disperse moderate amounts of many types of wastes (W) created by human production and consumption activities. The environment is in fact the ultimate sink for all the wastes created by human activities. When this environmental function is overwhelmed (i.e., $W > A$), pollution arises, which limits the ability of the environment to offer not only other ecological functions (e.g., natural capital regeneration) but also economic functions and thus diminishes human welfare. Because wastes are an inevitable by-product of economic activity (Pillet 1986), the question that naturally arises is, Are we exceeding the natural capacity to absorb pollution, and can we substitute artificial means for this capacity? In this case too, the answer depends on the scale of human activity. If it is small relative to the environment, the capacity of the latter to absorb wastes can be viewed as a free good. However, the scientific community has been warning us, for at least twenty years, of the change in the kind of pollution afflicting the environment. The latter has indeed evolved from being a local to a regional and a global problem. This means that the environmental capacity to absorb pollution is more and more jeopardized, from the local to the global scale. As the dimensions of these problems become larger, artificial means of purification become increasingly difficult to find and costly to implement (i.e., the replacement of the tropospheric ozone layer with human capital). For global pollution, natural functions cannot at all be substituted by man-made capital; therefore, solutions can be related only to shifts in polluting activities.

The third environmental function is final services to consumers, which are a direct source of utility (U). Such a function includes both amenities (e.g., recreational activities) and utilities (i.e., vital services), such as the proper functioning of the hydrological cycle. Since this function is provided by natural environments, there is no production technology other than natural processes that can reduce its scarcity (cf. Krutilla and Fisher 1985). The fundamental question that arises is, What is the carrying capacity of the environment, which ultimately enables human life on earth? The answer to this question is difficult, because the environment carrying capacity for animals can be considered almost entirely in terms of population, whereas for humans, population alone is not sufficient because consumption and technology change in time and across individuals (cf. Daly 1991a).[5] It is, however, clear that in this case too the scale of the human activity relative to the environment makes the concept of carrying capacity more or less important. If the scale of the human activity is small, we have some safety margin. However, one can note that the scale of our economies in terms of available space has grown to eliminate natural habitats for other species and thus reduced biodiversity (cf. Goodland 1991). In addition, the carrying capacity of a nation also depends on sources and sinks belonging to offshore ecosystems (Pillet 1991). As a matter of fact, the economic growth and power of many countries can be sustained only at the expense of ecosystems outside those countries. This is true for Switzerland, which is not living within the limits of its own environmental capital; for instance, imports are 3.5 times larger than exports on a solar-embodied energy accounting procedure (cf. Pillet and Odum 1984), while energy involved in Switzerland's economy is two to three times greater than that implicated in its biosphere (Greppin 1988). The fact is that the manifold increase in energy throughput that could be required to institute the Swiss environmental economic paradigm on a general scale would be ecologically impossible because of the total worldwide environmental and intergenerational consequences (Pillet 1991).

To summarize, in analyzing the environmental functions the physical environment provides to the economy, we stress the scale of the economy as a fundamental element in determining whether an environmental function can be sustained, that is, exploited by the present generation without reducing future generations' needs. It is, however, clear that if environmental functions cannot be provided at all in the long run, the problem of sustainability becomes one of survivability. Currently the exploitation of the environment by economic activities might be unsurvivable, because the growth of the economic system has reached environmental limits, thus seriously (and maybe irreversibly) diminishing useful and vital environmental functions. Goodland (1991) points to some important evidence that environmental limits have been reached: global warming (limits on absorptive capacity have been attained); land degradation (each year we lose 15 million acres of land—the regenerative capacity of the soil has been reached); destruction of the ozone shield; and loss of biodiversity. Whereas in the past much of the concern for environmental limits was about the use of the environment as a resource supplier, today's environmental limits result in particular from the use of the physical environment as a sink (including assimilative function) for human wastes (cf. Goodland et al. 1991; Nicolaisen, Dean, and Hoeller 1991). To take an example from Davis (1990), the amount of recoverable fossil fuel (10 trillion barrels of oil) is thought to be sufficient for another 170 years at present consumption rates, but the major problem will be the wastes resulting from the combustion of such a huge amount of resources. Therefore, availability of environmental functions is a prior consideration in comparison to availability of resources such as fossil fuel.

One of the major problems involved in sustainability requires therefore to ensure survivability, which results in defining the maximum scale of the economic system. When survivability is maintained, necessary conditions are ensured to define sustainability.

Once survivability is granted, sustainability requires definition of the optimal scale of the economic system. Nowadays, environmental economics is mainly based on microeconomics (Daly 1991a), as it refers to externality theory where optimal allocation problems are analyzed within a given scale. In contrast, as pointed out by Daly (1991a), the scale of the economy is a macroeconomic problem that deals with the physical size of the human activity measured by population times per capita resource use. Therefore, a macroenvironmental theory has to be constructed if we want to answer the question of sustainability (cf. Costanza 1991b; Pillet et al. 1990). A macroenvironmental theory should thus recognize that the maximum scale of the economic system is determined by physical constraints, but that the optimal scale depends on what is ethically desirable and economically achievable too. When an optimal scale has been chosen, microeconomic considerations can then be used to efficiently allocate resources. In other words, in a microenvironmental perspective, environmental decisions are based on cost-benefit analysis, which is grounded in exogenous individual preferences. However, exogenous individual preferences and market mimicking are not suitable to evaluate the optimal scale of the economic process. First, individual preferences are myopic. Second, social interactions shape individual values, and thus actual preferences are not exogenous. Third, future generations' preferences are endogenous to our decisions and to the environment we leave to them. Fourth, since society has a longer life expectancy than individuals, society has values that are likely to deviate from individual values—for example, those concerning the continuity of human life—which necessitates some environmental compatibility (Klaassen and Opschoor 1991). Here we can follow Page (1991) in his two-tier value theory, which says that some elements such as the institutional environment, property rights, macroeconomic prerequisites such as distribution of wealth, and sustainability represent the first tier, which provides the circumstances under which legislatures, courts, and markets (the second tier) operates. This theory is based on the belief that "the liberal state is a good but somewhat fragile thing, and will not survive and flourish under just any circumstances. It needs some nurturing conditions" (p. 68). These conditions are specified in the first tier, which contains generalized interests, not particular preferences of particular, identified individuals. Therefore, sustainability rules should be set forth before economic rationality is used to determine efficient allocation of resources.

Some Physical Measure of Survivability

Precise physical measures that indicate the maximum scale of the economy are difficult to define because of enormous scientific uncertainties about the precise linkages between the economic system and the biosphere. Actually, environmental issues related to survivability present precisely new tasks for the scientific community: "instead of discovery and application of facts, the new fundamental achievements for science will be in the work of clean up and survive" (Funtowitz and Ravetz 1990, p. 2). However, even if a precise scientific measure of the maximum survivable scale of the economy does not exist, this is not very important, because in every case approaching it, too much will not offer necessary resilience against unexpected changes. Indeed, defining a maximum scale for the economy would resemble the idea of establishing a safe minimum standard, proposed by Toman (1992). This means that defining a maximum scale for the economic system is not only a scientific problem but also a question of the level of risk that is socially acceptable.

Nevertheless, we have found in the literature three approaches concerning the definition of survivability. This will give us some order of magnitude of the scale of the economy relative to its possible maximum.

One index of the actual scale of the human economy is given by Vitousek et al. (1986, cit. in Daly 1991a, 1991b), who calculate that human appropriation of net primary production (NPP, which roughly indicates the basic food resource for everything on earth not capable of photosynthesis)[6] is 25 percent of total NPP or 40 percent of terrestrial NPP. Because it seems that it is not possible to increase the intake from oceans, the terrestrial figure is probably more relevant (Daly 1990). Assuming a constant level of per capita resource consumption,[7] the doubling of the world population and thus, the doubling of the scale of the economic system will approach human exploitation of terrestrial NPP near to 80 percent, which will represent a maximum scale for the economic process. Doubling time of the human population is actually on the order of thirty to forty years, but possibly a decline in population growth is expected seventy years from now (cf. Ridker 1992). This approach suggests therefore that we have half a century to steer our societies toward a survivable path.

A second approach to defining the maximum scale of the economy is made by Greppin (1978, 1988), who tries to exactly define the viability envelopes in which human life can exist. He stresses that the biosphere is a system that tends to a dynamic stationary equilibrium (climax) that naturally enables, but also constraints, life on earth. Actually, the biosphere operates on about 1 percent of the solar energy flow, the remainder being used to fuel the world's hydrothermic mechanisms. Human economy handles an equivalent of about 1 percent of solar energy (an amount amplified by the greenhouse effect), using, principally, nonrenewable resources. The scale of the economy is thus measured as equivalent to 10 percent of the biosphere, which implies that human action possesses the potential to greatly disturb the dynamic equilibrium of the biosphere and therefore to impair the existence of life on earth. In this context, Greppin (1978, 1988) calculates two measures that indicate a maximum allowable scale of the economy. The first is aimed at determining a maximum world population, based on minimum vital (subsistence) requirements for food, oxygen, land, clean water, and so on. He suggests a figure that says that survivability is ensured when the human population is between 10^{10} and 10^{11}, but not ensured when there is a population of more than 10^{11} at subsistence level. We believe that the lower bound for the population is very much compatible with measures presented earlier.

The second indicator proposed by Greppin results from the fact that to maintain the thermic equilibrium of the earth, it is necessary that the human system in his totality not produce more than 5×10^{18} kcal/year of heat (cf. T in Figure 7.1). Today's production of waste heat is estimated to be 0.08×10^{18} kcal/year (cf. Tsuchiya and Yano 1991), related mainly to the energy uses of human activities (especially industrial and residential electricity production). This indicates that the actual scale of the human activity is about one-sixth of the maximum possible.

The third indicator of survivability draws on the works of Faucheux (1990a, 1990b) and Pillet and Faucheux (1991). Unfortunately, only methodology can be presented here, because calculations are not available yet. The aim of this method is to determine the requirements for the physical reproduction of the economic system in the long run. Because this depends on the capacity of the biosphere to sustain the economic system, and because at the mere biospheric level the monetary dimension does not exist, only a physical approach is adopted. This latter is based on a particular form of energy analysis, namely, what is called the eMergy valuation procedure, which has been initiated by Odum (1971, 1983).[8] Various indicators of this procedure have been proposed (cf. Pillet and Faucheux 1991), two of which will be discussed here.

The first indicator relates to the finitude of the resource supplier function of the environment. It is called the available eMergy surplus (AES), which is perceived as the difference between the available energy and the amount of energy consumed by the system, both calculated through an eMergy valuation procedure. If $AES < 0$, the threshold of finitude is reached, and the economic system will enter (in the long run) a phase of decrease and contraction. If, however, $AES \geq 0$, there is an available energy surplus that would permit survivability and sustainable development. (If $AES = 0$, simple reproduction is allowed.) For survivability to be possible in the long run, the condition is therefore that the natural production rate of resources should not exceed their consumption rate. This analysis is, however, true only at the global level, because it appears that an economic system (such as Switzerland [cf. Pillet and Odum 1984]) may continue to exist while having a negative AES, because it can absorb the available eMergy surplus from other systems.[9]

The second indicator of survivability refers to the absorptive capacity function of the environment and thus to the limits imposed by entropy. Thanks to the entropic calculation developed by Murota (1984, 1985) and Tsuchida and Murota (1987), one may now measure the quantity of entropy discharged by a production system. Ideally, one can thus compare this quantity to the absorptive capacity of the biosphere, a difference that implies that this environmental function will be disrupted in the long run. However, such calculation is today impossible to accomplish, the only indicator at our disposal is that of the generation of minimum entropy, the set of existing technologies being given. The difference between effective entropy discharged by a system and minimum entropy may serve as an indicator to judge if the system is close to a survivable path.

Once survivability is ensured, ethical and economic considerations may be considered—the subject of the next section, which puts special emphasis on economic variables.

Appraising Sustainability

In what follows, we will describe the necessary elements to build a simple general model that takes into account the interactions of the economy with the environment. The purpose of this model is to set forth the elements that, once survivability is ensured, allow the economy to follow a path of sustainabillity We will then see that important criticisms to this approach can be addressed and that more measurable techniques are needed.

The economic literature now contains many models that theoretically analyze the interactions of the economy with some environmental function. Former economic models were interested in sustainable economic growth (i.e., growth in consumption goods; cf., e.g., Solow 1974; Stiglitz 1979) in the presence of nonrenewable resources; that is, the environment was considered only in its function as resource supplier. Nonrenewable resources were regarded as essential in production activities, and conditions allowing a positive consumption per head to be maintained (when population and technology are constant) are that the elasticity of substitution between exhaustible resources and other inputs is unity or bigger and that the elasticity of output with respect to reproducible capital exceeds the elasticity of output with respect to natural resources (Solow 1974, p. 11). In any case, the presence of backstop technologies allows the production process to be freed from the constraints imposed by dependence on exhaustible resources (cf. Nordhaus 1973). Indeed, scarcer nonrenewable resources imply higher prices, which will become, sooner or later, higher than the costs of using backstop technologies. At that point, production will switch from nonrenewable resource use to backstop technologies, that is, to resources that are available in unlimited supply. However, for this event to happen, certain conditions should be met. First, resource markets should function correctly by anticipating resource scarcities. If the market is myopic—that is, if it cannot forecast resource scarcities soon enough because of government intervention, demand and supply uncertainties, or market imperfections—prices will move upward too late. This will reduce the time available to discover and to adapt to the backstop technology. Second, it is clearly necessary that a backstop technology exist that can be effectively substituted for the nonrenewable resource. Third, when backstop technology is based on a renewable resource, consumption can in principle be sustained forever without the need for technological improvements or substitution phenomena, but this requires that the renewable resource not be depleted. From a private point of view it is rational *not* to deplete a renewable resource when interest rates are lower than natural regeneration rates and when property rights on the exploitation of the resource are well defined.[10] However, if interest rates are higher than natural regeneration rates or property rights are badly defined, even renewable resources can be depleted (if this is possible). In this circumstance, conditions for sustainable consumption become the same as in the nonrenewable case.

Recent economic models try to more completely incorporate the environment in the analysis, recognizing its multiple economic and vital functions (cf., e.g., Barbier 1990). In general, their structure is similar to former neoclassical models, but special emphasis is put on economic-environmental interactions (cf., among others, Pezzey 1989; Barbier 1990; Klaassen and Opschoor 1991). Sustainable economic development is usually considered as an additional constraint, generally requiring a nondecreasing utility level for a representative individual. In this case, environmental quality influences not only production processes but also utility, through the presence of natural resource stocks and pollution phenomena. However, environmental quality depends on economic activity, because economic systems extract resources and reject wastes in the environment. Economic activity can also in general invest in natural capital, through repairing and cleaning up reversible environmental damages, improving natural assimilation capacities, and producing pollution abatement capital goods. Issues about survivability can also be handled by introducing in the model some requirements for a minimum amount of natural resources to be preserved, a maximum amount of pollution, and a minimum level (subsistence) of consumption per head.

Figure 7.2 depicts a theoretical model that incorporates these considerations. In this chapter's appendix, we algebraically sketch the structure of the model, but even if relationships are kept simple, the model's specification is already too complex to be solved for precise solution. In a different context, we have, however, interpreted the conditions that lead to an optimal path.[11] Although such enlarged neoclassical models are good pedagogical instruments that permit powerful insights in understanding the variables governing the interactions between the economy and the environment, they are subject to important criticisms. First, reality is oversimplified because they consider well-behaved functions that enable mathematical solutions. Second, social well-being is reduced to the sum of individual well-being. Furthermore, individual behavior is reduced to utility maximization. Third, key variables are poor instruments to guide policy. This latter point is worth some comment. As Victor (1991) pointed out, neoclassical indicators of sustainable development are related principally to the physical environment as supplier of resources. These indicators are the elasticity of substitution, technological change, and prices. We have already discussed the first two indicators, concluding that possibilities of substitution are limited and that future technological change is uncertain. Because changes in prices (or rents) should reflect scarcity of resources, studies about the path of resource prices were undertaken, the most famous being that of Barnett and Morse (1963). Independently of the well-known results of these studies, we should remember that if resource markets are not operating as postulated in neoclassic models, prices cannot serve as indicators, since the assumptions under which they possess normative significance do not prevail (cf. Victor 1991, p. 201). Lastly, as noted by Pearce, Markandya, and Barbier (1989), the objective of these enlarged neoclassical models is to sustain utility, but this entity is not at all measurable, especially for a whole nation. Moreover, sustainable development implies a broader notion of welfare, and thus arguments in the utility function should be augmented to take into account not only the environment but also other elements such as wealth distribution, freedom,

Figure 7.2. A General Model of Economic-Environmental Interactions

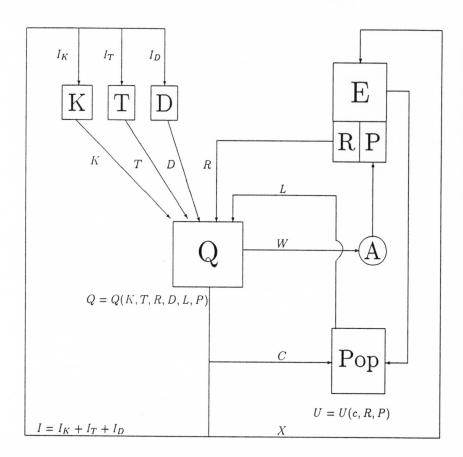

health, and security. Clearly, this extension will make the model quite messy. Moreover, sustainability in a broader sense also raises the philosophical issue concerning our rights over nature: Do we possess the right to exploit nature for our own benefits, even at the expense of species extinction (on this topic, cf. Bartolommei 1989; Forte 1991)? In neoclassical models, which are inherently utilitarian, it is difficult to find nonanthropocentric values, and thus nature does not have intrinsic rights.

In practice, to assess the consequences of past behavior on welfare, national income is used as a substitute for utility, because it can be measured by national accounts. There are, however, great difficulties in relying on national accounts to measure welfare (cf., e.g., Anderson 1991; Goodland and Ledec 1987). Indeed, national accounts are increasingly revised in order to reflect sustainable development, especially in relation to environmental issues (cf. Ahmad, El Serafy, and

Lutz 1989). Income is generally defined as Hicksian income, that is, the maximum amount available for consumption without consuming capital stock. If consumption is augmented at the expense of capital erosion, ability to maintain this level of consumption in the future is seriously questioned. In this restricted sense, if income is properly measured, it is thus sustainable by definition (El Serafy 1991a). Therefore, a measure of the capital stock of the economy is of fundamental importance in judging an economy performance with respect to sustainability.

The capital available to an economy is composed of the stock of goods with power of producing other goods or services in the future (El Serafy 1991b, p. 168). Capital goods are thus composed by man-made capital (machines, buildings, and so on) and natural capital (natural resource stocks that perform environmental functions). We have already seen that man-made capital is not always a good substitute for natural capital, especially because the latter performs multiple functions. Sustainability is thus sometimes viewed as a requirement for maintaining the natural capital stock (cf. Pearce and Turner 1990; Pearce, Markandya, and Barbier 1989). If this requirement is accepted, it is then possible to determine some rules of thumb that can be applied to the management of natural resources. For instance, it is possible to theoretically determine the conditions necessary to the existence of a steady state for *each* environmental function. For example, the use of renewable resources should not be greater than the natural regeneration rate; waste disposal should not exceed natural absorptive capacity (cf. Daly 1990). Rules concerning nonrenewable resource management are less straightforward, but sustainability is generally referred to the revenue resulting from resource extraction (cf. El Serafy 1991b; Hartwick 1977). Such revenue can be invested in other assets, and this reinvestment is sustainable if it can compensate for the decline in the receipts from the lower stock of resources.[12]

If sustainability requires maintaining the natural capital stock, this is a clear justification for implementing natural resource accounts to provide necessary information. These accounts can be included directly in the system of national accounts or considered in separate, satellite accounts. Significant difficulties are, however, involved in such a task. First, the state of the stocks is difficult to evaluate in physical terms, let alone in monetary terms.[13] Moreover, if stocks are evaluated in physical terms, they cannot be added together, and thus trade-offs cannot be judged (we are interested in total natural stock). However, stock evaluation in monetary terms is difficult to assess because environmental capital is often nonmarketed. In general, it is therefore necessary to evaluate the natural resource stock by willingness-to-pay measures, which is highly criticizable (on this topic cf., e.g., Pearce and Markandya 1989). Second, stock variations are even more difficult to calculate and to interpret, especially in monetary terms.[14] In effect, how can we interpret the monetary variation in the value of a stock due to a physical reduction in the stock if at the same time the price of the natural resource has augmented? Third, reductions in the stock of the natural resource result in an increase in both expenditures to clean up the environment and defensive expenditures. These expenditures are already contained in national accounts, but they are not easily isolated. For instance, defensive expenditures operated by firms are considered intermediate expenditures, whereas for government and households, they are considered final expenditures (Levin 1991).[15]

To sum up, although the construction of natural resource accounts will be of fundamental importance to economic planners interested in sustainable development, unsolved methodological problems and lack of data will postpone the use of this source of information. Therefore, if sustainable development is a pressing political objective—as actually seems—there is a need for more imperfect indicators, but more readily available instruments from a short-term perspective (cf. Kuik and Verbruggen 1991). In general, main indicators for sustainable development have for the moment a physical nature. From these indicators, a promising approach is the so-called AMOEBA model, applied by the Dutch Water Management Plan (for details, cf. ten Brink 1991). This model tries to measure sustainable development by the distance between the actual ecosystem and a reference ecosystem in which human manipulation is negligible. The assumption is that natural ecosystems offer the best guarantee of ecological sustainability, which is a basic element in sustainable development. Dialogue with the political sphere allows the maximum acceptable distance of this reference point to be fixed. An ecological Dow Jones index is then constructed, with the aim of aggregating in a single index all the measured differences between some target variables (arbitrarily chosen to characterize the ecosystem) and the reference point. This index is an element that can enter with others in the political decision-making process, where political weights will then determine its relative importance. Much research is, needed, however, to improve such indicators to include, for instance, the economic costs of attaining such a particular defined sustainable development.

Conclusion

This chapter has discussed some issues related to sustainable development. We have shown that sustainability has multiple implications resulting from its connection with very different domains. We have put special emphasis on the relationships between the economy and the physical environment. As pointed out, environmental limits have been reached because of the expansion of the scale of the economic system. We have therefore raised the question of the maximum tolerable scale, that is, what we call the survivability issue. We have noted that a precise answer to this question is not needed, because it does not seem a prudent strategy to develop the economic system to this maximum. Prudent behavior would dictate leaving some safety margin to respond to unexpected changes (surprises). With this fact in mind, we have presented three measures of the maximum viable scale for the economic system.

Finally, we have briefly analyzed enlarged neoclassical models of sustainable development, concluding that, although such models are useful from a theoretical point of view, they are highly criticizable from a practical one. In this vein, an analysis that prescribes the maintenance of a constant stock of natural resources appears more appealing. However, methodological problems and lack of data force us to rely on physical indicators that are imperfect and generally limited in scope.

In our presentation we have left out very important problems related to sustainability—as, for instance, distributional problems and North-South relationships—because we have concentrated on environmental issues. In this domain further research is called for, at both the scientific and the social science levels. For example, further research should deal with the inherent scientific uncertainty related to survivability and sustainability. Moreover, reflections on new institutions and new instruments that tackle globally interconnected problems are absolutely necessary.

Notes

1. Two well-known principles of thermodynamics are involved here. The first is the law of energy conservation, which states that energy (and matter) can be changed in form but neither created nor destroyed. In an isolated system, energy is thus constant. The second is the entropy law, which states that no energy conversion system is ever perfectly efficient. In an isolated system, energy thus irreversibly degrades to lower-quality forms (less capable of accomplishing useful work).
2. We will see later that substitution possibilities play a key role in sustainability, if production is dependent on natural resources at a rate higher than the natural regeneration rate, thus depleting the resource stock.
3. It is clear that at the micro or industrial level there are some substitution possibilities between man-made and natural capital, especially in the long run, even if it is difficult to prove it empirically (cf. the various articles in Berndt and Field 1981). However, we stress the fact that at the macro scale, the economy cannot physically create energy and matter. Therefore, there must be an ultimate limit to natural resource inputs for every produced good (including capital) and thus an upper limit to the extent that capital can be substituted for the input of resources (cf. Kamien and Schwartz 1982). Moreover, we will see in the discussion that follows that natural capital is different from man-made capital because of its multiple functions. Man-made capital might therefore be only an imperfect substitute for all the functions that natural capital provides.
4. The topic is closely related to what is called in the literature the quasi option value, that is, what a decision maker gains by delaying an irreversible decision of which the future consequences are not known with certainty (cf. Arrow and Fisher 1974; Henry 1974; Hanemann 1989).
5. A related question that is impossible to answer is, What is the ability of the human race to adapt to a changing environment?
6. More accurately, primary productivity indicates the fixation of solar energy by green plants (normally expressed in units of kilocalorie per square meter per time). Gross productivity indicates the total energy captured, and net subtracts the energy required for respiration (cf. Hall, Cleveland, and Kaufmann 1986).
7. Some would say that per capita resource consumption will be lower because of

technological resource-saving progress. However, we exactly adopt this extreme assumption to show the urgency of technological progress and the risk associated with relying only on technological progress to ensure survivability (cf. Table 7.1). Moreover, we should remember that in fact economic growth increases average per capita resource consumption and that pollution reduces NPP.

8. EMergy is shorthand for (solar) *embodied energy*. It is part of the ecoenergetic analysis, a procedure that enables comparisons between different forms of energy (commercial, but also nonmarketed energy) with respect to the energy required for their formation. In this context, it is therefore possible to establish a hierarchy of forms of energy according to the ability of each form to do useful (physical) work at the interface between environmental and economic systems.

9. It seems that if the Swiss economy used only its own renewable resources, its maximum population would be no more than 14 percent of its 1982 population (Pillet and Odum 1984).

10. Moreover, private exploitation of natural resources is socially optimal if the private discount rate is equal to the social rate of time preference and if all the (social) benefits resulting from the conservation of the natural resource and all the (social) costs of resource extraction are internalized.

11. Results and general discussion of the model will be available in Baranzini and Pillet (forthcoming). Unsurprisingly, optimal conditions require some kind of marginal cost-benefit rules for the variables that can be controlled by the social planner (i.e., production activity; consumption; investment in capital goods, technology, and pollution abatement capital; and environmental investment). It is also possible to determine from the program shadow prices for environmental functions.

12. From another point of view, Tinbergen and Hueting (1991) have proposed that nonrenewable resource stock depletion should be equal to the rate of efficiency growth in the use of energy.

13. France, among other nations, is developing a system of natural accounts in physical terms (cf. Ministère de l'Environnement 1986).

14. Value depreciation of a natural stock results from reduction in the physical ability of the capital to generate consumption, change in tastes, or change in interest rates (price) (cf. Peskin 1991).

15. Japan is creating a net national welfare index that corrects some of the problems of GNP when used as a measure for welfare (cf. Uno 1989). Welfare losses due to environmental pollution are subtracted from GNP and calculated as the cost of conforming to environmental standards.

References

Ahmad, Y. J., S. El Serafy, and E. Lutz., eds. 1989. *Environmental accounting for sustainable development.* Washington, DC: World Bank.

Anderson, T. L., and D. R. Leal. 1991. *Free market environmentalism.* Boulder, CO: Westview Press.

Anderson, V. 1991. *Alternative economic indicators.* London: Routledge.

Archibugi, F., and P. Nijkamp, eds. 1989. *Economy and ecology: Towards sustainable development.* Dordrecht, Netherlands: Kluwer Academic.

Arrow, K. J., and A. C. Fisher. 1974. "Environmental preservation, uncertainty and irreversibility." *Quarterly Journal of Economics* 88(2): 312–19.

Ayres, R. U., and I. Nair. 1984. "Thermodynamics and economics." *Physics Today* (November): 62–71.

Baranzini, A. 1990. Analyse économique de l'environnement: Orientations principales (Economic analysis of the environement: Principal points of view). In *Environne-*

ment—Economie. Analyse du rôle de l'environnement dans les macroprocessus économiques (Environment—Economy. Analysis of the role of the environment in economic macroprocesses), ed. G. Pillet. Berne, Report to the Swiss National Science Foundation # 1.378–0.86, pp. 384–454.

Baranzini, A., and G. Pillet. 1992. "A general neoclassical model of economic-environmental interactions securing survivability and sustainability." Forthcoming.

Barbier, E. B. 1990. "Alternative approaches to economic-environmental interactions." *Ecological Economics* 2(1): 7–26.

Barnett, H. J., and C. Morse. 1963. *Scarcity and growth: The economics of natural resource availability.* Baltimore: Johns Hopkins University Press.

Bartolommei, S. 1989. *Etica e ambiente* (Ethics and the environment). Milan: Guerini.

Berndt, E. R., and B. C. Field, eds. 1981. *Modeling and measuring natural resource substitution.* Cambridge, MA: Massachusetts Institute of Technology Press.

Bürgenmeier, B. 1993. Ethical Aspects of Environmental Protection, in J. P. Vernel, ed. *Environmental Contamination*: Studies in Environmental Science 55. Amsterdam: Elsevier, pp. 1–11.

———. 1992. *Socio-economics: An interdisciplinary approach—Ethics, institutions and markets.* Boston: Kluwer Academic.

Clark, C. W. 1990. *Mathematical bioeconomics,* 2d ed. New York: John Wiley & Sons.

Cleveland, J. C., R. Costanza, C. A. S. Hall, and R. Kaufmann. 1984. "Energy and the U.S. economy: A biophysical perspective." *Science* 210: 890–97.

Costanza, R. 1989. "What is ecological economics?" *Ecological Economics* 1(1): 1–7.

———. 1991a. "The ecological economics of sustainability." In *Environmentally sustainable economic development: Building on Brundtland,* ed. R. Goodland, H. Daly, S. El Serafy, and B. von Droste. Paris: UNESCO.

———, ed. 1991b. *Ecological economics: The science and management of sustainability.* New York: Columbia University Press.

Daly, H. E. 1974. "The economics of the steady state." *American Economic Review* 64(2): 15–21.

———. 1987a. "The economic growth debate: What some economists have learned but many have not." *Journal of Environmental Economics and Management* 14: 1–14.

———. 1987b. "Filters against folly in environmental economics: The impossible, the undesirable and the uneconomic." In *Environmental economics: The analysis of a major interface,* ed. G. Pillet. Geneva: R. Leimgruber.

———. 1990. "Towards some operational principles of sustainable development." *Ecological Economics* 2(1): 1–6.

———. 1991a. "Elements of environmental macroeconomics." In *Ecological economics: The science and management of sustainability,* ed. R. Costanza. New York: Columbia University Press.

———. 1991b. "From empty-world economics to full-world economics." In *Environmentally sustainable economic development: Building on Brundtland,* ed. R. Goodland, H. Daly, S. El Serafy, and B. von Droste. Paris: UNESCO.

Dasgupta, P. 1982. *The control of resources.* Oxford: Basil Blackwell.

Davis, G. R. 1990. "Energy for planet Earth." *Scientific American* 263(3): 21–27.

de Groot, R. S. 1986. *A functional ecosystem evaluation method as a tool in environmental planning and decision making.* Wageningen, Netherlands: Nature Conservation Department, Agricultural University.

Dryzek, J. 1989. *La razionalità ecologica* (Ecological rationalization). Ancona: Otium.

El Serafy, S. 1991a. "Sustainability, income measurement and growth." In *Environmentally sustainable economic development: Building on Brundtland,* ed. R. Goodland, H. Daly, S. El Serafy, and B. von Droste. Paris: UNESCO.

―――. 1991b. "The environment as capital." In *Ecological economics: The science and management of sustainability,* ed. R. Costanza. New York: Columbia University Press.

Faucheux, S. 1990a. *L'articulation des évaluations monétaire et énergétique en économie.* Doctoral thesis, Panthéon-Sorbonne, Paris.

―――. 1990b. "Sustainability in light of an eco-energetic analysis." Paper presented at the conference of the International Society for Ecological Economics, "The ecological economics of sustainability," May 21–23. Washington DC: World Bank.

Faucheux, S., and J. F. Noël. 1990. *Les menaces globales sur l'environnement* (Global threats to the environment). Paris: La Découverte.

Forte, F. 1991. *I diritti della natura.* Rome: Gallo.

Funtowitz, S. O., and J. R. Ravetz. 1990. "Global environmental issues and the emergence of second order science." Preprint paper, Commission of the European Communities, Institute for Systems Engineering and Informatics, Ispra. Varese: Italy.

Georgescu-Roegen, N. 1971. *The entropy law and the economic process.* Cambridge, MA: Harvard University Press.

―――. 1979. *Demain la décroissance.* Lausanne: Favre.

―――. 1982. *Energia e miti economici.* Torino: Boringhieri.

Goodland, R. 1991. "The case that the world has reached limits." In *Environmentally sustainable economic development: Building on Brundtland.* Paris: UNESCO.

Goodland, R., and G. Ledec. 1987. "Neoclassical economics and principles of sustainable development." *Ecological Modelling* 38: 19–46.

Goodland, R., H. Daly, S. El Serafy, and B. von Droste, eds. 1991. In *Environmentally sustainable economic development: Building on Brundtland. Paris: UNESCO.*

Greppin, H. 1978. Ecologie humaine et enveloppes de viabilité. *Médecine et Hygiène* 36(1306): 5–8.

―――. 1988. L'interface Homme-Nature. *Médecine et Hygiène* 46(1770): 15–19.

―――. 1988. "Environmental functions: An analytical framework for integrating environmental and economic assessment." Paper prepared for a workshop titled "Integrating environmental and economic assessment: Analytical and negotiating approaches." November 17–18, Vancouver (Canada).

Haavelmo, T., and S. Hansen. 1991. "On the strategy of trying to reduce economic inequality by expanding the scale of human activity." In *Environmentally sustainable economic development: Building on Brundtland,* ed. R. Goodland, H. Daly, S. El Serafy, and B. von Droste. Paris: UNESCO.

Hall, C. A. S. 1988. "An assessment of several of the historically most influential theoretical models used in ecology and of the data provided in their support." *Ecological Modeling* 43: 5–31.

Hall, C. A. S., C. J. Cleveland, and R. Kaufmann. 1986. *Energy and resource quality: The ecology of the economic process.* New York: John Wiley & Sons.

Hanemann, W. M. 1989. "Information and the concept of option value." *Journal of Environmental Economics and Management.* 16: 23–37.

Hartwick, J. M. 1977. "Intergenerational equity and the investing of rents from exhaustible resources." *American Economic Review* 66: 972–74.

Henry, C. 1974. "Investment decisions under uncertainty: The irreversibility effect." *American Economic Review* 64(6): 1006–12.

Hueting, R. 1990a. *New scarcity and economic growth.* Amsterdam: North-Holland.

―――. 1990b. "The Brundtland report: A matter of conflicting goals." *Ecological Economics* 2(2): 109–17.

―――. 1991. "Calculating a sustainable national income: A practical solution for a theoretical dilemma." Paper presented at the First International Conference of the European Association for Bioeconomic Studies, "Entropy and Bioeconomics." November 28–30, Rome.

Kamien, M. I., and N. L. Schwartz. 1982. "The role of common property resources in optimal planning models with exhaustible resources." In *Explorations in natural resource economics,* ed. V. K. Smith and J. V. Krutilla. Baltimore: Johns Hopkins University Press.

Klaassen, G. A. J., and J. B. Opschoor. 1991. "Economics sustainability or the sutainability of economics: Different paradigms." *Ecological Economics* 4(2): 93–115.

Krutilla, J. V., and A. C. Fisher. 1985. *The economics of natural environments,* rev. ed. Washington, DC: Resources for the Future.

Kuik, O., and H. Verbruggen, eds. 1991. *In search of indicators of sustainable development.* Dordrecht, Netherlands: Kluwer Academic.

Levin, J. 1991. Comment traiter l'environnement dans la comptabilité nationale? (How to treat the environment in national accounting?) *Economic Problems* 2225 (May 15): 30–32.

Meadows, D. H., D. L. Meadows, J. Randers, and W. Behrens III. 1972. *The limits to growth.* New York: Universe Books.

Ministère de l'Environnement (France). 1986. *Les comptes du patrimoine naturel.* Collection of the National Institut for Statistics and Economic Studies, No. 137–138.

Murota, T. 1984. "Heat economy of the water planet Earth: An entropic analysis and the water-soil matrix theory." *Hitotsubashi Journal of Economics* 25: 161–72.

———. 1985. "Heat economy of the water planet Earth: Part II. Revision and some new results." *Hitotsubashi Journal of Economics* 26: 181–85.

Nicolaisen, J., A. Dean, and P. Hoeller. 1991. "Economie et environnement: Problèmes et orientations possibles." *Economic Review of the Organization for Economic Cooperation and Development* 16: 9–49.

Nordhaus, W. D. 1973. "The allocation of energy resources." *Brookings Papers on Economic Activity* 3: 529–76.

Odum, H. T. 1971. *Environment, power and society.* New York: Wiley Interscience.

———. 1983. *Systems ecology: An introduction.* New York: Wiley Interscience.

Page, T. 1991. "Sustainability and the problem of valuation." In *Ecological economics: The science and management of sustainability,* ed. R. Costanza. New York: Columbia University Press.

Passet, R. 1979. *L'économique et le vivant.* Paris: Payot.

Pearce, D. W., and A. Markandya. 1989. *L'évaluation monétaire des avantages des politiques de l'environnement.* Paris: OECD..

Pearce, D. W., and R. K. Turner. 1990. *Economics of natural resources and the environment.* Hertfordshire, U.K.: Harvester Wheatsheaf.

Pearce, D. W., A. Markandya, and E. B. Barbier. 1989. *Blueprint for a green economy.* London: Earthscan.

Peskin, H. M. 1991. "Alternative environmental and resource accounting approaches." In *Ecological economics: The science and management of sustainability,* ed. R. Costanza. New York: Columbia University Press.

Pezzey, J. 1989. "Economic analysis of sustainable growth and sustainable development." Working Paper No. 15. Washington, DC: World Bank Environment Department.

Pillet, G. 1986. "From external effects to energy externality: New proposals in environmental economics." *Hitotsubashi Journal of Economics* 27(1): 77–97.

———. 1991. *Toward an inquiry into the carrying capacity on nations: What does over-population mean?* Report to the Coordinator for International Refugee Policy. Berne, Switzerland: Federal Department of Foreign Affairs. (Also available in French and German.)

Pillet, G., and S. Faucheux. 1991. "Alternative ecological-economic valuation procedures." Draft paper for the European Science Foundation Charmey Meeting, February 14–17.

Pillet, G., and H. T. Odum. 1984. "Energy externality and the economy of Switzerland." *Schweiz. Z. für Volkswirt. und Statistik* 120(3): 409–35.

―――. 1987. *E³: Energie, Ecologie, Economie* (E³: Energy, Ecology, Economics). Geneva: Georg ed.

Pillet, G., A. Baranzini, W. Hediger, S. Sandoz-Terraz, C. A. S. Hall, and H. Greppin. 1990. "Methods and models for valuing environments." Paper presented at the conference of the International Society for Ecological Economics, "The ecological economics of sustainability," May 21–23. Washington, DC: World Bank.

Plourde, C. G. 1972. "A model of waste accumulation and disposal." *Canadian Journal of Economics* 5(1): 117–25.

Ridker, R. G. 1992. "Population issues." *Resources* 106: 11–14.

Sachs, I. 1988. Notre avenir à tous—Notes critiques. *Futuribles* (March): 84–87.

Siebert, H. 1982. "Nature as a life support system. Renewable resources and environmental disruption." *Zeitschrift für Nationalökonomie* 42(2): 133–42.

Solow, R.M. 1974. "The economics of resources or the resources of economics." *American Economic Review* 64(2): 1–21.

Stiglitz, J. E. 1979. "A neoclassical analysis of the economics of natural resources." In *Scarcity and growth reconsidered,* ed. V. K. Smith. Baltimore: Johns Hopkins University Press.

ten Brink, B. 1991. "The AMOEBA approach as a useful tool for establishing sustainable development?" In *In search of indicators of sustainable development,* ed. O. Kuik and H. Verbruggen. Dordrecht, Netherlands: Kluwer Academic.

Tinbergen, J., and R. Hueting. 1991. "GNP and market prices." In *Environmentally sustainable economic development: Building on Brundtland,* ed. R. Goodland, H. Daly, S. El Serafy, and B. von Droste. Paris: UNESCO.

Toman, M. A. 1992. "The difficulty in defining sustainability." *Resources* 106: 3–6.

Tsuchida, A., and T. Murota. 1987. "Fundamentals in the entropy theory of the ecocycle and human economy." In *Environmental economics: The analysis of a major interface,* ed. G. Pillet and T. Murota. Geneva: Leimgruber.

Tsuchiya, H., and Y. Yano. 1991. "What we all own: Global resource balance." *Sunworld* 15(2): 22–28.

Uno, K. 1989. "Economic growth and environmental change in Japan: Net National Welfare and beyond." In *Economy and Ecology: Towards Sustainable Development,* ed. P. Archibugi and P. Nijkamp. Dordrecht, Netherlands: Kluwer Academic.

Victor, P.A. 1991. "Indicators of sustainable development: Some lessons fromcapital theory." *Ecological Economics* 4(3): 191–213.

World Bank. 1990. *World development report: Poverty.* Oxford: Oxford University Press.

World Commission on Environment and Development (WCED). 1987. *Our common future.* Oxford: Oxford University Press.

Appendix: A Model of Environment-Economy Interactions

The problem is the following (cf. Figure 7.2):

$$\max \int_0^\infty u(c, P, R) \, e^{-\delta t} \, dt \qquad (7.1)$$

The problem is that of a social planner who controls some variables with the objective of maximizing the present value of the utility of L-identical individuals. The arguments of the utility function are the following:

$c = (C/L)$ is the consumption per head; $U_c = \partial U/\partial c > 0$
P is the pollution stock; $U_P < 0$
R is the natural resource stock; $U_R > 0$
δ is the rate of discount.

The production function $Q(.)$ depends on:

K capital; $Q_K > 0$
L labour; $Q_L > 0$
Y (extracted) natural resource; $Q_Y > 0$
T technology; $Q_T > 0$
D waste and pollution abatement technology (e.g., air filters); $Q_D < 0$
P pollution stock, which reduces productivity; $Q_P < 0$.

The output can be consumed (C), used for environmental improvement goods (resource management, environmental cleanup) (X), and invested $(I,$ in: capital investment I_K; technological investment, I_T; waste and pollution abatement technologies, $I_D)$; thus the following identity holds:

$$Q = C + X + I \qquad (7.2)$$

The flow of wastes (W) creation is proportional to the produced quantity, depending on an emission-output ratio (α) that is a function of the investment operated in the abatement technology (I_D) (see Dasgupta 1982):

$$W = \alpha \, (I_D).Q \; ; \text{ we have: } \alpha' < 0; \; \alpha'' > 0 \qquad (7.3)$$

The environment possesses some capacity (A) to assimilate pollution which depends both on the pollution already existing (the pollution stock, because this capacity is assumed to be as a biological renewable resource) and on the effort the economy makes to clean up the environment. We assume that the flow of wastes does not interfere with this environmental function. Assuming separability, a very simple algebraic specification is:

$$A = A(P, X) = vP + sX \qquad (7.4)$$

where vP is the formula for radioactive decay (cf. Dasgupta 1982).

If the environment does not have this capacity (wastes are not biodegradable), then clearly $A = sX$.

The change of the stock of pollution over time $(\overset{o}{P} = \partial P/\partial t)$ is therefore:

$$\overset{o}{P} = W - A(P, X) = W - vP - sX \qquad (7.5)$$

Natural resources (R) in the environment possess some natural rate of growth $(G(R))$, but pollution (cf. Siebert 1982) and the rate of extraction diminish natural resource growth. If we assume separability, we have:

$$\overset{\circ}{R} = G(R) - \psi P - Y \tag{7.6}$$

Clearly, if there are nonrenewable resources, $G(R) = 0$; if there are nonbiological resources (e.g., an aquifer), $G(R) = F$ (F is a constant). Biological resources are generally assumed to follow a logistic growth pattern (cf., e.g. Plourde 1972; for criticisms, cf. Hall 1988).

Assuming no capital depreciation, capital growth is given by:

$$\overset{\circ}{K} = I_K = Q - C - I_T - I_D \tag{7.7}$$

Assuming no depreciation in the capital installed for waste and pollution abatement, we have that:

$$\overset{\circ}{D} = I_D = Q - C - I_T - I_K \tag{7.8}$$

Labor force variation is assumed to follow exponential population growth, thus:

$$\overset{\circ}{L} = \mu L \tag{7.9}$$

Survivability imposes three different constraints. First, because natural resources are essential to production and to human life, a minimum of environment has to be preserved:

$$R > R_s \tag{7.10}$$

Second, to guarantee human life, pollution cannot be higher than a definite level:

$$P < P_s \tag{7.11}$$

Third, consumption must be higher than subsistence level:

$$c > c_s \tag{7.12}$$

Sustainability implies then a further constraint, which may be defined as a non-decreasing level of utility over time, thus:

$$\overset{\circ}{u} \geq 0 \tag{7.13}$$

The program is thus to maximize equation (7.1), subject to the constraints shown in equations (7.5) to (7.13).

Part IV

The Policy Implication

8

JEAN-LOUIS LE MOIGNE AND MAGALI ORILLARD

Nearly Uncontrollable Pollution of an Agrarian System: A Socioeconomic Case Study

A rather typical, although still original, case study in the research field of the economic approach to environmental problems gives us a useful opportunity to appraise the resources of the socioeconomics paradigm. The case study also highlights some of the paradigm's epistemological foundations concerning the forms of the reasoning processes involved in such research.

**An Outline of the Case Study: Design and Management
of a Research Project Concerning an Agrarian System
Submitted to New Environmental Requirements**

First, let us introduce the summary of a recent article (Calvet, 1990, p. 89) describing this research project, often known as the AGREV (Agriculture, Environment, Vittel Project):

> How is it possible to maintain and to develop a highly efficient local farming activity able to control its effluent? That is the issue stated by an interdisciplinary group of scientists in Eastern France.
> The starting point of this research was the problem raised by increasing levels of nitrates in mineral water exploited by an industrial company. The scientists use a system analysis approach to investigate this issue in its ecological, economic and social dimensions. Articulations between the various scientific disciplines is achieved around three focal points of the program: modeling the way the farms operate; mapping the diverse spatial structures; concertation between the actors concerned by this issue within structures in which the scientists participate.

Some important developments of this ongoing research project, devoted mainly to the socioeconomic facets of the question, were published a few months late (AGREV Project, 1991). Its title characterizes the study's potential: Agricultural practices, underground water quality and research development project, "Modeling of nitrogen constraint in several farms." (This report, a first appraisal of the marginal cost of the mg/l of nitrates in bottled mineral water, considered the various types of soil and production systems) (Romp 1993).

Since the project's inception in 1988, the management team has clearly seen the systemic and multidimensional characteristics of the study and the need for some innovations in the methodologies to be used, particularly for its interdisciplinary formulation. But they know that they are starting from an initially rather well-structured problem: that the funding agency (the mineral water company) is expecting a practical solution to this problem.

Assuming that the increasing level of nitrates in the mineral water of a given area is coming mainly from the various agricultural and farming production systems active in this area (about twelve thousand acres, with about forty farms producing mainly cereals, breeding cattle, and milk), nearly all of which use nitrate fertilizers, the initial question was, "For the global socioeconomic system, what is the marginal cost of the mg/l of nitrates used by the farming system?" Once known, a fair compensation could be evaluated and offered by the local mineral water company to the farmers, who would be strongly incited to reduce or suppress the use of nitrate fertilizers and to adopt some specific techniques that minimize nitrates created by the breeding industry. This mineral water company is well-known for the "purity" of its products and is therefore ready to pay in order to maintain a very low level of nitrates. But to do so, it needs to know the right price.

As the research team had anticipated, the problem quickly appeared much more complex or ill structured. The sociocultural and political impacts of such a bargaining process with the farmers and the various professional organizations indirectly involved in the process (such as local offices of the department of agriculture, agricultural cooperatives, and agricultural unions) were very important—at least as important as the impacts of the behavior of the various French and European institutions concerned with establishing ad hoc norms for the rates of nitrates and other salts in mineral water.

At the same time, it appeared that the problem raised by this local mineral water company was a general problem, because many countries where the increasing rate of nitrates in water was also probably due to agricultural and farming systems were considering it a very important problem. In fact, the usual wait-and-see attitude no longer appears tolerable. No one within our familiar scientific disciplines—geologists, agronomists, sociologists, nutritionists, economists, or even ecologists—alone seems to be in a position to design a solution to the problem. And even multidisciplinary problem-solving teams of classical scientists have been unable to solve this rather practical problem in a purely scientific manner. The conflicts between experts proposing antagonistic solutions are rather permanent: taxes on fertilizers, administrative rules, lobbying to modify the norms, wait and see. Many uncertain solutions have been elaborated and firmly discussed by each expert.

The case was even considered desperate when geologists suggested a plausible hypothesis: that perhaps the nitrates are not coming through the ground from the agricultural production system, but from subphreatic levels, diffusing and growing up from deeper strata, thus polluting the mineral water level with nitrates and other salts at certain cyclical periods. Unfortunately, our present knowledge of this process is poor and very general. If this hypothesis were to be confirmed, the initial problem would completely disappear, but a much more difficult macroproblem would remain. For the time being, the geologists consider this hypothesis only plausible, and they don't expect to get any empirical confirmation for many years. Many other different assumptions, coming from chemists, or from zoologists or nutritionists, are still being formulated and all are plausible. But since none of them is certain, they have apparently complicated the problem by increasing its dimensions. But as will appear later, they constructively enrich at the same time the formulation of the problem offering, if not the final solution, at least some processes to consider.

At this stage, one may observe that the research team was wise to first increase the funding agency's confidence over the two years during which the team developed its diagnosis of the complexity of the problem. Starting from the initial, well-structured problem, they developed a rather original linear programming model that took into account various levels of admissible rates of nitrates and evaluated the global impact of some typical farming systems. This model, once adjusted to some empirical references, allows many sensitivity studies, and assuming that this initial, well-structured problem was the right problem, it leads to some well-argumented economic figures, mainly the marginal cost of the mg/l of added nitrates. This model quickly appears to be a rather powerful tool in the bargaining process between the various parties anticipating a deal. In practice, its usefulness appeared through the numerous discussions provoked by its results. The model induced a permanent reformulation of the problem, transforming it into not only an ill-structured problem, but also a richer one. Though there appears to be no simple and good solution, and it seems that various complex solutions could be developed and redeveloped endlessly, the approach nevertheless usefully leads in practice to what Simon (1981c) calls a sort of "designing without final goals."[1]

Some Espistemological Comments about This Case Study:
Are the Main Virtues of the Socioeconomics Paradigm Those
of "Procedural Rationality"?

This brief story of the ongoing research project AGREV easily confirms the need for an "alternative to the neo-classical paradigm for the study of economic behavior: socio-economics assumes that economics is embedded in society, policy and culture" (Calvet, 1990, p. 1). The behavior of the numerous and different parties involved in rather classical environmental problems cannot be definitively determined by the computation of a few marginal costs and values of externalities, as postulated by neoclassical economics, and if it ever were the case, one would clearly perceive the economic, social, and ecological perversity of such a rational behavior computed as the neoclassical paradigm postulates it (and, more generally, by the underlying positivist or neopositivist epistemologies). This argument appears particularly relevant in the case of the economic appraisal of environmental problems such as the nitrate pollution of mineral water.

Today, the need to complexify the formulation of problems perceived as ill structured (i.e., to enrich the modeling process of any complex problem) is explicitly taken into account by the project of the socioeconomic—or social self-organization (Lesourne 1991)—paradigm (and more generally by the underlying constructivist epistemologies). The designing processes of some intelligent representations of an ill-structured problem (such as a socioeconomic problem) are now perceived to be at the core of the "reasoning processes in human affairs" (Simon 1983). While the subjective expected utility (SEU) optimization model claims this possibility, the socioeconomic paradigm proposes no unique good model of a complex problem. Instead it proposes a modeling process, focusing on the problem's formulation more than on its solution. A complex problem such as an environmental socioeconomic problem is not a problem to solve, but a problem to deal with: The coding process is more important than the solving process (Orillard 1987, 1991). Through this collective dealing-with process—coding and recoding, reasoning and remodeling, naturally and artificially (Le Moigne 1989)—the perception of the problem is transformed, generating behavior modification in the process modelers: "Values other than pleasure and profit play a cardinal role in people's motivations".[3]

As Simon (1982) often underlined it, the change within problem solving from the neoclassical to the socioeconomic point of view has strong consequences for our cultural understanding of what good reasoning is: reasoning the understanding process and understanding the reasoning process. In human affairs, the basic question is not first what to decide, but how to decide what to do (Simon 1978a, 1982). The problem of mineral water pollution by nitrates, for instance, is less a problem solved through the computation of marginal utilities of certain externalities (as suggested by the neoclassical economic paradigm) than a problem formulation designed in a context that is both complex (many players, many criteria) and evolving. Assuming that the players' behaviors are related to their representations (and to the changes in these representations) of this context, we may rationally consider that some solutions (i.e., adequate behaviors[4]) will occur through these and other problem-setting and networking processes:

• transformation of an exclusive norm for the rate of nitrates in water into a complex norm for a mix of various salts

• development of new chemical processes for the manufacturing of fertilizers
• the selection of other types of cereals
• the definition of specific incentives through various forms of taxation and pricing.

From Substantive to Procedural Rationality in Socioeconomic Reasoning

Progress in the understanding of a multidimensional and evolving problem induces the progressive redesign of a number of alternative actions and a combination of actions (technical, legal, administrative, cultural, economic, fiscal, organizational, managerial, etc.). In order to model some plausible anticipation of expected (but not certain) models, these plans can be rationally and technologically designed, step by step. The reasoning process through which these design and expectation models are built can itself be understood and designed. We can develop a "science of design" (Simon 1981) that helps us to develop new forms of "Social Planning: Designing the evolving artifact" (Simon 1981b, 1981c). But to do so, we need to enrich our cultural understanding of rationality.

We need to understand that reasoning is not only deduction and that there are many other forms of logical reasoning than the syllogistical one. Our reasoning abilities are not devoted only to checking whether a final result is formally true or certain, but are, perhaps more so, devoted to imagining plausible and intermediate results through abduction, retroduction, transduction, and other forms of inductive reasoning that take into account the semantic and pragmatic characteristics of any system of symbols. Simon (1976, 1978b) has proposed to identify these two facets of rationality, that particularly pertain to socioeconomic reasoning:[5] "Rationality as a Process and as a Product of Thought" (Simon 1978b, p. 1) and "From Substantive to Procedural Rationality" (Simon 1976, p. 129). The key argument of the difference between the two forms of rationality raised by Simon is the definition of what we usually call logical, or scientific, rigor. Substantive rationality (formal deductive logic, syllogistical reasoning) is a priori neither more nor less rigorous than procedural rationality (dialectical reasoning, natural logic, argumentation). Both can be modeled through systems of physical symbols and through symbol-processing systems—both are programmable and teachable.

A rational behavior that is both substantive and procedural can be represented and simulated through the symbol-computing device known as the computer (or Turing machine) (Newell and Simon 1976). Correct and rigorous reasoning in socioeconomic affairs such as a complex environmental problem is much more a question of cognitive and behavioral processes than of economic evaluation. Simon (1976) distinguishes between the substantive and procedural aspects of rationality as follows:

SUBSTANTIVE RATIONALITY: Behavior is substantively rational when it is appropriate to the achievement of given goals within the limits imposed by given conditions and constraints. Notice that, by definition, the rationality of behavior depends upon the actor in only a single respect—his goals. Given these goals, the rational behavior is determined entirely by the characteristics of the environment in which it takes place.

PROCEDURAL RATIONALITY: Behavior is procedurally rational when it is the outcome of appropriate deliberation. Its procedural rationality depends on the process that generated it. When psychologists use the term "rational," it is usually procedural rationality they have in mind. William James, for example, in his *Principles of Psychology*, uses "rationality" as synonymous with "the peculiar thinking process called reasoning." Conversely, behavior tends to be described as "irrational" in psychology when it represents impulsive response to affective mechanisms without an adequate intervention of thought. (p. 131)

Among the numerous contributions of the socioeconomic paradigm to current scientific research in social planning, one of the most useful is perhaps the pragmatic development of many procedural forms of rationality—from Aristotelian rhetoric to contemporary systemic modeling (Le Moigne 1990). This epistemological discussion appears rather necessary in practice when a research team is involved in a complex research project such as the AGREV project. Although the neoclassical way of designing such a research program—computation of expected marginal utility—is undoubtedly based on substantive rationality (or formal deductive logic), the neoclassical model isn't necessarily better or more rigorous than other models. After all, is simplification—or "mutilation" (Morin 1991)—really a rigorous way of reasoning? The complexity of the modeling and reasoning system will lead to more rigorous and more lucid procedural reasoning because the aim is much more to understand and to invent plans than to verify the substantive logic of the plans (Wilensky 1983). In socioeconomic affairs too, the reward is in the journey.

Socioeconomic Planning: "Designing without Final Goals"

If the reward is in the journey, the goal of the journey is less important than the journey itself. Planners or problem solvers are much more concerned by the endless transformations of the problem than by the right substantive solution to the initial problem, not only because they cannot perfectly solve the initial problem (e.g., to determine the marginal cost of the mg/l of added nitrate in a phreatic layer for a given farming system), but mainly because the initial problem often appears to present a poor picture of the greater problem faced by the planner.

Even if this "poor well-structured problem" had been correctly solved (e.g., through a discussion of the linear-programming-model dual solution), this solution would not be easy to implement, for many rather understandable reasons: In the AGREV case study, some farmers had long since modified their production system in order to completely avoid any nitrated effluents. Understanding that the other farmers will get a substantial financial contribution from the mineral water company for reducing the level of nitrates in their effluent, they might conclude that they have a vested interest in returning to the previous nitrating production system, for they would get a specific antinitrate contribution evaluated in terms of the marginal cost per mg/l of added nitrates. Consequently, they would have an incentive to resume the use of nitrate fertilizers! When we study in some detail the practical consequences of straightforward, substantively computed economic solutions, we very often observe such counterintuitive effects.

The final goal of the planning problem, in the AGREV case study, is not to determine the marginal value of such an externality; it is probably to help the whole system—the farming system, interacting with the mineral water company, also interacting with various governmental and regional agencies—to deal with a rather complex problem, understanding that there is probably no final solution.

The problem is to endlessly transform and enrich the representation of the situation designed and redesigned by the people involved in this process. But can we "evaluate a design unless we have well-defined criteria against which to judge it, and how can the design process itself proceed without such criteria to guide it?" And is it not true that "to speak of planning without goals strikes one as a contradiction in terms?" March (1978; pp. 587–608) and Simon (1981c) propose to challenge such a theory of planning, which can be briefly summarized here in Simon's terms:

> A paradoxical, but perhaps realistic, view of design goals is that their function is to motivate activity which in turn will generate new goals. For example, when thirty years ago an extensive renewal program was begun in the city of Pittsburgh, a principal goal of the program was to rebuild the center of the city, the so-called Golden Triangle. Architects have had much to say, favorable and unfavorable, about the esthetic qualities of the plans that were carried out. But such evaluations are largely beside the point. The main consequence of the initial step of redevelopment was to demonstrate the possibility of creating an attractive and functional central city on this site, a demonstration that was followed by many subsequent construction activities that had changed the whole face of the city and the attitudes of its inhabitants.
>
> It is also beside the point to ask whether the later stages of the development were consistent with the initial one—whether the original designs were realized. Each step of implementation created a new situation; and the new situation provided a starting point for fresh design activity.
>
> Making complex designs that are implemented during a long period of time and continually modified in the course of implementation has much in common with painting in oil. In oil painting every new spot of pigment laid on the canvas creates some kind of pattern that provides a continuing source of new ideas to the painter. The painting process is a process of cyclical interaction between painter and canvas in which current goals lead to new applications of paint, while the gradually changing pattern suggests new goals. (p. 187)

We have quoted the entire page of Simon's chapter (1981c) on the concept of designing without final goals because it seems to characterize the new socioeconomic approach to the environment. We need to understand that the main aim of our socioeconomic studies is not to find the good solution to our environmental planning problems, but to collectively transform and enrich our representations of the problem that are inherent in the problem design process itself. We can't separate planning the problem from understanding the problem, and we always need to enrich our understanding of the solution (see Wilensky 1983). But to do so, don't we need some sort of understanding criteria? In practical terms, when we are engaged in a planning and understanding procedure, we must at each step answer a new question.

Among the possible new directions that appear to planners, they must not only identify all of them, but also choose one of them for the next step. To do so, if we don't agree to a randomly selected choice—and usually we won't—we need some sort of criteria. As far as socioeconomic environmental problems are concerned, it seems that the new criterion of sustainability of the consequences of each action is more and more being considered. But sustainability is still rather poorly defined, and we shall certainly have to work on it and with it during the coming years in order to improve its implementability.

In this perspective we should like to briefly evoke a sort of metacriteria recently argumented by Simon (1981) and, in a different context, by Von Foerster (1991) and previously by Gabor (1963): the criteria defined by the diversity of the next initial conditions.[6] "What we call *final* goals are in fact criteria for choosing the initial conditions that we will leave to our successors . . . what are good initial conditions for them?" (Simon 1981, p. 187). The answers to his question are perhaps also the first conclusions of our discussion of the epistemological lessons of our experience in modeling a socioeconomic environmental problem. Thus, the first feature of the criteria of sustainability will be the minimization of irreversibility: "one desideratum would be a world offering as many alternatives as possible to future decision makers, avoiding irreversible commitments that they cannot undo" (p. 187). The second feature is more the formulation of a research program for socioeconomics scientists than a teachable criterion: "A second desideratum is to leave the next generation of decision-makers with a better body of knowledge and a greater capacity for experience. The aim here is to enable them not just to evaluate alternatives better, but especially to experience the world in more and richer ways" (p. 187). Isn't the modeling of socioeconomic environmental problems the modeling of our experience of the world in "more and richer ways"? It is a rather stimulating research program on the methodological developments of complexity modeling (Le Moigne 1990).

Notes

1. "Designing without Final Goals" is a section in "Social Planning: Designing the Evolving Artifact," a chapter added in 1981 by Simon to the revised edition of *The Sciences of the Artificial* (Simon, 1981c).

2. Simon often said, in the 1960s and 1970s, that the status of the socioeconomic paradigm would be estabished by the end of the 1980s. See, for instance, the *New Palgrave Dictionary of Economics* (London: Macmillan, 1987) article "Behavioral Economics," pp. 221–25, and article "Bounded Rationality," p. 225.

3. Platform of the society for the Advancement of Socio-Economics, p.1.

4. Bourgine and Le Moigne in "Are Right Decisions Optimal or Adequate?" (in H. E. Bradley, ed. *Operation Research 90*, Pergamon Press, 1991, pp. 215–25) propose a discussion of the concept of Simonian "satisfying behavior."

5. See also Simon 1982, Models of Bounded Rationality, volume 2, MIT Press, Cambridge, Mass, p. 444–58 (the article was written and presented in 1973, in parallel with another article titled "Does scientific discovery have a logic?" This paper opened a still important controversy with K. Pepper about "the logic of scientific discovery."

6. Von Foerster (1991) writes, "Try to always act in order to increase the number of possible choices" (p. 51).

References

Brosinar, J., Benoit M., Fallouse, J. C., Gaury, F., Pierre, Ph., Communication presented at the 24th Seminar of the European Association of Agricultural economists, Viterbo, January.

Calvet, R., ed. 1990. English summary of a paper published in "Colloque Nitrate, Agriculture, Eau" (conference on nitrate, agriculture, water, in French. ed. INRA, written by J. P. Deffoutaine et groupe Agrev, (Researchers from various units of INRA: Institut National de Recherche Agronomique, Department "Systems Agraire et Developpements").

Gabor, D. 1963. *Inventing the future.* Hammondsworth, Middlesex: Pelican Books. Le Moigne, J. L. 1989. "Natural and artificial computing and reasoning in economic affairs." *Theory and Decision* 27 [Special issue: "Economic reasoning and artificial intelligence," ed. P. Bourgine] (July: 107–16.

———. 1990. *La Modélisation des systèmes complexes* (The modeling of complex systems). Paris: Dunod.

———. 1978a. "On how to decide what to do." *Bell Journal of Economics* 9(2): 494–507.

———. 1978b. "Rationality as a process and as a product of thought." *American Economic Review* 68(2): 1–16.

———. 1981a. *The sciences of the artificial,* rev. ed. Cambridge, MA: MIT Press.

———. 1981b. "The science of design." Chap. 5 in *The sciences of the artificial,* rev. ed.

———. 1981c. "Social planning: Designing the evolving artifact." Chap. 6 in *The sciences of the artificial,* rev. ed.

———. 1982. "Models of bounded rationality." Cambridge, MA: MIT Press.

———. 1983. *Reasoning in human affairs.* Stanford, CA: Stanford University Press.

Lesourne, J. 1991. *Economie de l'ordre et du désordre* (The economics of order and disorder). Paris: Economica.

March, J.G. 1978. "Bounded rationality, ambiguity, and the engineering of choice." *Bell Journal of Economics* 9: 587–608.

———. 1988. *Decisions and organization.* Oxford: *Basil Blackwell.*

Morin, E. 1991. *La Méthode* (The method). Paris: ed. du Seuil.

Newell, A., and H. A. Simon. 1976. "Computer science as empirical symbol and search." *Communication of the ACM* 19(3): 113–26.

Orillard, M. 1987. *Décisions de groupe: Coalitions et auto-organisation—Application aux processus de concertation et de négociation* (Group decisions: Coalitions and self-organization: Application to negotiation processes). Thesis, Université Aix-Marseille III.

———. 1991. "Representation of decision-making processes in a complex environment." *Revue Analyse de Système* 17: pp. 5–11.

Simon, H. A. 1976. "From substantive to procedural rationality." In *Methods and appraisal in economics,* ed. S. J. Latsis. Cambridge: Cambridge University Press.

Von Foerster, H. 1991. Ethique et Cybernétique du second ordre (Ethics and second order cybernetics). In *Systèmes, Ethiques, Perspectives en thérapie familiale* (Systems, ethics, perspectives in family therapy), ed. Y. Rey and B. Prieur. (Paris: Ed du Seuil.)

Wilensky, R. 1983. *Planning and understanding: A computational approach to human reasoning.* New York: Addison-Wesley.

9

BEAT BÜRGENMEIER

Environmental Policy: Beyond the Economic Dimension

Environmental policy is based on two kinds of measures that are often portrayed as conflicting. The first involves technical regulation, while the second consists of incentives founded on economic reasoning. However, for a number of reasons it is wrong to think of these two kinds of measures as being opposed. First of all, this suggests that they are substitutes for one another; yet in concrete applications such as the Emissions Trading Program proposed by the U.S. Environmental Protection Agency (Tietenberg 1989), they in fact complement one another. Second, this view ignores the fact that, whichever instruments are used, environmental policy ultimately depends on institutions, the underlying value system, and the prevailing balance of power, and that implementing such policies involves high consensus costs. And, finally, the claim that economic theory is conceptually capable of grasping the problem of environmental pollution smacks of economic imperialism (Swedberg 1990).

Thus, when it comes to environmental policy, we basically have a choice between two strategies. The first strategy views environmental protection as just one more aspect of economic policy. The essence of this approach is that economic thinking is derived from a science of scarcity whose purpose is optimal resource allocation (Danthine 1990). The second strategy, which sees environmental pollution as a consequence of our way of thinking, seeks to broaden the economic analysis by incorporating knowledge from other disciplines (Bürgenmeier 1992).

This second approach runs counter to mainstream economic theory, in which market forces are held to be the best means of dealing with the problems that now face us. This revival of classical economic thinking, whose basic premise is that the state and the market are diametrically opposed, insists that state intervention to protect the environment should involve instruments that do not conflict with market forces. In the resulting debate on the effectiveness of particular policies, a distinct bias in favor of incentives has emerged.

This call for a more market-based approach may be a logical response to the disappointing results of early attempts to control pollution through technical regulation. In the first part of this chapter, then, we shall discuss the advantages and disadvantages of the various environmental policy instruments. The second part will briefly review the main objections to a purely economic approach and will show how environmental policy must reconcile extremely varied states of knowledge whose complexity is only now starting to become apparent. The third part makes a case for a socioeconomic approach and suggests a number of ways in which the economic analysis can be broadened. Finally, some future trends in environmental policy are briefly sketched. Any comprehensive approach to the problem is hampered by the fact that our knowledge is currently split into highly specialized branches. We must therefore ensure that the various disciplines that serve as a basis for pollution control policies do not remain compartmentalized, and we must acknowledge the need to approach the environment from various different angles, thus allowing a multidimensional interpretation of human behavior. Such a strategy is clearly incompatible with the restrictive concept of economic rationality on which the economic model is based.

The Advantages and Disadvantages of the Various Instruments of Economic Policy Concerning the Environment

Economic theory (Baumol and Oates 1979) approaches the problem of environmental protection in terms of optimization, with social equilibrium being achieved at the point where the marginal disadvantages and the marginal net benefits of a given activity are equal. The environment is considered a public good and external to market forces. Accordingly, the environment is of concern to the economy only if its components generate a cost of which individuals are aware. Therefore, the primary goal of any environmental policy is to translate these explicit costs into monetary costs that can ultimately be expressed in accounting terms. However, there is no a priori legitimacy for such a policy. In order to justify state intervention in the market, market failure must be demonstrated to have occurred. The demonstration derives from the nature of a public good. Collective costs are dissociated from individual benefits. Since it is in no one's interest to bear the external costs, the state must do so. This familiar line of reasoning has become known as the prisoner's dilemma (Luce and Raiffa 1967). All that is then required is that the techniques used to internalize the external costs should abide by the polluter-pays principle. To avoid a conflict with market forces, state intervention must essentially be aimed at prices. However, the polluter-pays principle is by no means so easy to apply. First of all, the polluter cannot always be identified, and second, the pollution may come from several different sources, in which case it may not be possible to allocate the external costs properly, since the interactions between the various sources are not always known.

Table 9.1

Environmental Policy Instruments: Advantages and Disadvantages

	Advantages	Disadvantages
	1	*2*
Direct controls	Repair or containment	Relative prices
Regulations	of damage	unchanged
Technological controls	Applicability	Bureaucracy
Bans, fines	Practical experience	Arbitrariness
	Political logic	
	3	*4*
Incentives	Prevention	Problem of equity
Taxes, subsidies	Freedom of choice	Difficult empirical
	Condensed information	evaluation
Negotiable emission	through price changes	Impracticable in
certificates	Theoretical demonstration	the event of a
	Economic logic	disaster
Deposits		
Rights of ownership		

Source: Bürgenmeier (1992b, p. 452).

This may be the reason that, as countries grow more aware of environmental problems, they have usually attempted to tackle them by direct controls, which are claimed to be incompatible with market forces. Accordingly, in the debate on national environmental policy, direct controls and incentives are seen as being diametrically opposed.

Table 9.1 compares the chief advantages and disadvantages of the main policy instruments, which are extensively described in the literature (Frey 1972). Early environmental policy consisted of measures that came under the heading of direct controls (section of Table 9.1). As these direct controls began to take effect, their practical disadvantages also became apparent (section 2). Currently, we seem to be moving toward section 3, and as we subsequently discover the drawbacks of incentives, we will shift into section 4.

The table thus makes it clear that environmental policy must make use of both types of instrument. To favor one type at the expense of the other—which is what appears to be happening in the current public debate—is to miss the point. In most cases the source of pollution has remained, and state influence over the economy has tended to increase. Although the specific nature of intervention depends on the instruments used, inevitably our economic analysis is less in terms of exchange and more in terms of organization, at which point excluding the state ceases to be an option. Thus, the idea that the state and market forces are diametrically opposed is increasingly an obstacle to workable policies. Clearly, we need to accept that the market is merely one of a number of collective decision-making mechanisms, other examples being democracy and the civil service. The boundaries between these various mechanisms recall the distinction society makes between the private and public spheres. In years to come, this will undoubtedly be the central issue in the environmental policy debate.

Indeed, if we compare the various mechanisms, we can detect a tendency to favor collective decisions that emerge from private or public bureaucracies rather than from market forces or the democratic process. This shift toward a more bureaucratic type of collective decision making has been accompanied by a change in mentality: Not only are there new groups of voters, but society's image of the economy has changed. The market has yielded in importance to mechanisms that are more political in nature. It is therefore my view that the efficient-market model, as currently revived, is unacceptable as the sole frame of reference for environmental policy.

The Main Objections to Market-Oriented Environmental Policies

Table 9.2 lists the main objections to environmental policies whose sole frame of reference is the market-economy model. These objections are classified under a number of headings corresponding to the various scientific disciplines that bear on the issue of environmental pollution. The compartmentalization of these various disciplines makes it difficult to pull them together into a workable environmental policy. Interestingly enough, some of the objections actually derive from economic theory. They concern classic market failures such as problems of redistribution of income and wealth, imperfect competition, and the existence of a nonmarket sector of the economy that includes public goods (section A of Table 9.2). The idea of a competitive market as the best possible solution is purely theoretical; in practice, what we are faced with are second-best situations. Accordingly, environmental policy shifts the economy from one second-best situation to another, without this change being objectively assessable in terms of welfare. Such assessment can be based only on value judgments. Thus, environmental policy is essentially normative and is justified by a change in the value system on which it is based (Blackorby 1990).

Economic logic is also at odds with the logic of natural science, which emphasizes the limits to our knowledge (section B of Table 9.2). Science is unable to provide all the elements needed for a monetary evaluation of external effects on the biosphere. This may be one reason scientists tend to prefer a strategy that minimizes the source of pollution to one that seeks an optimum level of the kind proposed by economic theory.

However, such objections are insignificant in comparison with those raised by behavioral science, which point to the overrestrictive nature of the hypotheses behind the economic approach (section C of Table 9.2). According to this view, not only does a full grasp of the main interactions between the economy and the

Table 9.2

Objections to the Competitive-Market Model in Environmental Policy

A. Market Failures
    1. Redistribution
    2. Market structure (price elasticity of supply and demand) and degree of competition (product differentiation, limited price flexibility, etc.)
    3. The state and the environment as variables exogenous to the market (special nature of the environment as a public good that is hard to assess in monetary terms)

B. Environmental Science
    4. Currently incomplete knowledge of interactions between the economy and the biosphere
    5. Minimization rather than optimization

C. Behavioral Science
    6. Time frame limited to variables involved in economic calculus (durability of goods, rental and depreciation costs, etc.)
    7. Challenge to the behavioral hypothesis of economic rationality as a sole frame of reference
    8. Interdependence of supply and demand

D. Political Science
    9. The market as merely one of a number of collective decision-making mechanisms

environment require that the time frame be extended beyond purely economic parameters, but the very hypothesis of economic rationality as the sole frame of reference for human behavior is challenged; similar doubts arise when we examine the supposed independence of supply and demand. Clearly, then, economic problems are no longer so much matters of exchange as of organization, and environmental policy must take this into account by providing means of effectively supervising the communication and information networks that govern society. In that case, the market and the techniques it uses to internalize external effects can be understood only in relation to other collective decision-making mechanisms, whether democratic or bureaucratic (section D of Table 9.2).

These objections, which at present remain compartmentalized, are summarized in Table 9.2. The list is not exhaustive, but it does show that a purely economic approach is incapable of conceptualizing environmental problems. However, the economic dimension can be broadened only if these problems are approached in their entirety and not, as hitherto, with reference to specific details. Such a reversal of attitude, which scientists (for once in agreement with politicians) have themselves been crying out for, requires a revolution in the way knowledge is transmitted—a revolution that our institutions, prisoners as they are of the fragmented, specialized approach, are totally unprepared for. My thesis is thus quite simply this: Only a comprehensive socioeconomic approach will enable us to successfully analyze the problem of environmental pollution. If economics does not open the door to other disciplines, it will become irrelevant (cf. Olson 1991).

Broadening the Economic Dimension

In attempting to conceptualize the problem of environmental protection, economic theory presents the choice of an optimum pollution level as being the sum of individual choices between goods and between various periods of consumption. In order to take market failures into account, it proposes normative compensation mechanisms. Assuming that state intervention to adapt the institutional framework does not conflict with market forces, all that is then necessary is to encourage substitution between goods by altering their relative prices and to extend the time frame within which economic decisions are taken. In theory, this enables the utility of keeping the environment intact for future generations to be compared with the costs of pollution, taking permanent and cumulative effects into account. In practice, all it does is increase the uncertainty surrounding economic decisions. The problem of evaluating major risks will inevitably lead economics into a dead end unless it avails itself of knowledge acquired in other disciplines (Viscusi 1990). In the case of nuclear energy, for example, it is often claimed that those who oppose it are swayed by irrational feelings and that those in favor of it are motivated by economic rationality. Not only does this fail to take explicit account of the time factor, but it assumes that irrationality is unworthy of serious study as a causal factor. To quote Olievenstein (1988):

> Things which exist but cannot be fitted into a logical interpretation are either censored or, at best, contemptuously relegated to the nether world of the social sciences. . . . (p. 192)

We should therefore avoid clinging to a single kind of logic and should accept that there may sometimes be turning points in the development of society, at which our actions need to be reexamined. Environmental policies cannot simply be extrapolated from past experience. As Hirschman (1989) puts it:

> One of the major ideas in the social sciences is that, because of the limits to forecasting, human actions tend to have unexpected and far-reaching consequences. (p. 82)

Tomorrow's national environmental policies will be no exception.

Broadening Our View: Environmental Science

This approach involves radically reassessing the economic approach (Georgescu-Roegen 1979). Using an input-output analysis that is broadened to include flows between the economy and the biosphere, we can define a model of general equilibrium in real terms. This equilibrium derives from the first law of thermodynamics, according to which total energy within an isolated system remains constant. However, the quality of that energy when used within the economy deteriorates (the entropy of the system increases). Thus, economic laws are not independent of time. Far from being perpetuated ad infinitum by successive substitutions between factors of production, productive activity will eventually exhaust the available energy and natural resources. Environmental policies that seek only to internalize external costs in monetary terms fail to take this time dimension into account (Georgescu-Roegen, 1988).

The relevance of this line of reasoning tends not to be acknowledged by economists, who continue to believe in the unlimited substitution of capital and labor for nonrenewable resources. However, there are now those who realize that "in the substitution process, reference must be made to both economics and the law of entropy" (Solow 1974, p. 11). In other words, economics is not an exact science with laws that are immutable over time, but a social science that must come to terms with the unique historical development of our society. Writing in 1968, Habermas made the critical comment that science can be seen as an ideology underlying an implicit pact between technology and economics. Sooner or later, any workable environmental policy must reject this ideology and instead espouse ethical values that can be generated only by a democratic mechanism, not a market one (Seifert 1990).

Broadening Our View: Socioeconomics

In this section we will look at four different aspects of the socioeconomic approach, namely, psychology, law, sociology, and political science. All four seek to broaden the economic approach to environmental pollution with the help of motivation theories.

The social sciences—and in particular, behavioral studies—are concerned with the origins of preferences, which economic models take as given. The social sciences emphasize the role of unconscious motivation and attempt to identify the stages of cognitive development, which vary from individual to individual and are largely dependent on social context. This immediately challenges the concept of rational economic behavior that lies behind all environmental policies based on economic models.

Economic psychology. The branch of psychology that deals with economic issues has investigated the following three areas (Lea, Tarpy, and Webley 1987): (a) purchasing behavior, which is supposed to orient production toward (among other things) environmentally safer goods; (b) behavior in response to risks; and (c) intertemporal choices by individuals, which determine immediate and future consumption in a time frame extended by environmental concerns.

As regards purchasing behavior, economic theory sees market demand in terms of an order of individual preference, defined by the transitivity rule. However, psychological studies show that choices between a number of goods are nearly always stochastic. It is thus by no means certain that consumer behavior will respond as intended to incentives that alter the relative prices of goods whose production and consumption are either environmentally safe or hazardous. Moreover, average purchasing behavior is very stable, reflecting the influence of habit. Environmental policies must therefore overcome inertia, upsetting habits by recasting the institutions within which economic transactions currently take place.

As for individual choices made when faced with risk and uncertainty, psychological studies have failed to find an empirical indicator that would validate the hypothesis of rational behavior. The difficulty is that subjective probability is not identical to objective probability (as represented, for example, by actuarial statistics). The perception of risk and uncertainty varies so greatly from individual to individual that no obvious conclusions can be drawn from the studies. Finally, intertemporal choice—such an important guide to immediate or, through savings, future consumption—involves interactions between a number of factors that are difficult to evaluate. Psychological tests show that individuals have a marked preference for immediate consumption, which is a serious obstacle to any workable environmental policy.

There is thus no empirical basis for the hypothesis of economic rationality. Any policy implicitly based on this hypothesis would therefore benefit from closer collaboration between psychologists and economists, who both need to acknowledge that their hypotheses are essentially normative. Yet what are the alternatives to economic rationality?

Is human behavior simply random? That would imply that human behavior is too complex for us to understand. Is economic behavior determined by habit? Habit may have a perfectly rational basis in a social consensus of which the individual is not necessarily aware. Does irrationality exist, but depend on the importance attached to the economic decision? The objection here is that the degree of irrationality then depends on each individual's intelligence or education, which would merely underscore the importance of information and of controlling the communications media, which are required by environmental policies based on an economic approach that borrows from other disciplines. The central issue of environmental policy is an interdisciplinary one. To what extent does the individual exert influence on the economy, and to what extent does the economy shape the individual? This raises the issue of individual motivation, which in a purely economic approach is to some extent bypassed. Ultimately, if economic theory is to serve as a conceptual basis for state intervention, it must explain social reality and not merely remain consistent with its own logic.

It must then be acknowledged that society incorporates a number of different philosophical currents. To reduce all of these to utilitarianism and make this the sole basis for environmental protection smacks of ideology rather than pertinent analysis. There are at least two other relevant currents of thought. The first is based on a theory of justice (Rawls 1972) and can be traced back to the ideas of Rousseau and Kant, while the second, which is more recent, is based on the concept of bounded rationality (Simon 1947), which has inspired various organization theories, particularly in the field of sociology.

Law. The theory of justice is based on the notion of a social contract, which has profoundly influenced the development of Western society. According to Rawls (1972), the purpose of justice essentially concerns the basic structure of society, the distribution of fundamental rights and duties among individuals, and the benefits individuals expect from social cooperation. Action to protect the environment will undoubtedly upset the established pattern of distribution. This is therefore a suitable point at which to recall the three principles that govern the fair distribution of rights and duties.

The first is the principle of equal freedom, which is reflected in the democratic collective decision-making mechanism. In the economic sphere, this principle has led in turn to the principle of freedom of trade and industry and the system of private ownership of the factors of production. Seen in this light, a workable environmental policy is conceivable only if it distributes the new environmental rights and duties among all individuals while at the same time respecting rights of ownership, which then become essential in motivating individuals to protect the environment.

The second principle is the right to be different. Whereas the utilitarian approach prescribes that the same motivation lies behind all human behavior, the theory of justice stresses respect for different behavior. In that case, environmental policy must be nondiscriminatory and must take into account individuals' need to express their differences despite the new environmental constraints imposed on them.

Finally, the third principle is that of equal opportunity for all—that is, unrestricted access to education and information—which then plays a key role in individual awareness and motivation. Seen in this light, it is wrong for environmental policies to be devised by a few and then technocratically imposed on the whole of society; instead, such policies are everyone's concern.

But what if we compare these utopian-sounding principles with recent trends? What we then find is a growing tendency for businesses to concentrate (Sawyer 1987), which makes for imperfect competition, increasingly difficult access to private ownership (particularly of land), discriminatory practices, and attempts to manipulate information. Environmental policy cannot help being influenced by these trends, but if it actually encourages them, it will move away from the ideal of the social contract and will generate increasing consensus costs. This is one of the reasons we need to look at society in terms of organization rather than competition.

Sociology. Organization theories have arisen both in industrial economics (Jacquemin 1987), in which game theory is combined with traditional models of imperfect competition, and in sociology, in which emphasis is laid on the transaction costs generated by institutional change. These theories rely on the behavioral hypothesis of bounded rationality, which is more promising than the hypothesis of economic rationality as a basis for environmental policy. Bounded rationality acknowledges that, although human beings would like to be rational, they are only imperfectly so. In that case, the market is no longer the only way of expressing group strategy. Individuals who participate in a market but whose capabilities are limited will try to become more effectively organized. The problem of transactions is no longer purely a matter of market forces, but extends to the complex organizational structures that make up society (Bernoux 1985). The ways in which decisions are reached within complex organizations would therefore be a promising topic for research in the field of environmental policy. In stressing that economic decisions regarding the environment involve aspects of decision making and organizational power characterized by information flows, such an approach again broadens our economic analysis in the direction of political science.

Political science. The logic behind political collective decision-making mechanisms and market mechanisms is often quite different, although the theory of public choice attempts to prove that the neoclassical economic model applies to politics as well as economics (Brown and Jackson 1986). In the case of environmental protection, such mechanisms, whose purpose is to mark the boundaries between the private and public spheres, are accompanied by consensus and social costs. However, there is little point in trying to determine the relative importance of the various collective decision-making mechanisms. The point is not whether the market is preferable to other collective decision-making mechanisms, but how to devise policies that will be widely accepted. However, we can now observe a growing tendency toward normative assessment of economic problems, which are increasingly being examined from an ethical point of view (Ulrich 1990). This development reflects both the emergence of new technologies and the changes in motivation that can be observed in the labor market. A growing number of firms are therefore abandoning purely hierarchical systems of organization in an attempt to increase motivation by introducing new forms of employee collaboration, participation, and responsibility. Because such social shifts are probably due to technological change, there can be no doubt that, in political terms, the traditional worker is dying out and being replaced by a still undefined group of voters who will probably turn out to be more varied and individualistic. As far as environmental policy is concerned, the consequences of these changes are twofold: Traditional collective decision-making mechanisms are weakening, and the costs of achieving a consensus are increasing. At the same time, private and public bureaucracies are expanding, and the influence of pressure groups is growing (Olson 1968).

In response to such changes, governments tend to side with established pressure groups. However, the state is organized in a highly complex manner and accommodates a number of different decision-making processes. In simplified terms, the political and bureaucratic mechanisms are superimposed. Special interest groups then seek to influence both mechanisms, so that the state is also dependent on the private economic sector. Thus, instead of the state controlling the economy, the economy holds the state to ransom. Even though the state has a hand in virtually all economic decisions, it is relatively powerless and is trapped in a web of alliances and conflicts between the various pressure groups. In the field of environmental policy, the various interests are affected differently. Moreover, environmental policy does not have a single goal, but several, which diverge.

Politics, increasingly filtered through the media, likewise lends itself to expressing the value system of the majority of people in the country concerned. There are therefore attempts at manipulation in order to give particular pressure groups the external support they seek. Their specific interests must appear to coincide with the interests of most, if not all, citizens. Finally, the policy adopted must fit in with the collective memory as it has evolved through history. It must also be in keeping with both the domestic and the international institutional framework.

For all of these reasons, politics sheds a quite different light on the many recommendations that emerge from purely economic models. Not surprisingly, the policies adopted are not those recommended by economists (Frey 1991). In the case of the environment, this difference in interpretation has already been illustrated by the debate concerning incentives versus direct intervention in the first part of this chapter. Economic theory geared to concrete action cannot avoid analyzing the feasibility of its policy recommendations. It is therefore merely stating the obvious to suggest that economists and politicians should take a closer look at the links between their respective fields of endeavor.

In practice such links do exist and have resulted in tried and tested alliances between well-established special interest groups. However, in matters of environmental policy, these alliances must acknowledge the presence of disconcerting new pressure groups. The established alliances have traditionally acted as a channel for public opinion—which governments have not always perceived as clearly as they might—and have thereby helped the latter in determining their policy. Not only have governments relied on such alliances to popularize their policies, but the established pressure groups have relied on governments to accommodate them when deciding what policies to adopt. With the emergence of new groups of voters and pressure groups, governments have been deprived of this traditional policy guide and are therefore tempted to surround their decisions with extra precautions. The result is the proliferation of expert reports and environmental impact statements.

It is important to realize that politics consists of a network of relationships confronted with transaction costs that increase with the degree of consensus. In an institutional framework governed by democratic rules, the degree of consensus required is that of a majority of voters. The more that interests diverge, the greater the cost of achieving this degree of consensus. This approach is necessarily normative, since it attaches far more importance to the distributive aspects of a given policy than economic theory is willing to admit. It also remains subject to society's symbolic view of power. This last factor may serve to demonstrate the full extent of the lip service paid to the market economy system when compared with the way in which our economies are actually run.

The divergence between the economic and political interpretations of decision-making mechanisms can indeed be seen in the impact studies produced to disguise the increase in consensus costs. Let us take a look at some of the special interest groups that clash on matters of environmental policy.

Consumers are divided among themselves. Some call for a restrictive energy policy while continuing to consume energy and matter and to produce waste, and some are simply indifferent. Either they fail to understand the link between energy production and consumption, or they reject the whole idea of translating external costs into monetary terms. Both types of behavior may indicate market failure, in the sense that consumer sovereignty does not prevail, owing to a lack of information and transparency in the collective decision-making process. Such ignorance may result in hostility toward environmental measures as soon as they entail explicit costs.

Producers can be subdivided into three basic categories:

1. Producers who cause pollution remain opposed to environment policies as long as the costs of their existing plant are still being written off, and they often attempt to gain time by disseminating information that plays down the external effects.

2. Producers of services whose activities do not directly cause pollution are not opposed to environment policies, but insist on energy sources, communications, and infrastructure remaining available at a cost that does not affect their international competitive position.

3. Producers of environmental commodities (filters, treatment plants, etc.) have an obvious interest in the adoption of measures that will increase demand for such goods. They therefore tend to function as a new economic pressure group.

Each category calls in experts, politicians, and government experts to help assert its own particular viewpoint.

Governments are in no hurry to act as long as no clear majority emerges from the various alliances. Instead, they prefer to wait passively until a particular line of action crystallizes out of the debate. Naturally, the civil service produces documents that supposedly assist the decision-making process. However, in the absence of any clear political will, the civil service may itself end up concentrating its efforts on forming alliances. Furthermore, it may well be tempted to favor measures that it can easily supervise and that are likely to increase its influence.

In other words, the civil service will itself function as a pressure group unless the government takes specific steps to prevent it from doing so.

Conclusion: Future Trends in Environmental Policy

This discussion of the behavior of various special interest groups leads to the following three conclusions.

First, the longer decisions are delayed, the more the authorities will have to resort to blanket prohibition, which is hardly conducive to either creativity or innovation. Instead of changing relative prices in order to trigger a substitution process, state authorities will attempt organization of investment in research and development. Moreover, selective prohibition is unlikely to work, since it encourages alliances among the various minority groups, which, each for different reasons, consider such direct intervention as specifically unfair to them. What is needed, then, is a policy based on the transparency of interests of the groups concerned.

Second, economic analysis fails to take into account specific political factors. In the case of the environment, economic analysis favors the only two instruments that can really work, namely, taxes and subsidies. Both of these are classic political instruments that reflect the sovereignty of the state. Recommendations based on purely economic models thus cannot help impinging on political issues. The democratic rules that govern collective decision making must therefore prevail over economic rules.

Third and finally, our description of a number of special interest groups indicates the problems involved in organizing a network of relationships that explain the functioning of society more effectively than the market can. Accordingly, the notion of the bounded rationality of human behavior needs to replace the notion of strict rationality assumed by economic theory. While economic agents and politicians may believe they are acting rationally, in actual fact they are pursuing less laudable aims, and their behavior is influenced by the institutional dimension. What we are therefore dealing with is the sociological concept of organization theory rather than the economic concept of trade theory. Accordingly, the degree to which society effectively supervises its communications network will be crucial in shaping its environmental policy.

This chapter has thus attempted to show how important it is to environmental policy that economics should open the door to other disciplines. This approach reinstates economics as a social science and rejects a natural science interpretation. Unlike physics, economics is not value free (Solow, in Swedberg 1990). We are forced to acknowledge its normative content by the need to protect the environment. In order to grasp this dimension, the discussion of appropriate methodologies must move toward a realization that only an approach based on a combination of different methods is likely to find an answer to the problem of environmental policy. Economics, which is very much a deductive science, must allow more room for inductive methods.

Seen in this light, the emergence of contingent valuation methods (Mitchell and Carson 1989) is a sign of significant progress. At the same time, statistical observation must be greatly extended and systematized. Environmental policy is only in its infancy. Second-generation policies (OECD 1991) will undoubtedly put a strain on the internal cohesion of society. This institutional revolution will inevitably be accompanied by a reassessment of the value system on which society is currently based. To quote the report on the environment published by the Commission of the European Community (Funtowiez and Ravetz 1990):

> The political process regarding the environment must be accompanied by a *continuous debate* in which uncertainty, quality, politics and ethics are inextricably linked together. (p. 22)

Any attempt to isolate the purely economic aspects in a competitive-market approach is thus automatically doomed to failure. We cannot cope with the changes ahead by reviving outdated clichés based on an ideological interpretation of the neoclassical model. All that represents is a defensive attempt to maintain economic power that was acquired in the past and is now threatened by change. On the other hand, environmental policy should not yield to the temptation to reinforce paternalistic systems.

Future environmental policy must therefore be a combination of incentives that modify relative prices and direct controls that produce institutional change, so as to take into account needs that are increasing not only through force of circumstances but also as a result of our changing attitudes toward environmental values.

Such institutional change, and the resulting changes in our way of living, will be specifically reflected in legal terms. Only policies that are essentially democratic and based on the principle of individual freedom will be sufficiently acceptable to have a permanent effect on society's image of the environment. To quote one of the first people to predict "the great transformation" (Polanyi 1983):

> As long as [man] is faithful to his task of creating more freedom for all, he need have no fear that power or planning will oppose him and destroy the freedom which he is trying to build with their help. Such is the meaning of freedom in a complex society: it gives us all the certainty we need. (p. 334)

References

Baumol, W. J., and Oates W. E. 1979. *Economic environmental policy and the quality of life.* Englewood Cliffs, NJ: Prentice-Hall.
Bernoux, P. 1985. *La sociologie des organisations* (The sociology of organizations). Paris: Editions du Seuil.
Blackorby, C. 1990. "Economic policy in a second-best environment." *Canadian Journal of Economics* 23: 748–71.

Brown, C. V., and P. M. Jackson. 1986. *Public sector economics*, 3d ed. Oxford: Martin Robertson.

Bürgenmeier, B. 1992a. *Socio-Economics: An interdisciplinary approach—Ethics, institutions and markets* (particularly chap. 9, "The Environmental Debate"). Boston, Dordrecht, London: Kluwer Academic.

————. 1992b. *Analyse et politique économiques* (Economic analysis and policy), 4th ed. Paris: Economica.

Danthine, J. P. 1990. "Economie et ecologie" (Economy and ecology). *Revue économique et sociale* 48(1): 263–76.

Frey, B. S. 1991. "Is environment pricing so efficient after all?" Mimeograph. Zurich: University of Zurich.

Frey, R. L. 1972. Umweltschutz als wirtschaftspolitische Aufgabe (Environment protection: A task for economic policy) *Revue suisse d'économie politique et de statistique* 108: 453–477.

Funtowiez, S. O., and J. R. Ravetz. 1990. *Global environmental issues and the emergence of second order science.* Commission of the European Community, Preprint EUR 12803 EN. Brussels.

Georgescu-Roegen, N. 1979. *Demain la décroissance* (Tomorrow, the decreases of growth). Lausanne and Paris: Favre.

————. 1988. "Time and change in economics." In *Ökonomie und Zeit,* ed. E.K. Seifert (p. 22 ff). Frankfurt am Main: Haag & Herehen.

Habermas, J. 1968. *Technik und Wissenschaft als Ideologie.* Frankfurt am Main: Suhrkamp Verlag.

Hirschman, A. O. 1989. Deux cents ans de rhétorique réactionnaire: Le cas de l'effet pervers. *Annales ESC* 1: 67–86.

Jacquemin, A. 1987. *The new industrial organization, market forces and strategic behaviour.* Oxford: Clarendon Press.

Lea, S. E. G., R. M. Tarpy, and P. Webley P. 1987. *The individual in the economy: A survey of economic psychology.* Cambridge: Cambridge University Press.

Luce, D., and H. Raiffa. 1967. *Games and decisions.* New York: John Wiley & Sons.

Mitchell, R. C., and R. T. Carson. 1989. *Using surveys to value public goods: The contingent valuation method.* Washington, DC: Resources for the Future.

OECD (Organization for Economic Cooperation and Development). 1991. *The state of the environment.* Paris: OECD.

Olievenstein, C. 1988. *Le non-dit des émotions* (The unspoken side of emotions). Paris: Editions Odile Jacob.

Olson, M. 1968. *Die Logik des kollektiven Handelns* (The Logic of collectice acting). Tübingen: J. C. B. Mohr (Paul Siebeck).

————. 1991. *Umfassende Ökonomie* (The complete economy). Tübingen: J. C. B. Mohr (Paul Siebeck).

Polanyi, K. 1983. *La grande transformation, aux origines politiques et économiques de notre temps.* Paris: Editions Gallimard. (Trans. from the original English version, pub. 1944 as *The Great Transformation.*)

Rawls, J. 1972. *A theory of justice.* Oxford: Clarendon Press.

Seifert, E. K. 1990. Von der staatswissenschaftlichen zur ökologischen Kritik des Ökonomismus (From a political science to an ecological critique of the economy). In *Ökonomie und Ethik, Moral des Marktes oder Kritik der reinen ökonomischen Vernunft,* ed. C. Matthiessen. Freiburg: Hochschul Verlag.

Sawyer, M. 1987. "Merger: A case of market failure?" *British Review of Economic Issues* 9(21).

Simon, W. A. 1947. *Administrative behavior.* New York: Macmillan.

Solow, R. M. 1974. "The economics of resources or the resources of economics." *American Economic Review* 64: 1 ff.

Swedberg, R. 1990. *Economics and sociology*. Princeton, NJ: Princeton University Press.

Tietenberg, T. H. 1989. "Marketable permits in the U.S.: A decade of experience." In *Public finance and the performance of enterprises*, ed. K. W. Roskamp. Detroit: Wayne State University Press.

Ulrich, P. 1990. "The social contract theory, discursive ethics and political economy: Towards a critical conception of socio-economic rationality." Report No. 29 by the Institute of Economic Ethics. St. Gallen, Switzerland: Handelshochschule.

Viscusi, K. W. 1990. "Long-term environmental risk." *Journal of Risk and Uncertainty* 3: 311–14.

10

Charles Roig

The Challenge of Economics to Political Modernity: Some Views on the Limits of Collective Action and Power

Both the form and the content of socioeconomic problems in modern states are dealt with through two separate concerns. The first concern consists of the symbolic factors, which are just as much a determining factor in social choice and evolution as the material (economic, demographic, geopolitical, or other) factors that dominate most medium- and long-term studies. The second concern is a wish to take advantage of various provisional, localized results obtained in the basic stages of acquiring knowledge, in order to carry out a comparative textual investigation (inspired by the Hypertext system) of the processes leading to "the emergence of political modernity" (Roig 1989–90). These processes have been reconstructed by means of a retrospective, heuristic voyage guided by networks of lexical, polemical, factual, thematic, and random references and designed to establish relevant levels of inquiry and interpretation concerning the meanings and symbolic actions referred to in the texts.

In discussing these various points, I have used the concept of model making as a means of characterizing the sociosymbolic structures or systems whereby societies express and organize their ideas and portrayals of their own nature, destiny, and evolution. These are not concepts in the strict sense of the term, but combinations of both political and economic values, which may include the development of grammars expressing forms of cohesion and coherence, of conjunction and disjunction, of stability and evolution—the symbolic products that are an ongoing reflection on reality as it is experienced, perceived, and judged. This is well illustrated by Michael Barratt Brown's (1974) comments on the term *imperialism:*

> [Imperialism] cannot be reduced to a set of general equilibrium models; but it

has a long history as a framework for thought in political economy. The use of the word Imperialism, like Capitalism or Mercantilism, implies [the] need to combine political and economic analysis in explaining the unity of social phenomena. Where economic and political theory are combined in political economy, it is not only economic and political motives and institutions which are considered together but the economic and political theories that the men and women involved in social activity held (or hold). (p. 19)

Let me stress the totality of this perspective, in which "theory is as much a tool of apologetics as of scientific inquiry" (Brown 1974, p. 20). In the context of textology, however, this is no theoretical apriority, but the result of an investigation that, at the outset, was directed toward politics (the key words being *democracy* and *republic*) but soon acquired numerous links with the various manifestations of economic thought, which were often the deciding factor. In this connection, there can be no doubt that economics is an essential component of political modernity and is likewise the problem that political modernity has never succeeded in solving in the context of its own symbolic and conceptual creations. This persistent theoretical incompleteness primarily affects the study of the relationship between humanity and its environment insofar as this conditions the following factors: (1) the stability of political society, in what I refer to as the Third Enlightenment; (2) the harmony of social relations in industrial society, an issue raised in connection with the social question and the contrast between society and community; and (3) the survival of the species, in the context of contemporary ecology.

The Sources: Enlightenment Politics from Absolutism to the Market

My retrospective voyage through the texts in search of political modernity led me back to the Renaissance and the Reformation, revealing three distinct currents of political thought, which were to culminate in the Enlightenment. These currents were distinct in terms not only of their goals and dominant themes but also of the role they assigned to the economy, whose various transformations were very clearly perceived.

The mainstream of the First Enlightenment (Machiavelli, Locke, and Montesquieu) centered on the theological, theoretical, and technical aspects of political power following the break with the dogmas and practices of the Catholic church and the challenge to the concept of absolute monarchy by divine right. The main problem was thus how to create new sources of legitimacy and new forms of governmental organization. The dominant theme was the development of a mixed form of government, of which Machiavelli (1970) had the following to say: "Hence prudent legislators, aware of their defects, refrained from adopting as such any one of these forms [monarchy, aristocracy, and democracy], and chose instead one that shared in them all, since they thought that such a government would be stronger and more stable, for if in one and the same state there was principality, aristocracy and democracy each would keep watch over the other" (p. 109). This was the political combination that was to form the basis for the English constitution of 1688, as rationalized by Locke, and later the basis for the principle of the separation of powers, of which Hume (1948) was to write: "It may therefore be pronounced as an universal axiom in politics that an hereditary prince, a nobility without vassals, and a people voting by their representatives, form the best monarchy, aristocracy and democracy" (pp. 296–98). This current of Enlightenment thought was based on law or political science, seen as positivist science on a par with the natural sciences and even mathematics, whose logical rigor it shared.

The Second Enlightenment was an extension of the first. It was marked by two events that were to make economics an unavoidable issue: the American Revolution and the publication of *The Wealth of Nations*. The pivotal author here was Thomas Paine (1984), who also provided a link with the French Revolution and the principle of freedom of trade and industry. The changes wrought by this Second Enlightenment were considerable: In the political field, it put an end to the contradiction that had made Athenian-type democracy an unsuitable system of government for a large state. The example of the United States and the concept of democratic representation via elections encouraged the emergence of a new type of government, the democratic republic, which established itself as a credible alternative to the various kinds of monarchy. This was where economics became an integral part of political science, in both practical and theoretical terms. In practical terms, economics (and in particular the development of trade between the new American states) was one of the main themes of the negotiations that had led up to the adoption of the federal constitution. "The defect of power in the existing Confederacy to regulate the commerce between its several members, is in the number of those which have been clearly pointed out by experience" (Madison 1937, p. 274). The negotiations on the constitutional powers of the central government thus provided an opportunity to establish a market economy, a veritable constitution within the constitution that was to be of ever-increasing importance in American society. In theoretical terms, Paine demonstrated the link between the challenge to monarchy as an excessively authoritarian, interventionist, and costly—and therefore harmful—form of government and to the emergence of civil society with a solid, dynamic basis provided by freedom of expression and the free circulation of interest. "All the great laws of society are laws of nature. Those of trade and commerce, whether with respect to the intercourse of individuals, or of nations, are laws of mutual respect and reciprocal interest. They are followed and obeyed, because it is the interest of the parties to do so, and not on account of any formal laws these governments may impose or interpose" (Paine 1984, p. 165). Thus, in opposing absolutism, the Second Enlightenment ultimately reversed the relationship between economics and politics: The former was seen as the expression of natural laws, which the latter could only corrupt, thereby jeopardizing the spontaneous general equilibrium of civilized society.

The Third Enlightenment (More, Hobbes, Rousseau, and Robespierre) approached the same problem with a completely different philosophy, which was manifested as another reversal, this time in the context of a utopian social model. The emergence of political modernity was accompanied by the development of an urban, commercial, money economy in Western Europe. Various thinkers could not help pointing out the incompatibility between these two phenomena, whose effects and goals were contradictory. This resulted not only in the pursuit of alternative solutions in make-believe worlds and in the construction of exemplary utopian models but also in concrete—though seemingly desperate—political initiative (Robespierre). The Third Enlightenment had two essential characteristics. First, it asserted the autonomous constitution of politics—more specifically, the polity or political society—as the supreme human organization, which Hobbes was to identify with the body politic, Rousseau with the general will, and Sieyès and Robespierre with the nation. This was a rational creation by individuals who acquired citizenhood by adhering in one way or another to a social contract that imposed order and peace through universal constraint.

The second characteristic concerned the essential economic base, which had to be a subsistence economy—an indispensable condition for political order and social stability as defined, for example, in More's *Utopia* or Rousseau's *Projet de Constitution pour la Corse*. Rural life was seen as guaranteeing morality, solidarity, and stability in human relations by enabling life to be organized in an egalitarian fashion. This make-believe world was a manifesto against the capitalist trends of the time. Rural civilization was portrayed as a spiritual alternative to the supposedly degenerate life of the towns and cities; a regional barter economy as an alternative to an economy based on universal trade; labor, which guaranteed the basic necessities, as an alternative to money and extravagant expenditure, which created poverty; and tolerance as an alternative to the authority of the established churches and also of militant atheists. The consciously unrealistic nature of such models went hand in hand with a pessimistic propheticism whose historical outcome was the crackdown on racketeering and speculation during the Reign of Terror. But Robespierre had already vested his final hopes in a sort of redemption by the people who, as the ultimate sovereign recourse, were bound to have the last word. The Third Enlightenment went into a state of latency, until such time as the next opportunity for resurgence should occur.

Diffraction of the Enlightenment: Economics as a Science or a Political Choice

The end of the Enlightenment was marked by the fragmentation of knowledge into disciplines in which the positivist scientific model became the norm, into

diverging cultural trends that included the rise of nationalism, and into conflicting interpretations that reflected clashes of interest between various groups and
classes in what was now a rapidly urbanizing and industrializing society.

Politics—the focus of Enlightenment thinking—was at once both divided and
devalued. It was divided into a number of disciplines—public law, sociology,
economics, and political science—which together formed the social sciences and
could theoretically be evaluated by the same criteria as the natural sciences. At
the same time, it was devalued as a source of knowledge. As Fourier (1972, p.
162) was to ask: "What fatal circumstance has caused the modern sciences to
attain gigantic stature in physics and arts and to remain dwarfs in the subalternate
science of politics?" (p. 162).

The fate of politics had, of course, effectively been decided by Adam Smith
(1937, p. 651), who believed that the state had only three duties: to protect
society from external threats; to protect its members from injustice and oppression by getting rid of bad governments; and to build and maintain public works
and institutions that, though required by the community, could not be the subject
of remunerative trade. Such services could be provided only by public spending,
which in turn could come only from taxes levied on all members of society.
However, such spending had to be managed by rational methods so as to minimize the burden it placed on both producers and workers. This line of reasoning
allowed the state to be integrated into economic calculus as a political instrument
and a supplier of services and to be treated as simply one of a number of
parameters in what was henceforth seen as the only proper kind of government in
a civilized society. Following the publication in 1819 of his celebrated "Para-
ble," in which the most prestigious political authorities were reduced to a negligible quantity when compared with the finest "scientists, artists and craftsmen in
France," Saint-Simon (1951, p. 114) returned to the theme of economics and
showed how it had become a catchword in enlightened opinion: "The general
political inclination of the overwhelming majority of society is to be governed as
inexpensively as possible, to be governed as little as possible, to be governed by
those most capable and in a manner whereby public order can be altogether
guaranteed" (p. 114). Hegel (1952, para. 188) took much the same line in portraying political economy as a science that was the substratum of civil society
and that provided the latter with principles and concepts conducive to the satisfaction of needs, the defense of property, and the public defense of private
interests.

In short, political economy, seen as a scientific discipline, became the theory
and the basis for the best and cheapest possible form of government in a civil
society obeying identical principles and concepts that ensured and guaranteed the
equilibrium of the whole. Yet did such an economic conception of politics—
which reduced the latter to a minimal bourgeois state—ensure real equilibrium
and permit the harmonious development of society or, at least, reasonable hopes
to that effect? There was no evidence that it did, and indeed there were many

who challenged the whole idea, replacing scientific certainties with a new debate and reviving the persistent crisis in the relationship between authority and the market, between organization and free competition, between the state and civil society.

The minimal state was held to be a failure on the grounds that Smith's "invisible hand" could not make the market an effective substitute for the maximal state: It represented a symmetrical lack of management ability. This lack was noted by Sismondi (1971) back in 1819, who held that abstention from decision making, even to give free rein to natural laws, was simply another kind of decision making that could be just as effective or damaging as any other, depending on one's point of view. Since one was dealing with human relationships, which implies motives and aims, this dilemma was unavoidable. As Sismondi observed:

> We have seen that the rich can increase their wealth, either by new production, or by taking for themselves a larger share of what was previously reserved for the poor; and, to ensure that this share is legitimate and fair, we almost invariably resort to the kind of government intervention rejected by Adam Smith. We regard government as the protector of the weak against the strong, the defender of those who cannot defend themselves, and the representative of the permanent, yet peaceful, interest of the many against the temporary, yet passionate, interest of the individual. (p. 90)

This again raised the briefly obscured problem of politics seen as a governmental, economic, social, and ethical totality, whereas all a market economy could do was to reduce this complex whole to a series of problematic equilibrium situations. While the role of the economy was unquestioned, there was an unavoidable political choice involved in deciding on which model it should be cast. In fact, opting for the minimal state meant opting for an economy of selective scarcity and rejecting a more egalitarian economy of relative abundance, which, despite market laws, could also be seen as more rational. The governmental function was then reintroduced into the model, insofar as it protected the members of society from injustice and oppression. The social function implicit in such protection acquired a new dimension, running counter to the dogma of free, universal competition, which had led to "a prodigious development in the power of industry; but often, too, to a dreadful suffering among various classes of the population" Sismondi 1971, p. 90). This raised the social question, implying a need to reformulate politics as a totality. In this way the problem could be approached from a different angle, taking into account the extent to which knowledge also represented symbolic action.

Some decades later, Marx (1986) deepened our understanding of the problem by referring to the scientific nature of political economy but reinterpreting it from a materialistic point of view so as to give it a universal value independent of any idealistic bias. What was involved was the method of political economy and how it accounted for the construction of society on the basis of the superstructure or the infrastructure.

The 17th-century economists, for example, always started with the living whole, the population, the nation, the State, several states, etc., but analysis always led them in the end to the discovery of a few determining abstract, general relations, such as division of labour, money, value, etc. As soon as these individual moments were more or less clearly deduced and abstracted, economic systems were evolved, which from the simple concepts, such as labour, division of labour, need, exchange value, advanced to the State, international exchange and world market. The latter is obviously the correct scientific method. (pp. 37–38)

In this approach, politics as its expression in terms of the state appeared at two points in the argument: at the beginning, as an abstraction limited in terms of the symbols used (hence the criticism of the Hegelian approach, according to which knowledge was a deepening of thought through thought itself), and at the end, as a construction that followed a detour into the concrete, which itself was the result of a synthesis. Here the concrete was a series of implications involving the following stages, ranging from the material to the formal: (a) the degree of development, of material productive forces; (b) involuntary, determined relations of production; (c) the economic structure of society; and (d) the legal and political superstructure, with corresponding determined forms of social awareness.

"The mode of production of material life conditions the process of social, political and intellectual life in general" (Max 1986, p. 4). Thus, change could never originate in the political or social sphere, since these were determined rather than determining. Change could only be the product of contradictions at the most concrete levels and, more particularly, between the development of material productive forces on the one hand and the existing relationships of production—or their legal expression, the relationships of ownership—on the other. "This opens up an era of social revolution. The whole of the enormous superstructure is sooner or later upset by the change in the economic basis." However, this change occurred at two levels: a fundamental material upheaval (revealed by scientific analysis) and an ideological and political breach in which "men become aware of the conflict and fight to the very end."[1]

At this stage of the reasoning, there arose once more the dilemma referred to earlier and the resulting alternative in the two fields of understanding and action. One could opt for absolute determination of the formal by the material, in which case any symbolic action or indeed any autonomous political thought became futile, not to say irrelevant. But one could also infer the existence of a third political movement: the very awareness whereby those concerned became involved in the conflict, that is, in a revolutionary process. In his *Communist Manifesto,* Marx had already opted for this second interpretation with its idealistic bias. Indeed, it was an act of propaganda and an exhortation that implied that people could be motivated and mobilized by symbols with autonomous illocutionary force. However, this merely increased the uncertainty attached to political action in the Marxist conception of medium- and long-term historical development. As we know, this uncertainty split the movement and its main leaders (Engels, Bernstein, Kautsky, Trotsky, and Lenin), who had to solve the dilemma on the basis of their own plans and according to circumstances.

The Effects of the Diffusion of Modernity and Societal Polarity

The effects of the diffusion of political modernity and of economic thought must be seen as manifestations of the cultural dynamics that became a destabilizing factor, first on a European and later on a world scale, from the eighteenth century onward. In this chapter I cannot more than briefly give a few general pointers before moving on to a more detailed review of the theoretical problems raised by the societal polarity inherent in modernity. These problems, already heralded by the Third Enlightenment, were to become crucial in the nineteenth century, in a number of forms, which included the more theoretical form propounded by Tönnies (1979).

First, let us recall that Britain and (with something of a time lag) the United States were the countries that, within the framework of their respective institutions, were most successful in devising a form of political management compatible with the market economy and industrialization. Relative political and social stability was achieved through legitimacy of power and constitutional reform. Economic development was made more acceptable by territorial expansion, which encouraged commercial and demographic movements. This confirmed the validity of Smith's and Ricardo's theories. Yet in the same period Robert Owen was to set up a countersociety in the form of a model community, which was inspired by utopian models and offered an ideological and political alternative: the principle of free trade and the minimal state.

In France, on the other hand, the adaptation process was much more lengthy and difficult, for both historical and sociological reasons. France inherited from the Revolution three kinds of legitimacy, which continued to compete and which gave the country's constitutional development a repetitive threefold rhythm: autocratic legitimacy (monarchic, imperial, circumstantial); representative legitimacy (elected bodies, parliaments); and popular legitimacy (revolutions, miscellaneous movements). The dilemma surrounding the political management of the new economy was accompanied by a polarity aggravated by, among other factors, the survival of a powerful farming class, the persistence of a strong civil service, and the virulence of religious antagonisms. In their diversity, eclecticism, and radicalism, the writings of Fourier (1972) typified the ideological resistance to, and rejection of, false values represented by "politics which vaunts the rights of man but fails to guarantee the first right and the only useful one, which is the right to work" (p. 159) and by "economism which promises wealth to nations but only teaches the art of enriching financiers and leeches, the art of doubling taxes . . . and of neglecting all research into domestic association, the basis of the economy" p. 160).

The farther a country was situated, both geographically and culturally, from the European sources of Enlightenment thinking, the greater the polarization caused by resistance to what was seen as a threat to its deep-rooted cultural, national, and ethnic identities. This was particularly true of the major empires— Austro-Hungarian, Russian, Ottoman, even Chinese and Japanese. In political terms, the force of tradition became an inability to adapt and reform, other than by processes that proved to be lengthy, complex, and fraught with difficulty. In economic terms, these traditional sociopolitical institutions—to borrow Marx's terminology, these *forms*—do indeed appear to have paralyzed economic structures and prevented the development of productive forces, except through the local and sometimes damaging intervention of foreign capital, subject to the whims of political or military power.

The intensity and scale of the response to the effects of diffusion and polarity, conceived as a symmetrical relationship, are admirably illustrated by passages from Dostoyevsky (1960), written in 1863 after a journey to Western Europe, which he describes in none too flattering terms in winter notes on summer impressions. He wrote of Westerners, and Frenchmen in particular, who sought to create a brotherhood that was bound to elude them, since it could not be created: "[Brotherhood] is obtained, is found in nature. Yet, in the nature of the Frenchman in Western nature in general, it is replaced by the particularist principle, the principle of reinforced self-preservation, of personal activity, of self-determination in one's own self, of opposition of this self to nature and to all of society". For a Slavophile, on the other hand, personality could be created only by "the voluntary sacrifice, which is perfectly conscious and in no way imposed, of all one's being for the benefit of all." This was "the law of nature [to] which men of morals are inclined", and "it is then wrong to make the slight calculation for one's own personal advantage". As for socialism, which preached this vanished brotherhood in the West, he proclaimed: "Liberty, equality, fraternity or death. In that case, discussion is at an end; and the triumph of the bourgeois is complete".

These thoughts and intuitions must now be incorporated in a totally revised model. Investigation of the above themes very soon led me to focus on Tönnies's work *Gemeinschaft und Gesellschaft* (1887, 1979), whose attempt to define the basic categories of pure sociology established a number of concepts built up by processes of opposition, substitution, and competition. The term *community (Gemeinschaft)* refers to a social bond imposed by natural living conditions, which, although they evolve, do so in an organic context determined by reciprocal knowledge, empathy, and concord.

> The community of blood, as a unit of being, develops and tends towards the community of place, which finds its direct expression in shared dwelling, and in turn develops and tends towards the community of mind, as shared activity and administration operating in the same direction, in the same sense. . . . All

three kinds of community are closely linked [in] both space and time, and thus in all these individual phenomena and their development, and more generally in human culture and its history. p. 12, my translation).

The key concept is harmony born of this conjunction between space, time, and shared life, as created and fertilized by kinship, neighborhood, and friendship. Since such harmony is not static, it is liable to be extended to ever larger groups if the development starts from a center that symbolizes the unity of the whole. At a given level of complexity, a hierarchy may be established in the form of dignities, that is, qualities that are universally acknowledged (paternity, age, strength, wisdom, etc.) and are accompanied by responsibilities. In this context, a domestic economy may include the organization of community trade involving the family, the village, the city, or the region. At this point, moreover, there is the risk of a drift toward the concept of trade seen as the mere circulation of goods.

Tönnies states further: "The theory of society (*Gesellschaft*) posits a group of people who, while living and dwelling peacefully alongside one another, as in a community, are not essentially linked but are essentially separate; whereas, in the community, they remain linked in spite of all separation, in society they remain separate in spite of all links" (p. 39, my translation). As a result, there is no a priori unity from which to derive the activities of individuals: "Each man exists only for himself and in a state of tension with all others. . . . No-one will do anything for another, no-one is prepared to grant or donate anything to another, except in return for a service or gift which is judged to be at least equivalent to one's own" (p. 52, my translation). This is a statement of the intrusion of market laws, which implies that everything should be considered an object for private appropriation. A shared good can exist only through the construction of a fictitious shared subject with an imaginary will, to which the shared value can be related. This, then, is the challenge faced by politics in society: That which is provided organically by the community must be artificially reconstructed by mutual agreement and against the grain of individual wills.

Society, states Tönnies, develops by a shift from "general domestic economy to general commercial economy and, closely linked to this, from supremacy of agriculture to supremacy of industry. This shift may be considered as though it were governed by a plan in which, with ever-increasing success within each people, merchants (capitalists) and capitalists (as merchants) force their way to the front and appear to unite as though with a shared purpose. This purpose may be referred to as 'trade' and its ultimate framework is the world market" (p. 55). This is a further challenge to politics, forced to operate in a field that is largely beyond its control.

Societal polarity and its effects are summed up by Tönnies as follows:

1. Definition based on opposition between characteristics of community and society:

Community Society

Community	Society
Essential will	Elected will
The self	The person
Possession	Wealth
Land	Money
Family law	Law of obligation

2. Definition based on evolution and competition: "To conclude this general examination, there are thus two opposing eras of major cultural development: the era of society, which follows the era of the community. The latter is characterized by the social will as concord, custom and religion, the former by the social will as convention, politics and public opinion" (p. 235).
3. Definition based on substitution: The will of the state operates in society through justice and policing rather than custom and religion. However, "once dead custom and religion cannot be revived by constraint or teaching of any kind; in order to create or allow the development of moral forces and moral individuals, the state must create the necessary conditions, the necessary soil, or at least eliminate opposing forces. The state, as the reason of society, should resolve to destroy society, or at least renew it in a different form. Such efforts are extremely unlikely to succeed" (p. 235).

An alternative model involves a Marxist-type process, in which the working class—which is the most numerous and the most underprivileged—"can only use its strength to revolt" (p. 14) in order to be "rid of its misery" (p. 39). Furthermore, "The class struggle may destroy the society and the state which it wishes to reform. And, since the entire culture has been transformed into social and political civilization, the very culture will perish in this altered form, unless its scattered seeds survive and the essence and ideas of the community, being re-nourished, secretly develop a new culture within that which is perishing" (pp. 235–36).

What we have here is an attempted systematic interpretation of the crisis in politics caused by the shift from community to society and the resulting destabilization of the latter. One could find no better expression of the recurrence of this theme in numerous forms, which, however, have three basic issues in common: the destabilization of (state) politics when faced with the dilemma raised by the overall management of an industrial market economy, scientific and existential uncertainty about the implications and consequences of the crisis, and prophetic extrapolations ranging from scenarios of total disaster to possible rescue or redemption by some historical force or hazard.

Tönnies's analysis raises the following additional comments. First, as regards the theoretical implications of the definition based on opposition between community and society, this definition covers phenomena that are far more numerous, rich, and complex than the author suggests. The subsequent development of the social sciences has revealed the value of these categories in the study of numerous phenomena in which the same kind of polarity occurs in a manner that may be complementary, antagonistic, or a mixture of the two. This applies, for example, to primary groups and secondary groups, to hierarchical relations and relations of exchange in social organizations (bureaucracies), to reproduction (family, status of women, demography) and production (labor, technology, communications), to family socialization and institutional education of the young, to latency and resurgence of sociosymbolic trends and systems (religious or secular beliefs), and so on. These examples are sufficient to show that, while societal polarity can be perceived and examined in its entirety, it may occur in fragmented, provisional forms, thereby providing alternatives and potential choices that avoid the fundamental dilemma. At the very least, such an interpretation would account for the survival of nation-states and, at best, for the fluidity and adaptability of many sociopolitical and socioeconomic systems that act as buffer systems, owing in particular to their symbolic properties, which deserve closer examination.

Furthermore, this interpretation then makes it possible to avoid treating the opposition between community and society as a zero-sum game, as suggested by the viewpoints set forth above. In fact, politics is a means of managing numerous combinations of elements from both community and society as defined by Tönnies; this is done at the expense of conflicts and compromises that may be sustainable and controlled, or acute and damaging, to various degrees, depending on the choices, cultures, and circumstances that accompany the disruptive effects of the diffusion of modernity. At this level, a decisive role may be played by constitutional, economic, and symbolic processes—classic examples being the New Deal and the policies proposed by Keynes. Nevertheless, any nation-state in which politics is supposed to act as a shock absorber may find itself in an impasse or else sliding disastrously out of control. Tönnies has proved prophetic as regards certain extremely costly experiences—among them totalitarianism—which will be discussed below.

The Costs: Politics in Crisis, Loss of Control, Countereffects

This last section will briefly present two relevant levels of inquiry and interpretation concerning the information used as the basis for the textological investigation in which the original key word was *democracy* (Roig 1989–90).

The term *totalitarianism* immediately became part of the reference system by virtue of its regular occurrence in twentieth-century political writings and factual data. In both respects, moreover, it is linked to Tönnies's (1979) writings in a striking and unfortunate case of self-fulfilling prophecy. *Gemeinschaft und Gesellschaft* was published in Bismarck's Germany and was rejected because of its references to Marx, which were held to be pernicious. It was republished—only this time in order to produce an illocutionary effect—in Hitler's Germany (1935) because of its supposed exaltation of the community, the *Volk*. In an additional preface, the author was forced to state that he did not, "either now or fifty years ago, intend this book to be an ethical or political treatise and that, in [his] initial preface, [he] issued a strong warning against erroneous interpretations and ostensibly sound applications" (1979, pp. 1–2). Such information must be taken into account when drawing textological inferences.

Retrospective reconstruction of the origins of totalitarianism was rapidly brought to a halt by World War I, which introduced a major innovation in political management of the economy in the industrial age: the war economy, the planned administration of resources, and the translation of these into acceptable political language and principles. The intertext network leads us specifically to the economic problems that confronted general staffs—and in particular, the German high command—when the war lasted longer than expected and nation-states began to encounter difficulties in mobilizing, producing, and allocating human and material resources. Clausewitz had already suggested a relationship between war and politics when he described the former as the instrument of the latter in the international sphere. Ludendorff (1937) rejected this idea as too restrictive and instead proposed the concept of total war, which—above all, domestically—implied total politics. This definition was the basis for the plan issued by the German general headquarters in September 1916. The plan rejected both capitalism and socialism; instead, in accordance with ancient Germanic law, "the forces of all belong, in time of war, to the state" (Ludendorff 1920, p. 360). This was the source and the matrix for later political grammars of totalitarianism, including those formulated by Ludendorff (1937) himself and, in his wake, by Hitler. Here are some of the main elements:

> ... The State, by which I mean total politics and the leaders of total war must take special measures including, for example, the most rigorous censorship of the press ... the prohibition of meetings, the arrest of at least the leaders of the "malcontents" ... (pp. 31–33)

> Opposition parties or harmful saboteurs, either operating on their own or influenced by enemies of the war or by the representatives of international powers, the Jews and Rome ... must likewise be actively attacked ...

> A profound source of discontent, or of danger to the cohesion of the nation, is the potential economic outlook before and after the war. The truth of this is only too clearly confirmed by the rift which the social-democratic and communist doctrines have caused among the people ...

Management of the war economy remained the weak link in this program. Experience had shown that bureaucratic centralization "deprived everyone of all creative initiative and of all responsibility" (1937, p. 56) and that dishonesty and corruption shook "the people's trust in the fairness of an economic system based on constraint—a system which, on account of the restrictions it imposes, must inevitably be rejected by any private initiative and any productive force" (1937, pp. 56–57). Yet no solution was offered to reconcile economic efficiency with the cohesion of the nation. It was Hitler who found the solution in the form of "war capitalism."

Clausewitz and the German war experience provided the framework for a different totalitarian political grammar—that proposed by Lenin and the Bolsheviks. In his *Notebooks on Clausewitz,* Lenin (1945: p. 72) noted: "The whole: politics," "Is politics the main thing?", and "N.B. Marxist approach". Specifically, in becoming total, the Great War exposed the fundamentally dictatorial nature of capitalist states—bourgeois equivalents of the dictatorship of the proletariat—and also the dialectical relationship between international war and the revolutionary class struggle. This interpretation justified the establishment of a symmetrical relationship between capitalism and socialism, allowing the latter to borrow from the former those policies and techniques that had already proven themselves. This constituted both the practical and the doctrinal origin of war communism and of Soviet economic policy up to the introduction of the New Economic Policy (NEP). This was also the experience that served as the inspiration for the planned economy and the all-out industrialization program launched in 1928; the same applied to foreign policy up to the era of peaceful coexistence, truly the first step in the disintegration of a form of totalitarianism that, in the absence of a credible state of war, was deprived of its sociosymbolic basis (see Roig 1980, p. 153; 1988, p. 439).

Another relevant level of political inquiry worthy of mention is that raised by the issue of decolonization in the form of a theory of political development as conceived and expanded in the 1960s, in relation to the theory of economic growth whose prototype was Rostow's book *The Stages of Economic Growth* (1960). Under totalitarianism, political management of the economy was based on controlled scarcity; the aim of political development, on the other hand, was to combine pluralist democracy with an economy of abundance. There were various alternative approaches, which are worth examining. In its initial version, this liberally oriented political theory of economic management was based on the following elements: (1) The unit of analysis was the nation-state, conceived as a system of interdependent structures and functions, whose success was evaluated on the basis of two parameters: its duration and its ability to adapt both internally (democratization) and externally (foreign trade, security, diplomacy). (2) The performance of nation-states was evaluated according to a number of parameters: authoritarian or democratic development, level of economic growth, and weight in world equilibrium. (3) The theory presupposed an ideology of progress, the model for which was provided by the United States and which was dominated by such values as individualism, tolerance (secularity), rationality (in the Weberian and technological senses), liberalism, and competition. At the same time, the theory played down community values as defined by Tönnies (1979), adverse effects (such as monoculture and debt at the local level and pollution at a more global level), and the resistance this engendered in political, cultural, or religious contexts.

The theory of linear political development thus rationalizes practices that create their own limits in a world where the resources available to humankind are reduced. The need to protect the environment is a concomitant acknowledgment of these limits, presupposing a redefinition of politics as the guarantor and protector of the public interest at this crucial stage in world history. In *Economics and the Public Purpose,* Galbraith (1975) sets forth this line of reasoning in three theses, which may be summed up as follows: First of all, the answer cannot lie in adapting the rules of the market by means of a formula requiring those responsible for pollution and damage to pay for it. Such a moralizing approach is unrealistic, since the offending activities bear little relation to the scale and gravity of the potential consequences. Nor can the answer lie in such radical measures as the authoritarian restriction of economic growth, perhaps even zero growth. By perpetuating existing national disparities and social inequalities, this would create an unstable and potentially explosive situation. All that is left is the political solution: "to continue economic growth but to specify by legislation the parameters within which it can occur" (p. 306).

Textological research reveals the recurring nature of this approach, which is based on the principle of precedence as set forth by Galbraith: "In the past, when the divergence of some private or planning purpose from the public interest (with environmental or other effect) became intolerable, it was the practice to specify the broad legislative purpose and to pass enabling legislation" (p. 307).

Here again we see political action conditioned by the balances of power, compromise, and uncertainty inherent in its development in the context of the state, elected institutions, and bureaucratic organizations, whose effectiveness is limited by the action of private groups and by public opinion as conveyed via the media, not to mention by national frontiers that guarantee sovereignty. Once again, politics can be interpreted as an uncertain attempt to manage global phenomena that are inaccessible to rational methods, since it is a form of thinking that constantly adapts in an effort to guide and control the random changes that mark the development of increasingly complex societies. Textology sets up as a relevant level of inquiry two aspects of politics that are the source of a recurrent contradiction that sustains an ongoing ideological debate: (1) the identification of politics with the action of a state whose rationality can in principle be defined and (2) the intrusion into such action of processes that it cannot control and that may even render it counterproductive. Yet surely such a situation demands that politics be seen for what it is: a forecasting function of society at its highest level of generality, which is constantly shifting and which thus forces it to redefine itself under conditions of more or less total uncertainty.

This process, I believe, needs to be seen as totally determined by a given state of the world. It can be briefly sketched as follows: (1) Political action is a process of identification and acknowledgment of a need or a threat that is successively seen as a problem, debated, and politicized (for example, measures to combat a source of pollution). (2) The process itself provides the appropriate treatment of this need or threat by creating structures that correspond to this new function, circumscribed by information that may necessitate very lengthy research. Such structures also depend on technical factors (organization), territorial factors (jurisdiction) and symbolic factors (cultural or ideological resistance). (3) Politics is the political rationalization of a new sphere of action that implies a challenge to the principle of precedence and the existing order, as perceived in its various forms (legitimacy, law, institutions). In this sense, political action is perceived as a cost that is almost always high, owing to two inevitable constraints:

1. the time involved in carrying out the necessary reforms, which delays intervention and renders it ineffective or even harmful (leading to criticism of democratic or diplomatic processes)
2. the adoption of premature or radical measures whose effects are negative (leading to criticism of authoritarian, totalitarian processes and unfair treatment).

These costs, which are hard to avoid, represent setbacks for politics, which is thereby discredited in regular cycles that are brought to light by textological research. However, the same analysis reveals that this type of discourse can also be interpreted as an important element in the process of adaptation to global change, by providing data, criticism, and the means of disseminating information and mobilizing resources in the critical situations that increasingly confront us as the century draws to a close. The environment can thus be seen as just one of a number of parameters shaping new political models and adding to the specific costs of politics. The following key points may be mentioned.

First, the preferred unit of analysis should be the world in its totality, seen as a system made up of autonomous subsystems linked together in various configurations. In any case, the disappearance of the balance of fear and the collapse of the totalitarian regimes impose this global perspective, which needs to be conceptualized on a new basis. The principle of sovereignty of nation-states is starting to be qualified and adapted in order to ensure effective protection of other existing or future entities, examples being the right of intervention in the event of natural disasters or emergencies of the same order that justify humanitarian escape routes. In the economic sphere, we are witnessing similar developments designed to adjust markets and international trade flows; in this connection, debt reduction policy is a revolution in financial and banking practice, quite apart from being a reassessment and rectification of economic management in North-South relations. Traditional distinctions such as those between national and international law are tending to become blurred or even vanishing altogether. Politics is reconquering ground lost after the Enlightenment, when it was at least its acknowledged duty to resort to reason (in its various senses) in order to prevent the often irreversible adverse effects of ill-considered decisions or situations based on narrow, overspecialized points of view.

Second, the study of the complex interrelationships between the various subsystems (states, groups of states, multinational firms, stock exchanges, etc.) is becoming a matter of priority. Political and economic processes and their various combinations are not necessarily linear or even exponential; they also display cycles (for example, in the relationship between economic recessions and authoritarian regimes), alternations (for example, in balances of power and domination breakdowns, as in the collapse of entire economic subsystems such as postwar Latin America or, more recently, the Communist bloc), and survivals or revivals (for example, in the sociopolitical function of ideologies or religion such as Islam and in the growth in the number of communities of various kinds). The concept of special interest or pressure groups seemingly no longer suffices to explain the implications or the impact of such processes.

Finally, the kinds of reason that must be reconstructed or created by politics as an instrument for the management and coordination of the world economy and environment are related to bounded or weighted rationality, the main aim of which is to foresee and establish procedures that can become institutionalized at world level (e.g., the G7, the Brundtland Commission of the UN) or at regional level, increasingly in geographical areas where the values of European modernity no longer prevail (the Arab-Islamic world, Southeast Asia, North and South America, for example). The limitations of state sovereignty are lending credibility to the idea of an international police force under the supervision of the United Nations. The complex process of federalization and defederalization merits particular attention as a process of peaceful change and orientation. While historical experience makes clear that this process is not immune to violence (see the examples of Switzerland and the United States), once it has started it contains the potential for solutions or compromises that can be achieved by extensive negotiation. Politics can thus be seen as the study and implementation of adaptation processes that—given the diversity of the situations encountered—are often precarious and diffuse, such as sustainable development and ecology, rather than as the analysis of institutions with precise, stable legal forms. Retrospective reconstruction of the creation of political modernity therefore means changing our epistemic viewpoint, so that politics can be seen as a process of constant questioning in a world that we must try to regulate but that we can never completely control.

Note

1. From a preface added by Marx in 1859 (Marx, 1986, p. 4).

References

Brown, M. B. 1974. *The economics of imperialism.* Harmondsworth, U.K.: Penguin Modern Economics Texts.

Dostoyevsky, F. M. 1960. *Oeuvres littéraires* (Literary works), 4. Lausanne, Switzerland: Editions Rencontre.

Fourier, C. 1972. *The utopian vision of Charles Fourier.* London: Jonathan Cape.

Galbraith, J. K. 1975. *Economics and the public purpose.* Harmondsworth: Penguin.

Hamilton, A., T. Jay, and A. Madison. 1937. *The federalist* [1787–88]. New York: Modern Library.

Hegel, G. W. F. 1952. *Philosophy of right* [1821]. Oxford: Clarendon Press.

Hume, D. 1948. *Moral and political philosophy.* London: Haffner Press.

Lenin, V. I. 1945. *Cahiers sur Clausewitz* (Notebooks on Clausewitz). In *Les fondements théoriques de la guerre et de la paix en U.R.S.S.* (Theoretical foundations of war and peace in the USSR), ed. B.C. Friedl. Paris: Médicis.

Ludendorff, E. 1920. *Souvenirs de guerre* (Recollections of war). Paris: Payot.

Machiavelli, N. 1970. *The discourses.* Harmondsworth, U.K.: Penguin.

Madison, J. 1937. *The federalist.* [1787–88]. New York: Modern Library.

Marx, K. 1957. Contribution à la ethique de l'économie politique. Paris editions sociales. Foreword added in 1859.

Paine, T. 1984. *Rights of man* [1791–92]. Harmondsworth, U.K.: Penguin.

Roig, C. 1980. *La grammaire politique de Lénine. Formes et effets d'un discours politique* (The political grammer of Lenin: Style and effects of a political speech). Paris: L'Age d'Homme.

———. 1988. A propos de *perestroika* de Mikhail Gorbachev. Légitimité et changement en Union Soviétique (A propos of Mikhail Gorbachev's perestroika: Legitimacy and change in the Soviet Union). *Revue Française de Science Politique* 38(3): 439–43.

———. 1989–90. *L'invention de la modernité politique* (The invention of modern politics) (2 vols.). Geneva: Recherches et Travaux, Département de Science Politique de l'Université de Genève.

Rostow, W. W. 1960. *The stages of economic growth.* Cambridge: Cambridge University Press.

Saint-Simon, H. 1951. *Textes choisis (Selected readings).* Paris: Editions Sociales.

Sismondi, J. C. L. 1971. *Nouveaux principes d'économie politique* (New principles of political economics) [1819]. Paris: Calmann-Lévy.

Smith, A. 1937. *The wealth of nations* [1776]. New York: Random House.

Tönnies, F. 1944. *Communauté et société. Catégories fondamentales de la sociologie pure* (Community and society: Fundamental categories of pure sociology) [1887, 1935] (trans. J. Leif). Paris: PressesUuniversitaires de France.

———. 1979. *Gemeinschaft und Gesellschaft. Grundbegriffe der reinen Soziologie* [1887]. Darmstadt, West Germany: Wissenschaftliche Buchgesellschaft.

Index

A

Ability, 55
  habit, 61–63
  recyclying, 61–64
  task knowledge, 63–64
Absorptive capacity. See Assimilative
  capacity
Acid rain, 84
Advertising, 33
AES. See Available energy surplus
Affluence, 32–33, 37, 45
AGREV (Agriculture, Environment,
  Vittel Project), 165–72
American Revolution, 193
AMOEBA model, 154
Anamnesis, 107
Aristotle, 111–12, 115n.17
Assimilative capacity, 144–45, 149
Attitudes, and behavior, 40, 67–68
Available energy surplus (AES), 149

B

Backstop technology theory, 79–81, 150
BCSD. See Business Council for
  Sustainable Development
Beckerman, W., 123–24, 125–26
Behavior, 178–79, 181
  and attitudes, 40, 67–68

Behavior *(continued)*
  recycling costs, 59–60
  and regulation, 41
Behavioral fix, 41–43, 45
Bernstam, M., 128–29
Biodiversity, 145, 146
Bioecology, 46
Bioeconomics, 107–13
Bioengineering, 39
Biosphere, 4, 77–78, 89, 148
Bounded rationality, 183, 184, 187
Britain. See Great Britain
Brown, Michael, 191–92
Brundtland Commission, 127–28, 131,
  139–40
Business, 128
Business Charter for Sustainable
  Development, 128
Business Council for Sustainable
  Development (BCSD), 128

C

Capital, 80, 82, 153–54
Capitalism, 31, 33, 34, 35, 204
Carrying capacity, 145
Chrematistics, 112
Civil service, 186–87
Class struggle, 201

Climate change, 130
Cognitive fix, 39–40, 43
Cognitive psychologists, 21, 22
Collection effectiveness, 62–63, 66,
   69n.11
Collective action, 191–207
Commoner, Barry, 29, 31, 32
Communism, 204
Communist Manifesto (Marx), 197
Community, 199–200
Complementarity, 142–43
Computers, 39
Consumers, 40, 186
   behavior, 36–37, 55, 181–82
   discrete versus continuous choice,
      20–23
   values, 37
   waste, 52
Consumption, 33, 145, 153
   and economic growth, 130–31
   energy, 98, 130
   and survivability, 148
Contingent valuation (CV) studies,
   11–12, 23, 188
   and consumer choice, 20–23
   embedding, 12–16
   framing, 16–18
   probability, 18–20
Corporate producers, 36–37
Cost-benefit analysis, 85–88
Culture, 34, 35, 38
CV studies. See Contingent valuation studies

D

Daly, H.E., 125, 127, 141
Dasgupta, P., 81
Decision making, 184–856, 196
Declining block rate system, 41

Decolonization, 204
Defensive expenditures, 132, 154
Democracy, 193
Denmark, 51, 53–55
Development, economic, 100, 140
Direct controls, 177, 188
Disasters, 15
Discount rate, 87–88
Dose/response ratios, 86
Dostoyevsky, F., 199
Dryzek, J., 141
Duncan, Otis Dudley, 30–31
Dutch National Environment Policy
   Plan, 130
Dutch Water Management Plan, 154

E

EABS. See European Association for
   Bioeconomic Studies
Ecoenergy analysis, 77–101, 181
   and entropy management, 96–101
   and management of finitude, 89–96
   of production function, 90–94
Ecological complex, 30–31, 33, 35, 37,
   44, 47n.1
Ecological economics. See
   Environmental economics
Ecological unsustainability,
   140
Economic analysis
   and environment, 79–88
   and pollution management, 84–88
Economic growth, 139–40, 150
   and environmental deterioration, 34
   limits to, 121–29
   overall benefits of, 125
   social costs of, 126
   and sustainable development, 121–34

Economic psychology, 181–82
Economics, 35
  and biosphere, 77–78
  and ethics, 107–13
  historical school, 108
  optimal scale of, 146
  political, 195–96
Economics and the Public Purpose
    (Galbraith), 205
Economic unsustainability, 140
Efficiency, 42, 81, 95, 123
Ehrlich, Paul, 29, 31, 32
Embedding, 12–16
Embodied energy. See Emergy
Emergy, 91, 92–93, 94, 149,
    156n.8
Emissions Trading Program, 175
Energy, 128, 142, 181
  consumption, 98, 130
  efficiency, 42, 92
  reductionism, 78
  solar, 124–25
  technologies, 38–39
  See also Ecoenergy analysis
Enlightenment, 192–94
  diffraction of, 194–98
  ethics and, 110–11
Entropy, 81, 124–25, 149, 181
  management, 96–101
  quality of production, 99–100
  valuation procedure, 99
Environment
  and economic analysis, 79–88
  and economy, 3–4
Environmental activists, 27
Environmental economics, 4, 46, 100–101
  socioeconomic elements of, 77–101
  See also Bioeconomics
Environmental functions, 142–47

Environmental policy, 85–88, 175–88
  economic dimension of, 180–87
  future trends in, 187–88
  instruments of, 176–78
  objections to market oriented, 178–80
Environmental problems, 27–47
  causes of, 29–38
    socioecological perspective, 30–35
    socioeconomic perspective, 35–38
  distributional impact of, 45
  impact of, 44–45
  solving, 38–43
  See also Pollution
Environmental science, 180–81
Environmental services, 15
Environmental sociology, 29–47
Equilibrium, 181
Ethics
  and economics, 107–13
  and Enlightenment, 110–11
  judgment, 125
Etzioni, A., 36–37
European Association for Bioeconomic
    Studies(EABS), 107
Exergy, 90–91
Existence values, 125
Expectations, 81–83
Expenditures. See Defensive
    expenditures
Experience, 56

F

Finitude, 89–96, 149
Fossil fuels, 98, 124, 146
Fourier, C., 195, 198
Framing, 16–18
France, 198

Freedom, 183

G

Galbraith, J.K., 205
Georgescu-Roegen, N., 112, 124
Germany, 132
Gesellschaft und Gemainschaft
    (Tonnies), 202–03
Global warming, 146
GNP. See Gross national product
Goodland, R., 146
Government, 192–93
Great Britain, 198
Greenhouse effect, 85, 86, 97
Greppin, H., 148
Gross national product (GNP), 132–13
Gross productivity, 155n.6
Growth. See Economic growth

H

Habermas, J., 181
Habit, 61–63, 182
Happiness, 36
Heal, G., 81
Hegel, G.W.F., 195
Heilbroner, Robert, 111
Hicksian income, 153
Hirsch, F., 126–27
Hirschman, A.O., 180
Hotelling, H., 79–80
Hueting, R., 132
Human exemption paradigm, 28
Hume, D., 193

I

Imperialism, 191–92

Incentives, 68, 175, 177, 188
Incineration plants, 51
Inclining block rate system, 41
Income, national, 152–53
Industry, 68–69n.1
Information, 19, 63–64, 68, 182
   context of, 17
   technologies, 39
Interdisciplinary research, 11–24
Interest groups, 184–87
Intergenerational equity, 45, 82, 83
Intergovernmental Panel on Climate
   Change (IPCC), 130
Internalization theory, 79
International institutions, 141
IPAT equation, 32
IPCC. See Intergovernmental Panel on
   Climate Change
Irreversibility, 85

J

Judeo-Christian ethic, 34
Justice, 183

K

Kahneman, D., 14–15
Keynes, John Neville, 109–10
KLEM models, 80, 83
Knetsch, Jack L., 14–15
Knowledge fix. See Cognitive fix
Kummel, R., 98, 99

L

Lacy, M.G., 32–33
Land degradation, 146
Laws, 40–41, 183

Lecomber, R., 123, 124
Legitimacy, 198
Leipert, C., 132
Lenin, V.I., 204
Lesourd, J.B., 81
Lifestyle, 37–38
Ludendorf, E., 203–04

M

Machiavelli, N., 192–93
Macroenvironmental theory, 146–47
Marx, K., 196–97
Matching, 21–22
Materialism, 36
Meadows, Donella and Dennis, 121–22, 123
Media, 27
Mishan, E.J., 126
Morality, 12, 127
Motivation, 55, 57–61, 184
  attitudes and, 58
  behavior costs, 59–60
  financial costs, 58
  public benefits, 60, 67

N

Nationalism, 195
Needs, 34, 36, 131
Negative externality, 84
Net primary production (NPP), 148
Nitrates, 166–67
Nonuse values, 11–24
Nordhaus, W.D., 80
NPP. See Net primary production

O

Odum, H.T., 91–92

OECD. See Organization for Economic
  Cooperation and Development
Olievenstein, C., 180
Opportunity, 55–56, 64–66, 183
Optimization, 176
Organization for Economic Cooperation
  and Development (OECD), 52,
  68–69n.1
Our Common Future, 127–28
Overpopulation. See Population
Owen, Robert, 198
Ozone layer, 85–86, 97, 146

P

Paine, Thomas, 193
Parsons, Talcott, 33
Passet, R., 101
Payment vehicles, 17
Pearce, D.W., 88
Peer pressure, 58
Personal gain, 68
Personality, 34, 35
Pieters, Rik, 58
POET model, 31, 32
Polarity. See Societal polarity
Political modernity, 191–207
  effects of diffusion of, 198–202
  and Enlightenment, 192–98
Political science, 184–85
Political system, 35
Pollution
  of agrarian system, 165–72
  economic analysis and management
    of, 84–88
  global, 84–88, 97, 145
  polluter-pays principle, 176
Population, 29–32, 34, 35, 37, 38,43, 46
  carrying capacity, 145

Population *(continued)*
  predictions, 130–31
  and survivability, 148
Poverty, 31
Power differentials, 36–37
Precautionary principle, 87
Preferences, 37, 86, 147, 181
Prices, 78, 151, 187
  and expectations, 81–82
  and resource management, 80
  shadow, 86
  signals, 42
Primary productivity, 155n.6
Prisoner's dilemma, 176
Probability, 18–20, 182
Problem solving, 168
Procedural rationality, 170
Procedure invariance, 22
Producers, 36–37, 186
Production, 33, 81, 131–33
  and ecoenergy analysis, 90–94
  entropic quality of, 99–100
  factors, 80
  treadmill mill of, 33
  See also Net primary production
Productivity, 155n.6
Profit, 33
Prominence hypothesis, 22
Property rights, 11, 150
Protestantism, 35
Psychology, economic, 181–82
Public benefits, 60, 67
Public choice theory, 184
Public good, 176
Punti, A., 93

R

Rationality. See Bounded rationality;

Rationality *(continued)*
  Procedural rationality; Substantive
    rationality
Reasoning, 169
Recycling, 51–68
  ability, 61–64
  behavioral science frame of reference,
    55–57
  collection effectiveness, 62–63, 66,
    69n.11
  motivation, 57–61
  municipal policy in Denmark, 53–55
    attitudes toward, 54–55
    participation, 53–54
  opportunity, 64–66
Referendums, 17
Regulations, 40–41, 175–76
Religion, 35
Renewability, 93–94
Rescue operations, 15
Resources, 89, 129, 142–43, 150, 151
  allocation of, 82, 123–24, 147, 175
  as capital, 153
  exclusion of specificity of, 79–84
  national accounts, 153–54
  nonmarket, 89
  paradox of, 94–95
  theory of, 79
Revealed preference, 37
Risk, 16, 19–22, 47n.4, 144, 182
Rural life, 194

S

Saint-Simon, H., 195
Schmidheiny, Stephan, 128
Schmoller, Gustav von, 108–09
Schnaiberg, A., 31–32, 33
Sen, A., 107–08

SEU. See Subjective expected utility
Sismondi, J.C.L., 196
Smith, Adam, 110–11, 195
Socialism, 199
Social organization, 31, 33, 34, 46, 128
Social sciences, 27, 181, 195
Social welfare, 131–33, 140, 152
Societal polarity, 200–202
Society for Studies on Entropy, 99
Socioeconomics, 35–38, 46–47
  case study, 165–72
  and environmental economics, 77–101
  and environmental policy, 181–87
  planning, 170–72
  of sustainable development, 139–55
Sociology, 29–47, 183–84
Solar energy, 124–25
Solow, R.M., 81–83
Source separation. See Recycling
Sovereignty, 206–07
Spillover effects, 123–24
Structural strategies, 40–41, 43
Subjective expected utility (SEU), 168
Subsidies, 187
Substantive rationality, 169–70
Substitution, 123, 142–43, 155n.3, 180,
  181, 187
Survivability, 142–47, 154
  physical measures of, 147–49
Sussex University, 122
Sustainable development, 77–78,
  100–101
  achieving, 129–33
  appraising, 149–54
  and business, 128
  defined, 3
  and economic growth, 121–34
  implications of, 139–42
  neoclassical indicators of, 151–52

Sustainable development *(continued)*
  socioeconomy of, 139–55
Switzerland, 145–46

T

Taxes, 187
Technology, 29–32, 34, 35, 37, 43, 46,
  82, 123, 128
  energy, 38–39
  payoff matrix, 144
  and survivability, 143–45
  See also Backstop technologytheory
Thermodynamics, laws of, 81, 82, 124,
  155n.1, 181
Tonnies, F., 199–200, 202–03
Totalitarianism, 202–04
Tradition, 199
Transformity, 92–93
Translog functions, 83–84

U

United Nations, 207
United States, 198
Utility, 18, 91, 145, 151
  See also Subjective expected utility

V

Values, 37, 38
  crystallized, 17
  "two-tier" theory, 147
Viability envelopes, 148

W

Wants, 34, 36, 131

War, 203–04
Waste, 144–45
Waste handling. See Recycling
Wealth of Nations (Smith), 193
Weber, Max, 35
Welfare. See Social welfare

Willingness-to-pay (WTP) value, 12, 16–18, 20, 24n.5, 86–87
World Commission on Environment and Development, 139
WTP value. See Willingness-to-pay value

Contributors

Andrea Baranzini is a research fellow on the faculty of Economic and Social Sciences at the University of Geneva.

Gardner Brown is professor of economics in the Department of Economics at the University of Washington in Seattle.

Beat Bürgenmeier is professor of economics at the University of Geneva.

Riley E. Dunlap is professor of sociology in the Department of Sociology at Washington State University in Pullman.

Paul Ekins is a research fellow in the Department of Economics at Birkbeck College in London.

Sylvie Faucheux is professor of economics in the Centre Economie-Espace-Environnement of the University of Paris I, Panthéon-Sorbonne, Paris.

Jean-Louis Le Moigne is professor of systems sciences and director of GRASCE at the University of Aix-Marseille III in Aix-en-Provence, France.

Loren A. Lutzenhiser is assistant professor of sociology in the Department of Sociology at Washington State University in Pullman.

Magali Orillard is professor of economics with GRASCE at the University of Aix-Marseille III in Aix-en-Provence, France.

Gonzague Pillet is head of the Section for Environmental Economics of the Environmental and Systems Analysis Laboratory at Paul Scherrer Institute in Switzerland.

Charles Roig is professor of political science at the University of Geneva in Aix-en-Provence, France.

Eugene A. Rosa is professor of sociology in the Department of Sociology at Washington State University in Pullman.

Eberhard K. Seifert is a senior fellow at Institut For Environmental and Energy in Wuppertar, Germany.

John Thøgersen is professor in the Department of Marketing at the Aarhus School of Business in Aarhus, Denmark.

About the Editor

Beat Bürgenmeier is professor of economics at the University of Geneva. His main contributions in the field of socioeconomics are *The Case of Socioeconomics* (in French, Paris: Economica, 1990) and *Socioeconomics: An Interdisciplinary Approach—Ethics, Institutions, and Markets* (Boston, Dordrecht, London: Kluwer Academic Publishers, 1992). He is also the author of *Economic Analysis and Policy,* 4th ed. (in French, Paris: Economica, 1992).